A Farmer and His Dog

A Farmer and His Dog

By the same author

Adam's Farm: My Life on the Land
Like Farmer, Like Son

A Farmer and His Dog

Adam Henson

BBC
BOOKS

1 3 5 7 9 10 8 6 4 2

BBC Books, an imprint of Ebury Publishing
20 Vauxhall Bridge Road
London SW1V 2SA

BBC Books is part of the Penguin Random House group of companies
whose addresses can be found at global.penguinrandomhouse.com

Penguin
Random House
UK

First published by BBC Books in 2017

www.penguin.co.uk

A CIP catalogue record for this book is available
from the British Library

ISBN 9781785942471

Typeset in India by Integra Software Services Pvt. Ltd, Pondicherry

Printed and bound in Great Britain by Clays Ltd, St Ives PLC

Penguin Random House is committed to a sustainable future for our
business, our readers and our planet. This book is made from Forest
Stewardship Council® certified paper.

MIX
Paper from
responsible sources
FSC
www.fsc.org   FSC® C018179

To all the wonderful dogs who have been
my loyal companions over the years

Contents

Introduction   viii

1   Childhood Friends   1
2   Carlo and Co   15
3   Nita   29
4   My Aussie Mates   47
5   Three Wonderful Dogs   75
6   Finding Peg   95
7   Other Kinds of Sheepdog   109
8   My Kind of Dogs   137
9   Have You Thought About Hungarian
    Wire-haired Vizslas?   175
10   Losing Dolly   199
11   Dogs at War   213
12   Assistance Dogs   237
13   How Bright Are My Dogs?   257
14   They Also Serve ...   273

Afterword   299
Index   301

Introduction

There are very few times in my life when there isn't a dog near to me. Sometimes I'm watching an intelligent, hard-working border collie handle my sheep at the far side of a field. Sometimes I'm sitting in the kitchen reading with a furry body pressed against my legs. Sometimes I'm bumping across the fields with the back of my truck loaded with four dogs – the collies Peg and Pearl and our Hungarian wire-haired Vizslas, Boo and Olive. Sometimes, when I'm away from home filming for *Countryfile*, I'm meeting other remarkable dogs whose relationship with their owners goes way beyond simple companionship.

Not that I ever underestimate the powerful beneficial effects of having a dog in the house simply as a pet. One in four households in Britain today is home to a dog and there's plenty of research to show that dog owners are fitter, healthier, and suffer less from depression than those who don't have them. Children growing up with pets learn so much, and also gain that simple, unconditional love that irons out so many worries and anxieties. There is nothing more reassuring for a youngster than cuddling up with a dog, who never asks questions about what kind of day you had, never judges you for not doing homework or not getting good grades, who is always in your corner when other friends are more fickle. Yes, just having a dog in the family is a wonderful thing, and our household always feels very empty when one of our much-loved dogs dies.

Although I understand the relationship between a family and its pet, I love the fact that dogs have evolved over millennia to be so much more than companions. Peg, the border collie sheepdog whose kennel is next to the back door of the farmhouse, is my partner when it comes to all the shepherding work I have to do. She makes my work possible in a way that no mechanical aids or extra humans could, and it is a role that dogs like her have filled more or less unchanged over centuries, even thousands of years. When I watch her working the flock I know there is a connection that goes right back to the evolution of dogs from their wolf ancestors: my work with Peg is something that a Bronze Age shepherd, rounding up his goats or sheep, would recognise. It was Peg's ancestors who made it possible for men to stop hunting to feed their families and start cultivating their own land and animals. They were there at the birth of civilisation as we recognise it today.

For me, the bond I have with Peg is priceless; she gives me a wonderful devotion and loyalty that is a real privilege, as well as making an enormous contribution to my farming life. Every morning when she bounds out of her kennel, eager to greet me and to get on with the work I have lined up for her, I know how very lucky I, and thousands of other shepherds and farmers, are to have these extraordinarily bright, enthusiastic dogs at our side. And we, who work the land and our flocks, are not the only beneficiaries of the extraordinary relationship between man and dog.

If Peg's ancestry goes back to the early days of dogs working happily alongside humans, there are many other dogs whose roles have evolved more recently to fit in with our changing times. There are gundogs, like the Labradors I grew up with, and the Hungarian wire-haired Vizslas like Boo and Olive who live with us now. There are assistance dogs, whose skills involve understanding modern life so much they can use cash machines, load and unload washing machines, and save the lives of their owners on a regular basis when they have serious health problems. There are guard dogs, search and rescue dogs, sniffer dogs – the list goes on.

In this book I want to introduce you to my own dogs, but also to some of the many others I have met through *Countryfile*, and whose stories have reinforced my belief that we humans owe an enormous debt to our wet-nosed, tail-wagging, snuffling, four-legged friends.

CHAPTER 1

Childhood Friends

The fairy godmother who stood guard over my cot when I was a baby, protecting and loving me in a way that only a dog can, was a gentle black Labrador called Chemmers. Chemmers was my first real experience of dogs, but I'm sad to report I have no clear memory of her. She died when I was three years old, but for those three years she felt her role in life was to look after me and my three older sisters, Libby, Lolo and Becca. Her main devotion was to Mum, who had been given her as a twentieth birthday present by a boyfriend she had before she knew Dad. In those young, single days Mum took Chemmers everywhere with her, including sailing down at Weymouth, which they both loved. Chemmers' unusual name came from one of the buoys they had to sail round.

Luckily for me and my sisters, the boyfriend didn't last long. However, Chemmers did, and when Mum met Dad it was a matter of 'Love me, love my dog'. This wasn't something Dad had a problem with, as he adored dogs from his own childhood days during the war, in particular, a Great Dane called John and a bull terrier called Barney. Sometimes Mum joked that he married her for the dog: that's a long way from the truth, but he was certainly very happy to share her with Chemmers. They met in Cheltenham, where Mum was working as a teacher, and after they married Chemmers moved with them to the first farm Dad managed. When he got the tenancy of Bemborough Farm, where I was born and live to this day, Chemmers was very much part of the family, and because Mum was very attentive to her small brood of children, Chemmers joined in with her, treating us as if we were her own puppies.

It's a pity that I don't remember her, because according to Mum and my oldest sister Libby she was a truly wonderful dog: gentle, kind, well-mannered and everything that the very best Labradors can be. She accepted the rough and tumble of young children, the tiny sticky hands grabbing at her fur, the small, tottering steps taken by us as we clung to her back.

Mum got her into pup with a local dog, Barney, a promiscuous yellow Lab with a bit of a reputation as a Lothario; everyone in the neighbourhood with a female dog had to be on the lookout for Barney when their bitches were in season. He was remarkably agile, even jumping through an open kitchen window in pursuit of a mate at one neighbour's home. On this occasion he was officially sanctioned to breed with Chemmers, and he made the most of it, fathering a beautiful litter of puppies.

People who don't have Labradors are often surprised that when different coloured dogs and bitches are mated together, they sometimes produce litters with all three standard Lab colours – black, yellow and brown – among the puppies. (Incidentally, brown Labradors used to be called 'liver', but they were renamed 'chocolate' to increase their popularity.) I don't want to get all scientific about it, but it's down to genes. In the Labrador world, black is the dominant gene, but there are other genes in the mix, and depending on the combination different mixes of pups can occur. Nowadays breeders are able to have their dogs genotyped, if they are prepared to pay for it. Without the testing, the only things we know for sure is that two yellow Lab parents will always produce yellow pups, and a brown and yellow pairing will produce yellow or brown pups – sometimes both in the same litter – as will two brown parents. Pairings involving a black parent can produce a litter with all three different coloured pups in it, in all possible combinations. On this occasion, even though Barney was yellow, the pups were all born black.

Chemmers was an instinctively good mother to her litter. She was so relaxed that she accepted Libby curling up in bed with her puppies: like I said, I think she thought we were all her offspring, whether we had four legs or two ...

When Chemmers died, at a good old age, Dad took Libby with him to see a litter and to help him choose another black Labrador puppy. He and Mum both thought that a house needs a dog to really be a home and they both loved black Labs. Besides, when you are living in a fairly remote farmhouse, even though there is a sheepdog in a kennel outside, having a house dog gives a great sense of security. Although Labradors are, on the whole, a placid breed, they have a surprisingly stentorian bark. A recent survey by an insurance company tested reactions to recordings of dogs barking and, without being able to see which dog it was, the one that was voted as having the scariest bark was to everyone's surprise the Labrador, with more than half of all those canvassed guessing the Lab bark belonged to a Rottweiler. Next on the list of most scary was a Weimaraner, with the Rottweiler coming in third out of ten breeds that were tested.

So Labs make really good house dogs, and police and insurance companies believe the presence of any noisy dog is a great deterrent. Certainly, owners of dogs make fewer insurance claims for theft than non-owners, and surveys of burglars (yes, some burglars do co-operate when asked what would deter them ...) show that a noisy dog is top of the list of things they would avoid when sizing up a break-in.

The puppy Dad and Libby chose was named Tassle. The end of most Labradors' tails has slightly longer hair with a twist in it. This particular puppy had a very long twist to the end of its tail, like a little tassle, hence her name. Libby, who was six years older than me and nine at this time, adored her. Sadly, like many other pure bred animals, Labradors as a breed have inherent problems. One of the most common with Labs and retrievers (and other large breeds like German Shepherds) is hip dysplasia: it is, in fact, the most common orthopaedic disorder in all dogs. It means abnormal growth of the hip, with the ball and socket less functional than they should be, the socket restricting the normal movement of the ball. Muscles and ligaments around the joint can also be too lax to support it, so eventually the joint becomes arthritic and painful.

It's very hard to detect this problem in a small puppy, it only becomes obvious between six and 18 months old, and sometimes much later. Some dogs with dysplasia don't have much pain, but their legs are stiffer and they may become lame. Others, sadly, are badly disabled and in constant pain, irritable, not wanting to exercise. They can be treated with physiotherapy or anti-inflammatory drugs, and as an extreme resort, surgery, including hip replacement. Nowadays responsible dog owners only breed dogs with good hip scores. The score is a system of assessing the hips, and allocating each with a number. A perfect 0:0 is not very common in Labs, but the important thing is to keep the total as low as possible, with each hip being more or less the same as its pair. The highest score is 53 each side, so a total of 106, but this dog would probably be chronically disabled. The average total for both hips in Labradors is 12.

The score cannot be done until the dog is at least a year old, when a vet will X-ray the hips, and then a good breeder will decide whether the dog can be used for mating. Hip dysplasia is largely inherited, so scoring the parents is the only good way to avoid it. There are other factors, like how overweight the dog is (and Labradors never stop thinking about their stomachs and will eat everything ...) Of course genes are tricky things and a puppy whose parents have great hip scores can still have dysplasia from a throwback gene. However, responsible breeding means that the number of dogs with lifelong debilitating conditions is being reduced.

The British Veterinary Association and the Kennel Club – the organisation dedicated to promoting the welfare of all dogs – jointly introduced hip scoring in 1984, quite a few years after we got Tassle, but it was already well known that breeding from a dog with dysplasia was irresponsible. Sadly, Tassle became lame and Mum and Dad decided to have her X-rayed. It was then that it became apparent that she was suffering from mild hip dysplasia and they knew that they would never allow her to have a litter because of the high risk of passing her problems on. With that decision made, it was sensible to have her spayed. After all, they didn't want an enthusiastic rogue like Barney coming in pursuit of her ...

This is where the story becomes very sad, especially for my sister Libby. At the age of three, Tassle went to the vet for a routine spaying op, which obviously meant a general anaesthetic. Tragically, her heart gave out under the anaesthetic and she died on the operating table. In retrospect, perhaps it was for the best: the dysplasia would have eventually caused her pain, and she clearly had a heart problem, too. However it's impossible to be that rational about the death of a much loved family pet. I was only six, so any memories I have are brief snapshots, and not many of those. But for my sisters, especially Libby, this was terrible news, and for a few days the whole household was cast in gloom. Tassle may have died young, but she is remembered as a gentle, loving dog who fitted in with the family very well.

Labradors were now well and truly established as a Henson family institution, and the next one that came into the farmhouse was an older, well-trained gundog called Trudy. Along with a springer spaniel called Ben, she came from a mate of Dad's who was emigrating to Australia. The friend, a Mr Hidcote who lived near to us at Hawling Manor, was a shooting companion of Dad's, and when Dad heard that the dogs might have to be put down when he left the country Dad offered to have them. Trudy was five at the time, and in the prime of life, and Ben, a liver and white springer, was 11, so already an old boy. Mr Hidcote was convinced the dogs would not take to anyone else as he had bonded so closely with them. It took quite a lot of persuasion on Dad's part for him to agree to let Dad try. The dogs were duly delivered to our farm, and in a moment of inspiration Mr Hidcote included his own old shooting jackets and waterproofs. He was roughly the same size as Dad, and when Dad wore the clothes the dogs trotted happily at his side, quickly becoming completely devoted to him.

I know the smell on the clothes helped, but I'm not sure it is always as hard to rehome dogs as their owners like to think. We love to imagine we have a 'one person' dog, an animal that belongs just to us. And it's true that sometimes within a family a dog will have its 'preferred' owner – the person it relates to best and feels, on its own terms, that it belongs with. But dogs are pragmatists, they have a strong instinct for self-preservation, and generally they will go with anyone who feeds and loves them. That's not to say they will desert an owner for anyone who offers them treats: they are very loyal. But if their owner vanishes from their life (and, sadly, owners do sometimes die before their pets), it is, in almost every case, possible to rehome them.

A friend I know who works for a charity rehoming dogs has three dogs of her own, and she said to me: 'I always imagined that if anything happened to me, two of my dogs would adapt and go to new owners. But my little Jack Russell, I was sure, would pine away and die without me. Now I have been doing this job for a few years I no longer believe that. Dogs do miss people, and sometimes they do become withdrawn and sad when they lose an owner. But with sympathetic treatment they can all be successfully rehomed.'

There are, of course, loads of stories of very loyal and faithful dogs, some who spend years waiting for their masters to come back to them. But their loyalty always also involves being fed and looked after. There's a famous story about Greyfriars Bobby, a Skye terrier who kept guard over his master's grave in Greyfriars Kirkyard in Edinburgh for 14 years until his own death in 1872. Bobby became a popular tourist attraction and was rewarded with a meal from a local café every day, the café benefiting enormously from the trade it attracted. But, of course, the dog knew nothing of this, only that it had a place to stay and food. How much memory he had of his master after 14 years, I really don't know. But the public loved the story of Bobby's loyalty, and there was even a statue erected to him after his death (although cynics say the real dog died and was replaced with a lookalike, to keep the tourists coming).

It's a familiar story across many nations and cultures: dogs who wait by graves, or at the place they last saw their owner. Like Fido, a street mongrel from Italy who turned up at the bus stop for 14 years expecting the man who adopted him to get off the bus, when sadly he had been killed in a wartime air raid. Or Hachiko, an Akita, who made his way to a train station in Tokyo every day for nine years, at the time his master, who had died, would have arrived home. Like Greyfriars Bobby, these dogs have had statues erected to them as a tribute to their fidelity. And like Bobby, they were well cared for and fed; their devotion became part of their routine, and I suspect they would have moved on if nobody had been looking after them.

Ben and Trudy took to Dad and did not seem to miss their old owner – although, I daresay if he had walked back into their lives they would have been overjoyed to see him. Ben, in particular, became devoted to Dad, even following him up and down the rows when he was turning hay with the tractor and haybob. Old when he came to us, he grew noticeably older, as his gait stiffened and he no longer ran about the place. But he still loved being out with Dad, and one hot summer's day Dad sat down at the base of a drystone wall to eat his lunchtime sandwiches. Ben came and lay next to him, his head on Dad's legs. He fell asleep and he never woke up, dying very peacefully in the best place, in the lap of the man he loved and who loved him. If there is such a thing as a perfect death, Ben achieved it.

Although I remember Ben, I was still very young when he arrived in our household, and because of his age he was only with us for a couple of years. Yet I loved the look of him, that proud springer stance, his soft mouth, his unflagging enthusiasm. My parents noticed how much I took to him, and it put down a marker for my future ...

Trudy was much younger than Ben, and she is the first of the house dogs of whom I have clear memories. I loved taking her for long walks and she was a perfect companion for a young boy. Most of all, I was really happy when Dad went pheasant shooting, and I was allowed to go along, holding on to her until the order came for her to retrieve. It was wonderful to be trusted to be Dad's companion, and to spend time with him, and Trudy was the ideal gundog for me to learn with.

Before Trudy died, Mum and Dad returned to their first love, black Labs. They bought another puppy, Jemima. She was a very traditional-looking Labrador, with short legs, a barrel chest and an insatiable appetite. Labradors love their food, but it's really important for their health not to let them become overweight. Carrying extra pounds creates all sorts of health problems for dogs, from arthritis to diabetes, through to breathing and heart problems. A study of Labradors over many years has shown that slimmer dogs live on average two years longer than their overweight peers, have fewer visits to the vet because of health problems and need less prescribed medication. The fatter labs have an average age of 11, the thinner ones of 13.

That alone is a good reason to keep their weight down. But it's not just the length of life, but the quality of it. I feel so sorry for fat dogs waddling along with their owners. They are not enjoying life to the full, unable to run and jump, miserable on hot days because they find it harder to regulate their temperature and can struggle to breathe.

I appreciate how hard it is to keep the weight of some dogs down, and Labradors in particular have a well-deserved reputation for being greedy. But where throwing them a titbit when they look at you with those imploring brown eyes may feel like a kindness, it can actually be cruel. Dad always had a firm rule that dogs were not allowed near the table when we were eating. Our dogs were fed once a day and left alone to eat. This is especially important with visiting young children in the house, because even the friendliest of dogs can be protective of their supper and a growl can easily be followed up with a bite. I continue with the same rules in our house today. But even the most disciplined of owners can find their rules thwarted.

A friend of mine had a large extension built, so the builders were around for a few months. One young builder took a shine to the family Lab and was convinced the dog loved him above all others. What she actually loved was his sandwiches, which he shared with her every lunchtime. He also gave her chocolate biscuits until my friend realised and pointed out that chocolate can be deadly for dogs. In the time it took to do the building work, the Lab's weight increased dramatically, and my friend was firmly told to get a grip on it by a tough, funny nurse at her local vet practice, who said: 'That's a dog, not a coffee table. I could balance my mug on her back, she's so fat. Bring her back in four weeks to be weighed and if she hasn't lost weight I'll put you against the wall and shoot you ...'

Of course, Jemima never got overweight, because life on a farm involves a lot of exercise. But we were all aware that, given half a chance, she'd be sticking her nose in the bin or a bucket of pig nuts, and if anything got spilled on the floor she'd be there licking it up. Not all dogs need the same amount of food. Of course, working dogs eat more than house dogs, as a rule. But even with two dogs of the same breed leading the same lifestyle, food has to be individually tailored, as one will be able to eat more than another without piling on the pounds.

Jemima was a great friend and companion for me as a young boy. I first went away to boarding school at the age of eight and wasn't happy there. The school rules said I couldn't contact home for the first three weeks – a rule devised to help new boys acclimatise. I felt bereft, away from my family and away from my beloved Jemima. She was high up the list of things I missed, along with my family and all the routines of the farm.

I never told Mum and Dad quite how miserable I was. I knew they sent me away to school because they wanted the best for me. I was the sort of carefree, distracted child who had not followed my sisters' academic success at the local primary and they felt I would learn more in a more structured environment. So I never wanted to disappoint them, and they were right that being away from the farm made me concentrate on my studies more. But Mum knew, as she dropped me back at school in floods of tears, that I missed home more than I could say.

When I did come home for a weekend or for the holidays, Jemima seemed to sense that I needed comfort. I could bury my face in her shiny, black coat, stroke her silky ears and share all my fears and worries with her. She was an uncomplicated, loving friend: that's the wonderful gift that a dog can give to anyone, but particularly to a young child.

It was my close bond with Jemima that made Mum and Dad aware that dogs meant so much to me and it was at this time that I started to ask them if I could have a dog of my own. Jemima was a brilliant companion, but she related most of all to Dad, and I longed for my own, special four-legged friend.

CHAPTER 2

Carlo and Co

When Carlo lifted his top lip to show his teeth, you never quite knew why: to me and the rest of my family it was a smile of welcome. To anyone he didn't want to see, or was suspicious of, it was a snarl of warning. Maybe there was a subtle difference in the two expressions, but I never really saw it. All I know is, I'm really glad Carlo was on my side ...

Carlo was a very tough sheepdog. He was the dog Dad had when I was young and the first one that I remember watching at work, turning a flock of sheep and bringing them back to where he wanted them. Carlo was also a great guard dog and quite a few visitors to the farm were trapped in their cars until he was told they were 'friends' and allowed to be there. Woe betide them if they didn't wait for clearance, though! One land agent turned up to inspect the farm buildings but didn't have the sense to ring up first, or to call at the farmhouse before he started his inspection. Instead, he started wandering around the barns, unaccompanied, clipboard in hand. What was a dog to think? Carlo was in no doubt that this was an intruder, and it was clearly his job to protect the farm from him. A swift nip to the back of the man's leg sent the agent hobbling to the farmhouse, obviously expecting tea and sympathy from Mum and a fierce reprimand for Carlo. Instead, he was told in no uncertain terms how stupid he had been. What's the point of a guard dog if it doesn't guard? The dog, she told him, was only doing his job, and should be praised, not criticised, for apprehending a stranger who was inside the farm buildings without permission.

Carlo was always lovely with us four kids and would happily lie in the garden in the sun while we played, but if there was ever an opportunity to chase something he was up and away. It's an instinct with sheepdogs. He felt it was his duty to control anything that was moving as if it were an errant sheep. This meant he was forever chasing the postman's van, biting at the tyres, and even nipping the postman if he was foolhardy enough to jump out when Carlo was around.

One day Carlo was actually knocked over by the van. It clipped him as he ran alongside, sending him flying. He got up, shook himself, staggered as if dazed for a moment, and then normal service was resumed as he carried on chasing it. It didn't teach him a lesson.

Carlo was a black and white border collie with long hair that always seemed to be caked in mud and sheep muck. He didn't mind being so unkempt, but from time to time it was decided that Carlo needed to be tidied up. He hated the process, which involved cutting off the matted straggly bits which Dad referred to as his 'diggy-dags'. The only way to get rid of them was to muzzle him and then attack his coat with the sheep shears, and as soon as I was old enough the job seemed to fall to me. Although Carlo clearly hated it he didn't hold it against me, and as soon as he'd been released and unmuzzled he was his usual friendly self, just looking a bit tidier – although it was no poodle parlour job.

Dad was a brilliant farmer. He understood livestock, and could assess an animal at a quick glance. He had a great eye for a good animal to buy and was equally good at spotting, from a distance of 200 yards or more, if one of our animals was sick and needed help. I miss his guiding hand, and I always will.

However there was one aspect of farming where Dad was not perfect, or anywhere near it. And that was working a sheepdog. He loved his dogs and they adored him, and they worked well enough for him, but he was not a natural at training them. He'd probably never really been shown. My dad didn't come from a farming background. Dad's father was a famous actor and comedian, Leslie Henson, and his mother was a chorus girl and dancer. His younger brother, Nicky Henson, followed them on to the stage, but as a young man Dad turned his back on his family's showbusiness traditions and followed his own dream, to live on the land and to run a farm. So I think he simply devised his own way of training a sheepdog, which wasn't orthodox or, I'm forced to admit, particularly good. His success as a shepherd owed a lot to the dogs' enthusiasm to work and their instinctive grasp of what they had to do.

It was a different matter with the Labradors he schooled as gundogs: they were generally very obedient and well trained, but the sheepdogs were always a bit unruly. They were OK at doing what he wanted, which was usually fairly routine, but if they ever got it wrong he could be heard shouting at them, losing his rag. It was the only time I ever knew him to lose his temper: with us children and with the gundogs he was patient and kind. But a badly behaved sheepdog would be subjected to a rant – which meant not a thing to the dog except that it got the general idea it was in trouble.

So working sheepdogs wasn't his biggest skill, and as the farm grew in size he took on a succession of stockmen who did most of the shepherding. Some of them were quite good, but some were in the same league as Dad, so I didn't grow up with a really brilliant sheepdog mentor either. The stockmen often had their own dogs, so I could go out with them and I picked up the basic commands. While watching them work the sheep, I think I learned early on that Dad's approach – endlessly shouting at the dog – didn't help.

Carlo was one of the few male dogs we have ever had at Bemborough Farm – Dad preferred bitches, and so do I. I love the look of male dogs, they are very handsome animals. But when you are out with them they have an overriding interest in any nearby females who may be in season, constantly sniffing any bitches they come across, and if they get the scent it is all they can think about. They also stop and pee on almost every gate post and thistle to mark their territory. It drives me mad!

I know that a lot of top sheepdog trainers prefer dogs because in some ways their temperament is more reliable – bitches can be a bit unpredictable when they are in season. Also, there's some evidence that dogs are more competitive, and that's important in high-level trialling. If you look at the results of field trial championships, 80 per cent of the top awards go to dogs, not bitches. Breeders who make a living from their working dogs often prefer a male, which can be put out to stud at a high fee as often as he can cope with, whereas a bitch can only (responsibly) produce one litter a year, and she cannot compete in trials while in the latter stages of pregnancy or when she is nursing her puppies.

However, I don't pretend to be up with the best sheepdog trainers and I don't go trialling, so a bitch suits me better. Farmers and shepherds hardly ever have dogs castrated or bitches spayed: there's a deep-seated belief that they work better, and are tougher, if they have all their bits and pieces. There may not be any evidence, but it's generally believed that a sheepdog may become lazier and fatter if it is neutered. Personally, I like to leave my dogs the way nature intended them to be: it feels right. But here on a farm there is plenty of land for them to roam on, and I do understand why pet owners living in very different circumstances need to have the operation carried out, and as long as it is done properly at the right time the animals thrive.

The name 'collie' for a sheepdog can probably be traced back to the same root as 'coal' and 'collier', because they were originally black, or predominantly black. They have a very long history: dogs attached themselves to humans as soon as our ancestors settled in groups, scavenging for food, and soon taking on their first important role as guard dogs. But their next role came as soon as men began herding flocks of animals. Most experts believe that the instinct to herd – and it is an instinct, and one that saved Dad many times when his orders were confusing – is a natural extension of their innate need to hunt. Instead of hunting to kill and provide their own food, they learned that their best bet was to help the humans who would take care of their needs.

The work they do, and the different terrains and climates in which they have done it over the centuries, means that sheepdogs are superbly fine-tuned, with good feet, weatherproof coats, astonishing hearing (I'm always amazed at how a hill shepherd can control a dog with a whistle from three fields away with a mound between them) and excellent eyesight. They are functional dogs, not bred for their looks but for their herding skills, although to me no dog looks better than a well-set collie. But for farmers and shepherds, the reason to check a dog's pedigree is to see whether he comes from good working stock, not how photogenic he is.

There are different kinds of collies, but generally we have borders at Bemborough. After Carlo, Dad had, for a very brief time, a Welsh collie called Megan. He had been to the LLeyn peninsula in North Wales, probably to look at and buy some Welsh black cattle, and when the farmer mentioned that he had a dog for sale, already trained, Dad happily bought her, as he needed a replacement for Carlo who had died peacefully at the end of a long working life.

Welsh collies are longer legged, broader in the chest and generally have wider muzzles than border collies. But it's not the difference in appearance that matters: they have, over centuries, been bred for a different purpose. They were historically droving dogs, that were used to take sheep or cattle to market, rather than being herding dogs used to round up flocks of sheep. It's a subtle distinction, and nowadays with the need to move flocks to market by droving gone, many Welsh farmers have switched to border collies. But it's important to keep the breed going, and there are plenty of enthusiasts.

In terms of working the dogs, the difference is in what sheepdog trainers call 'the eye'. Border collies have 'a strong eye', which means they stare hard at the sheep and keep them in order by never taking their gaze from them. A 'loose-eyed' dog like a traditional Welsh collie, glances at the flock and runs around it more and is usually able to work more independently, making its own decisions. It is generally more mobile, constantly on the go rather than commanding the flock with its stare.

A loose-eyed dog is vital to move cattle, which are big beasts and can easily step on and damage a dog that doesn't get out of the way of their hooves. That's why small dogs, like Welsh corgis, were also traditionally used to move cattle; they could dart in and out.

So the Welsh collie was invaluable when the flock was being taken in one direction (along a droving road to market, for example), allowing one man and a good dog to move large numbers of animals, sometimes for miles in a day. However they were less useful in terms of splitting a flock, bringing them back, penning them. That's not to say there haven't been some absolutely brilliant Welsh collies working sheep, but for most top trainers, taking part in sheepdog trialling, the border collie is the preferred breed.

The problem with Megan, though, was not her 'loose eye'. I don't think Dad ever got far enough with her to discover whether she was any good at herding sheep or not. The problem was much more fundamental. She spoke Welsh! She had been trained in Welsh, all the commands she knew were in Welsh. No amount of yelling commands at her in English produced any response. A sheepdog only knows a limited number of commands (a family pet knows even fewer) and it certainly isn't bi-lingual. Poor Megan was as confused as I would be if someone was talking to me in Chinese or Polish. When Dad realised the problem, he knew he couldn't keep her. Even though she was a sweet-natured dog, he didn't have the time or patience to re-train her in English or to master her commands in Welsh. So Megan was returned to North Wales, where no doubt she flourished in the land of her fathers, with an owner fluent in her language.

Pat was our next sheepdog, a black and white smooth-haired border bitch. She had one big advantage over Carlo – no diggy-dags. No matter how muddy the ground, she seemed to self-clean when she got back into her kennel. She worked well, and even had her own moment of TV stardom. Dad appeared on television fairly regularly throughout my childhood, starting after he opened Cotswold Farm Park where he housed a collection of rare breed farm animals, a passion of his which I share. The farm park is on land adjoining Bemborough Farm, but with its own entrance. Due to my work on *Countryfile*, I'm away from the farm and the farm park a lot and rely on my business partner, Duncan Andrews, and our great team of managers and staff. Whenever I'm home, I spend as much time as I can working with the livestock and meeting visitors at the farm park. I'm thrilled that the farm park attracts many visitors to see the work we do, preserving traditional British breeds. When the farm park opened, Dad was interviewed by lots of journalists from newspapers and television stations. He was a natural: he had clearly inherited the family showbiz gene from his parents; something of his background remained, and it was clear he was at home in front of the cameras.

So he was recruited to do slots on Johnny Morris's popular children's programme, *Animal Magic*, and also to take part in other farming programmes. In one, called *Barnyard Safari*, he demonstrated how difficult it is to round up the ancient and rare Soay sheep we keep on the farm. Rather than flocking together, they have an instinct to scatter, confusing a dog that is used to dealing with more biddable flocks. Pat starred as the dog whose job it was to attempt to round them up.

When Pat died, Dad was given an ex-trialling dog called Queen by a retired shepherd from Northleach. She was brilliantly trained, a champion trialler with a great pedigree. She was a tri-colour – black and white with little ginger bits on her chin and above her eyes. She was a beautiful dog, well behaved and a brilliant worker. She took to Dad instantly, and was definitely the best sheepdog he'd ever had, although perhaps she secretly wondered what she had come down to, from working sheep at a very high level at trials to doing a basic shepherding job at our farm ...

When I was about 13 years old I was standing with Dad in a field while he talked to some people who were interested in buying some sheep. He cast Queenie out, gave her the simple command 'come by' and with great skill she skirted the edge of the field, making sure she picked up every sheep, and brought them to him without another command, and without him ever stopping his conversation. The potential buyers were very impressed by her, raving about what an amazing dog she was, and left with a trailer full of sheep.

Tragically, after only a couple of years with us, Dad let her out of her kennel one morning and she dashed through a gap in the hedge on to the farm drive, just as the assistant stockman was driving past in the farm's Land Rover. She went straight under the wheels and was killed immediately. We were all very upset, but Dad was devastated, as was the chap who ran her over although there was nothing he could have done to avert the accident. Queenie was so easy to work with, and at the same time a good-natured dog who really loved Dad.

The same stockman was leaving us shortly afterwards to run a flock in Saudi Arabia, and he gave Dad his own sheepdog, Bill. Bill was a big, shaggy-haired, thick-headed black and white collie, more like Carlo in temperament and attitude. He didn't work well for Dad, who was constantly exasperated by him, and could be seen running up and down the field yelling 'Bill, Bill!' with little success in getting him to do what was needed. Again, he could perform the basic functions of a sheepdog, but nowhere near the brilliant Queenie.

Although I really love sheepdogs – there's nothing better than watching a collie working well, and a dog that loves its work makes a great companion – sheepdogs are not the best choice as a family pet in an urban environment and sadly a large number end up having to be rehomed. Collies as a breed have high levels of energy, stamina and enthusiasm. They are also intelligent, and need mental stimulation almost as much as physical exercise. Owners who don't choose a pet carefully may find that a sheepdog with that inbuilt instinct to round up will chase whatever it can uncontrollably. They may also find if the dog is cooped up all day it becomes stressed and agitated, developing bad habits like chewing, barking and nipping.

There are three main reasons why collies end up in an animal shelter. One is that they were bought by farmers and shepherds to work with sheep but simply do not have the right herding instincts. These dogs can make good pets when they are sympathetically rehomed. They still need lots of exercise, but they can make happy, well-balanced family dogs.

The second common reason for them being rehomed is that they don't necessarily fit in with little children. A small child running down the garden is like a sheep escaping the flock to a collie, and its instinct is to round the child up by running in front and turning to stare at him, perhaps barking. This can frighten the child, who tries to run away, and the dog instinctively runs after him, perhaps even nipping at his heels. Disaster! The family assumes it has a nasty dog, but in fact the dog is only behaving in the way its nature tells it.

But the biggest reason collies end up looking for new homes is that their owners find them 'hyper'. According to Border Collie Rescue, the charity which helps rehome unwanted border collies and collie crosses: 'Most people are not willing, prepared, or able to put in the large time commitment it takes to adequately exercise a border collie ... Herding sheep is an all-day activity and often entails miles of running and sprinting across uneven farmland.'

I visited the charity for a *Countryfile* programme, and was shown around by Ben Wilkes, a retired policeman who has spent many years volunteering for the Trust. When I was visiting, there were 26 dogs on site.

'We see so many dogs, coming from a variety of sources,' Ben told me. 'Sometimes it is a bereavement, sometimes families find they have a child who is allergic to the dog, sometimes it's a matter of people having to work long hours and not having enough time with the dog, and in recent years we've seen a steep rise in people moving into rented accommodation where they're not allowed to keep a dog.'

Often it is simply because a collie needs so much mental and physical stimulation that they are not an ideal pet unless owners can devote time and energy to them.

'Farmers breed for their own needs, not for the characteristics that a domestic dog owner is looking for. People buy on impulse, and then the problems develop later,' said Ben.

The Trust does an amazing job, looking after these very special dogs, and I'm a great supporter of their work. There will always be collies that need rescuing, often for very good reasons. But the work of the Trust would be easier if families looked more carefully at what they want from a pet dog, and what they can offer the dog.

My advice to any potential dog owner is always: find a pet who fits in with your lifestyle. If you live near open land and have time to get your collie out there for an hour or two a day, he may be the perfect pet for you. If you want a dog to train for agility classes (see chapter How Bright Are My Dogs?) a collie may be the right choice. But there are many other breeds which require far less exercise and are better adapted to living indoors with young families.

Choose your dog carefully.

CHAPTER 3

Nita

It was Christmas 1974, and I was eight, nearly nine years old. My older sisters and I were, like all kids on Christmas Day, scarcely able to contain our excitement. As per usual in most farming households, we children had to wait for our present-opening session until Dad had finished seeing to the stock. Animals first: they had no idea it was a special day, and needed to follow their usual routine of being fed and checked to ensure all was well.

My sisters and I would often go with Dad and the dogs to help out. I am not sure whether we were more of a hindrance than help, but it was great fun and gave Mum some space in the house to prepare the Christmas feast. Once back, washed and changed, we would settle down to the main event. Not the big lunch, which was always great as Mum was such a fantastic cook but, of course, the presents. That year was a Christmas of special presents for all of us. Mum and Dad had decided to push the boat out and give us all a larger, more expensive gift than we were normally given. There was a bike for Libby – hard to wrap up so we had a good idea it was coming. Lolo got a flute, which she had been learning to play at school, and Becca a saxophone, as she loved Ska music.

As they were all oohing and aahing over their presents, I looked around the room wondering where mine was, but trying to be brave and not make a fuss. There was nothing left under the Christmas tree, and the room was awash with colourful discarded Christmas wrapping paper and the sound of the girls trying out their instruments. The only object that wasn't normally in the room was a battered old tea chest in the corner – a big, square plywood box, bound on the edges with metal. The top was covered with a sheet of bright red Christmas paper.

'And here's your present, Adam,' said Dad, a broad smile on his face. I went to the chest, not sure what it could possibly be, tore off the wrapping and there, nestled at the bottom on an old blanket, was the best present I could have dreamed of: a small liver and white puppy, looking up at me with as much wonder in her big brown eyes as I had in mine. As we looked at each other I felt a rush of love for this tiny creature, and I believe she recognised it and felt the same. It was love at first sight for me.

She was eight weeks old and tiny: probably the smallest from the litter. Mum and Dad knew I wanted a spaniel, because I'd always said I liked them and I still do: they are fantastic dogs.

Dad was very fond of his aunt Benita, so in honour of her, and partly for Ben, his old spaniel, Benita became the puppy's registered kennel name, but she was always known as Nita. I can still remember the moment when Dad lifted her out of the chest and put her into my arms: she instinctively snuggled against my chest. Later I had to be reluctantly separated from her to join in with the traditional Christmas lunch, but no amount of crackers, turkey and pudding could distract me from her, and as soon as was decently possible I left the table and joined Nita on the floor.

There were strict rules in our house about dogs: they were not allowed on the furniture and they were definitely not allowed upstairs. Only one dog was ever allowed to break this rule – Nita. On the first night, when she was bedded down in the kitchen, I reluctantly went to bed. But I could not sleep for thinking about her, and when I heard her whimpering, I sneaked silently down the stairs, took her in my arms – whispering to her to keep quiet – and carried her up to my bedroom. She was soon snuggled up next to me and we both fell fast asleep. Mum found us the next morning, and I pretended to be asleep in fear of getting told off. She didn't have the heart to lay down the law thankfully, and neither did Dad: from that moment on, when I was home from school, Nita shared my bed. Dad pretended to be disgusted by a dog on a bed, but he always let me get away with it.

I'd been at boarding school for a year by the time Nita came into my life, and although I hated leaving my family at the start of every term, I was growing more used to it and had settled into the life of the school. But leaving Nita was agony, and I extracted firm promises from Mum and Dad about how she was to be looked after while I was away (as if they needed any advice on caring for dogs!) Phone calls home were always peppered with questions about her, and the most thrilling dates in the school calendar were the rugby fixtures when Mum and Dad came to watch me play. Of course, I was delighted to see them as I missed them badly. But I was delirious with happiness when they brought Nita with them. It was wonderful to see her on the touchline.

I know Nita loved and bonded with me above all others, but I also know that when I wasn't at home – and there were long spells when I wasn't – she was happy with Mum and Dad and my sisters looking after her. But when I was there, it was my legs she snuggled against when I sat down, and at night she took up her usual place at the bottom of the stairs, waiting to be invited up to share my bed, which she always was.

There's a very special relationship between children and dogs, and I first experienced it with our black Lab Jemima, and then, in spades, with Nita. I'm not surprised that we hear so many stories of dogs helping children with problems, whether it's conditions like autism, Asperger's, family break-ups, or terrible traumas. You can bury your face in the coat of a dog and feel accepted and loved, whatever is happening in the rest of your life. Not that I needed Nita to make me feel loved, but I know that wonderful feeling of emotional completeness that a dog brings. Everyone has times of being sad, angry, excited, happy: a dog shares it all. Nita was my best mate, always enthusiastic about trailing around the farm with me, full of energy, but also there, cuddled up to me, if ever I needed reassurance.

Jemima was firmly established as the house dog when Nita arrived. After the usual stand-off between an older dog and a puppy, she came to accept the little one. It's always difficult introducing a new puppy into a home with other dogs and even when they are bitches you should never assume that the maternal instincts of older dogs will kick in. The best advice is to monitor them, never force a puppy on another dog and let them establish their own relationship. After snapping at Nita once or twice to put her in her place and to instil due respect for her elder, Jemima and Nita settled down happily together.

Like all springers, Nita had an incredible energy and enthusiasm and a brilliant sense of smell. Once when I was in my early teens, I took a shotgun to go pigeon shooting. Pigeons can be a real problem on the farm, particularly when they eat young oilseed rape plants, and from time to time we try to deter them by shooting. Nita was never the sort of dog to sit patiently in the hide with me: she was so inquisitive that she couldn't resist nosing around, which would scare off the pigeons before I had chance to take aim. So I left her at the farmhouse, shut into the kitchen. I walked half a mile down the farm road, then skirted around the boundary of several fields carrying my shotgun. I erected a simple camouflage hide, put out some decoy plastic pigeons to attract the real birds, and settled down to wait.

Looking back towards the farmhouse I saw an amazing sight. Someone must have left the door open, because Nita was out and she had one mission: to find me. I could see this small liver-and-white splash of movement. I watched her, nose to the ground, go out of the farmyard, down the drive, turn left at the gate, up along one hedge, round another hedge, along the top of a big field, following my scent. Then she was at the hide, and she knew I was inside despite the camouflage. She'd achieved her target, finding me, but I didn't achieve mine: needless to say, I didn't bag any pigeons that day ...

But if she stopped me shooting the pigeons on that occasion, she was very useful on conventional pheasant shoots. I took her with me when I was working as a beater. She would flush the birds out of even the thickest of brambles and then retrieve them for me.

Nita actually spent more of her long life apart from me than with me. I was away at boarding school until I was 16, then I had two blissful years when I was studying A-levels locally, when she was welded to my side whenever I was out and about on the farm. I was no different from most boys of that age: I hated getting up in the morning. No longer at boarding school, I discovered the joys of beer and girls so, after arriving home in the early hours, I was even more reluctant to be dragged from my warm, comfortable bed. Nita was my ally. Whenever anyone came into the bedroom to rouse me, she would growl protectively and not let them near me. I owe many a good lie-in to Nita's guard dog instincts.

After A-levels, I spent a year working on the Chatsworth Estate in Derbyshire. Then I was at agricultural college in Devon for three years, and only home in the holidays, and after I went travelling for a year with my good friend (and now my business partner) Duncan Andrews. But despite all these long separations, Nita knew she was my dog. She was fine with everyone else, and didn't seem to pine for me, but the minute I was back she related totally to me. She lived with our separations, accepting that I would come and go, and adapted her life to my absences. Going upstairs to sleep on a bed only happened when I was home: she never presumed to try it with anyone else and accepted without question that she slept in the downstairs toilet the rest of the time.

The downstairs loo at Bemborough Farm always seems to have a dog bed in it, that's why I point guests upstairs when they visit! There is a flagged passageway entrance to the farmhouse, leading into the kitchen, with the loo off it. When dogs track mud into the house (and they do all the time when you live on a farm), then the passage and loo are a good place to confine them until they dry off. Otherwise Mum would have spent her whole time mopping mud from the kitchen floor. Spaniels have large, well-feathered feet – in other words, very hairy, and a real sponge for picking up mud and debris. Nita was very used to plopping down on her bed until she had dried off, when she would be allowed into the kitchen.

Springers have a very long history as gundogs, and although they were not recognised as a Kennel Club breed until the early twentieth century, there's lots of evidence that they, or very similar dogs, have been around for centuries. The name 'spaniel' is generally accepted to come from the word used by the Romans for Spain, Hispania, or perhaps the French term 'chiens d'Espanol', which means they almost certainly originated in the Iberian peninsula. But they spread across the globe long before anyone started to categorise dogs. There's a reference to spaniels in the 1576 book *The Treatise of Englishe Dogs*, but it was not until 1801 that springers and cockers were separated into two types: 'the springing, hawking or starter' and the 'cocking or cocker' spaniel.

At that time there was no attempt to breed them separately. It was simply a matter of sorting through a litter and making the small ones 'cockers', their name coming from hunting woodcock, and the larger ones 'springers', who could spring and flush out birds to be caught by hawks or falcons, and later by men with guns. Nita was certainly a springy dog, always ready to jump up and take part in anything that was going on.

There are some highly questionable references to springer spaniels in history, including a tale that one travelled to America with the Pilgrim Fathers. I love the story that William Wallace, that icon of Scottish history played by Mel Gibson in the film *Braveheart*, had a springer by the name of Merlin MacDonald way back in the thirteenth century. But there's no real evidence as to the type of dog he had (or even that he had one), and the film makers left Merlin out of their Hollywood blockbuster, much to the annoyance of some springer fans. But though the dog wasn't in the film, I was. Dad was asked if he could provide some traditional-looking livestock for the movie, including a pair of longhorn oxen to pull William Wallace's dead father's body back from the battlefield. An old college mate joined me and, dressed up in kilts and ginger wigs, we worked with the actors to control the oxen, so my claim to fame is that I have been directed by Mel Gibson. You'll have to look closely to spot me, but it was good fun.

What we do know, reliably, about the history of springers, is that when George Stubbs, famous for his paintings of horses and dogs, painted a 'land spaniel' at the end of the eighteenth century, the dog looks more like a liver and white springer than a cocker, although not quite the same around the ears.

There are lots of other variations on the spaniel breed, notably the King Charles and Cavalier King Charles (much smaller dogs bred by mating small parents, and for other distinctive characteristics like their flat noses). Others are known by their place of origin: Norfolk, Sussex, German, Russian spaniels, and Irish water spaniels.

Naturally, the type of spaniel that appealed to me – and to my dad – was a springer, because of their ability to retrieve, as well as to flush. They have beautifully soft mouths, like all good gundogs. This is important so that they don't crunch down into whatever they are carrying, as often the shot prey is for human consumption. They have an easy temperament, are quick to learn and like working hard, all of which makes them the perfect dog for hunting with, but also a great companion.

As well as working as gundogs, the sniffing ability of springers, which I saw first-hand when Nita tracked me through the fields, has been recognised – alongside that of Labradors and other breeds of spaniel – and they are used by police forces and military organisations across the world in drug and explosive detection. Jake, a springer working with the Met police, was deployed to search for explosives after the London bombings in 2005. Another springer, Buster, is estimated to have saved more than a thousand lives in his work as an explosives detection dog, serving with the RAF in Bosnia, Iraq and Afghanistan, earning a chest full of campaign medals. I'm happy to say he had a happy retirement with his handler, and died peacefully at the age of 13.

Jemima died peacefully at a good old age and I think Nita missed her old house mate. Dogs are unpredictable when it comes to mourning their companions. Some dogs take the departure of a familiar friend without showing any sign of grieving. On the other hand, sometimes some dogs are so closely bonded that one deeply pines when the other dies, perhaps going off their food and becoming lethargic. I've known a dog lie on the bed of her departed friend for hours, a place she never previously went, and I've heard of a dog who escaped the garden of her home at every opportunity to lie on the front door step of the house next door, the place that her best friend had originally lived before being adopted into her family eight years earlier. She still seemed to believe he would come bounding out to greet her.

Mostly, dogs appear to be able to move on without too much disturbance. Mum, though, missed her gentle black shadow and was very happy when Dad suggested we get another puppy. That's how a bundle of black fur called Raven came into our lives. She was given her name while she was in the litter: the breeder insisted all the puppies born that year should have names beginning with the letter R. The Guide Dogs for the Blind Association, which is the world's largest breeder and trainer of working dogs, follows the same rule, choosing names with the same initial letter for each litter of puppies.

Nita, by now a stately middle-aged lady, was a little bit apprehensive about the boisterous ball of energy who invaded her space, especially as Raven was allowed to sleep curled up in front of the Aga while she was confined to the passageway and loo. Not fair! And the new arrival seemed to be getting a lot of attention: there's nothing cuter than a Labrador puppy, so there was a lot of fuss from visitors. Nita's nose was out of joint at first, but she soon mellowed towards the puppy and accepted her into the family.

Raven grew to look like a replica Jemima, with a round body that looked podgy even though she was very fit, and she loved working as a gundog. All our house dogs are able to roam freely around the farm yard. We are lucky enough to live a long way from the road and they quickly learn to avoid tractors and other farm vehicles, so they are fairly safe. If we want them home, then shouting their name, or a whistle, soon brings them trotting back. Like Jemima, and most of her breed, Raven loved her grub to the point of being gluttonous, which sadly, led to her early death when she was only eight years old. While out and about around the farm buildings she unfortunately came across some spilt rat poison, which she snaffled down. Farms need to control vermin, but Raven's death underlines how important it is not to leave poisons in an accessible place.

It's not just poisons: there are lots of innocuous-seeming human foods that are dangerous to dogs. Most people know that chocolate, especially dark chocolate, should be kept well away from pets, and increasingly, more and more pet owners are aware that grapes (and raisins) can be a serious problem. A friend of mine had a greedy Labrador/springer cross that managed to eat half of a Christmas cake. If he hadn't been very, very sick, and vomited the whole thing out, he would have needed to have his stomach pumped.

Other foods that are dangerous to dogs include avocados, coffee, alcohol, onions, garlic and the kind of synthetic sweetener often used in low-calorie chewing gum. Responsible owners have a duty to keep all human foods out of reach of their dogs, but these in particular. Even the best-behaved dog will be tempted if left alone with the enticing smell of something that is well within his reach.

I firmly believe dogs should be fed a very good quality food designed for them. I was fascinated to find, when I made a programme for *Countryfile*, that the first pet foods came on to the market in the 1860s. Before that dogs and cats lived on scraps and anything they could scavenge, and naturally their lifespan was much shorter. The first proper dog food was made by an American electrician called James Spratt, who saw dogs scavenging for food in the London docks when he arrived in this country. He realised there was a market selling food to the rich English gentry for their shooting dogs and came up with a complete dog food that combined wheat meal, vegetables and meat all bound together with beef blood.

Today the pet food industry is vast, with £3 billion spent in Britain every year. Dog trainer Richard Clarke demonstrated to me for the programme just how important it is to check the quality of the food we give to our dogs. He showed me a tin of appetising-looking meaty chunks in gravy, only to reveal that actually the tin contained 80 per cent gravy and a lot less meat than I expected from the picture. He also poured out a portion of complete dry dog food with bits in green, brown and beige.

'Dogs are colour blind: the colours are designed for the owners, and the colours are artificial additives. The same additives and preservatives are in this food as are in a can of fizzy drink.' he said.

We talked about how a poor diet can affect a dog's behaviour, as well as its general health. Going to a supermarket and looking at the array of dog foods on sale can be, we agreed, a bit of a nightmare.

'It's about balance,' Richard said. 'The cheaper the food, the cheaper the ingredients. Look at the list of ingredients on the label: the one that comes first will be the one that accounts for the biggest proportion, so if it is cereal, avoid it.'

My dogs are a vital part of my working life, but I know that even if they were just family pets I would feel the same: I want to fuel them well. Just as I know my children need a balanced diet, so do my dogs. I also know the risks of feeding them titbits and extras: in a survey of 2,000 dog owners, Forthglade pet foods found that 60 per cent of owners fed their dogs part of their Christmas lunch, even though over half of all owners know that human food is harmful to pets.

I was shocked to be told that 15 per cent of all dog owners needed to take their pet to the vet, or get advice from a vet, on Boxing Day. Spurred on by this alarming statistic, I made a film for Forthglade to make owners aware of the problems their dogs face if they are too indulgent. It may feel like you are giving them a treat, but it is much better to be cruel to be kind, and ignore those pleading eyes. It is far better to treat your dog with an extra helping of affection and some play.

It's also important to check that the food you give your dog is appropriate for its age: puppies, adult dogs and senior dogs have different dietary requirements.

If Nita felt a bit put out by Raven's arrival in the family, another intruder, Tammy, caused a much bigger upset. Tammy was also a liver and white spaniel, although not identical to Nita because she had patches of ginger fur above her eyes. Technically, that made her a tri-colour spaniel. She belonged to my sister Libby, and was a bit of an impulse buy. Mum and Libby had been to visit our Auntie Nancy in hospital, and on the way back they saw a sign on a gate: 'Spaniel puppies for sale'. On the spur of the moment, they made the rash decision that it was time for the Henson household to have another springer, and this time it would be Libby's.

Tammy was a typical puppy, full of beans and into mischief, which didn't go down well with Nita, who regarded her as a tiresome nuisance. The puppy was not particularly well trained, mainly because Libby soon went travelling and then worked in America. Tammy grew up to feel that she was in no way subservient to

Nita, and the two jostled to be top spaniel. If I was around, the position automatically went to Nita, and then in my absence, when Libby was in residence, Tammy would strut around as top dog. There was no natural head of the pack, which normally happens when dogs live together.

The most difficult time was if both Libby and I were there together. On one occasion, the dogs started to fight, both determined to exercise their authority. Libby blamed Nita for the scrap and started shouting at her. This was a red rag to a bull for me, as I was definitely on Nita's side. In the end, as Libby and I railed at each other, I settled the argument by picking Libby up bodily, carrying her out into the farmyard and dunking her in the water trough. Luckily, we can look back on it now and laugh, although I'm not sure Libby was laughing at the time ...

When I returned from my travels with Duncan in Australia, New Zealand and America, which was the longest continuous time I was away from Nita or my family, the change I saw in her was dramatic. Within that year, she had aged: she was 14 when I got back, which is a good age for any dog, and particularly for a springer (their average age is 10, and only a few live to 14). Nita looked like a real old lady. I realised, with a lump in my throat, that while I was growing up, she was growing old.

She was thrilled to see me, shuffling to me as fast as her stiff old legs would allow, pushing her way to the front of the reception committee of family and friends who welcomed me home, and her tail never stopped wagging for the first couple of days. She followed me as I worked in the yard, always by my side, snuffling at the familiar scents, and brushing her unkempt coat against my legs every so often to remind me that she was there. I fondled her shaggy head, and made a note to myself to give her a makeover: I resolved to groom her and cut her nails. Her coat was duller and curlier than before, and there were grey hairs around her muzzle. Although she was slow and no longer had that spring that gives the springer its name, she was so happy to be with me, pottering about the farm.

One thing she could not manage on her arthritic legs was to come upstairs to my bed, and she accepted this, no longer waiting at the bottom of the stairs for my summons. So at times, as if to even the score, I got down and cuddled her on her bed. We both felt the same, unbreakable bond we made when our eyes first met as I peered into the tea chest. She was mine, and I was hers, but I realised sorrowfully that our time was running out.

Three weeks after I came home I found her one morning, peacefully curled up on her bed. She did not respond to the sound of my feet or my voice gently calling her name. I crouched down and realised she had died in her sleep: like Ben, she had the kindest and most peaceful death any dog can have. It was the perfect way to go, and I was grateful for it. She had lived well beyond the usual span for a springer, and it was as if she had kept herself going until she saw me again. Some uncanny sixth sense let her know that I was heading for home, and she waited for me. Then, having renewed our old, deep companionship, she allowed herself to go, happily and quietly.

The tears poured down my cheeks as I dug her grave at Buttington Clump, a group of trees not far from the farmhouse where all our family dogs are buried, and lowered her shaggy body into it. I knew I was saying farewell to the best and most faithful friend any young boy could ever have. I have now said goodbye to many wonderful dogs, but Nita was the first dog that was so personal to me, and I still well up when I think about her.

CHAPTER 4

My Aussie Mates

B ob is a dog who made a huge impact on me. I met
Bob during my gap year, when I was travelling
around the world with Duncan. Duncan and I met at
agricultural college and became great friends, and we
now work together as business partners at Bemborough
Farm. Back in 1988, though, we were young lads with
no responsibilities, who decided to see a bit of the
world before we settled down to full-time work. Being
farmers was a great help: it's not too difficult to find
jobs on farms if you are happy to be a labourer and
get stuck in. If you add in some skills, well, you can
earn enough to keep funding your travels when you
move on.

That's how we arrived in Katanning, a small town
two hours' drive from Perth, Western Australia. We'd
worked ourselves into the ground for six weeks with a
sheep-shearing gang, travelling to different farms to
help the shearers. It was exhausting, hot and pretty
relentless work.

So we were hoping for something a bit easier as we
rattled into Katanning in our beaten-up, ancient Ford
Falcon XB (a model only made in Australia) and made

our way to a farm which we had been told was looking for seasonal staff. The farmer had one question for us: did we prefer livestock or machines? It wasn't difficult to answer. I, like my dad, have always been a livestock man. Duncan is the arable man, and that's the machine part of farming (it's how we still divide up the farm work to this day). On this occasion Duncan certainly made the right call, and found himself having an easier time than I had working with the sheep. He spent all day driving a huge, state-of-the-art combine harvester, with a lovely air-conditioned cabin.

I, on the other hand, was asked to drench 16,000 Merino sheep. That number may not mean much to a non-farmer, but if I say I have a flock of 700 sheep at Bemborough now you get an idea of the scale of these outback farms or 'sheep stations'. (The largest has about 60,000 sheep – imagine going to sleep counting that lot!) Drenching was a familiar process to me: you have a pack on your back full of the necessary liquid worm treatment and a pipe with a gun on the end with which you squirt a dose down the throat of every sheep. But 16,000? I couldn't imagine any flock so vast.

Nowadays drenching is scientific; we take dung samples from our sheep that are dissolved into a solution so they can be examined under a microscope to assess what is known as a faecal egg count. An expert is then consulted on exactly how much of what chemical to use to treat our sheep. Back then, it was a matter of getting a dose of worm treatment into every single sheep, and without Bob I simply wouldn't have been able to do it. It would have been a two, or possibly three, man job, so Bob, who worked for nothing more than his daily feed, definitely earned his keep for the farmer. Bob was an Australian sheepdog, known as a kelpie. He was not the first I had seen on my trip, as the farmers rounding up their flocks for the shearing gang used them to help pen the sheep, and I'd watched in awe as these agile, enthusiastic dogs moved the sheep around quickly and expertly.

Kelpies are great yard dogs, handling huge mobs of sheep (the Australians talk about 'mobs', not flocks, and, with the numbers they handle, it's a good word ...) Kelpies are brilliant at moving the sheep and packing them into pens. They can bark on command and when they are penning the sheep they jump up on to their backs, moving from the front to the back of the mob barking and packing the animals in tighter.

At every sheep station we went to with the shearing gang, the farm owner (known in Australian slang as 'cockies', because the early settlers, like the cockatoos, made their homes along the edge of water courses) used their own dogs to get the sheep into the sheds for shearing. The shearing sheds over there were purpose built, with stands for as many as ten shearers (we generally have shearers who bring their own mobile stands, with a maximum of two or three). As roustabouts, or unskilled labourers, we had to do everything apart from the actual shearing: picking up the fleeces as soon as they were off the sheep, lying them flat on a table, picking out the dirty bits, then rolling them up and throwing them into the right bin for their grade, which was determined by a professional grader. It was hard work keeping up with the shearers, but if there was ever a pause we were expected to sweep up the shearing area, so that it was spotless and clear of any locks of wool.

The cockie would use his border collies to bring the sheep in from the paddocks, and Duncan and I would push the sheep into the catching pens. That was when I first saw a kelpie jump on to the back of the sheep. I'd heard about it, but never seen it. They squeezed the sheep in, but with pens containing as many as 500 sheep the dog had to be brought out quickly: if his presence made the sheep rush to one side they could crush each other.

I was fascinated and really impressed by the dogs' skill and hard work. Kelpies look a bit like dingoes and lots of Australians believe they are indeed descended from the ancient wild dogs that have lived on the Australian continent for at least 3,500 years. However, it's actually more complicated than that. Kelpies are almost certainly descended from collies brought over by early settlers, but there is scientific evidence that dingoes interbred with them, probably way back in the early nineteenth century when Australia was newly colonised. The interbreeding may have been accidental at first, but seeing the result some shepherds and farmers probably deliberately bred dingo into the mix. There is no real way of knowing because keeping dingoes or dingo-cross dogs was illegal, so nobody ever owned up to doing it. When sheep were introduced to Australia the dingo found them easy prey, and was therefore public enemy number one. There was a bounty for killing them, and a hefty fine for any farmer keeping a dingo cross. So naturally farmers were deliberately vague about their dogs' pedigree.

But DNA tests in recent years have shown that modern kelpies have 3–4 per cent dingo genes. That's only a small percentage, but perhaps enough to account for the differences between traditional collies and kelpies. Bill Robertson, a well-known breeder who organised the DNA testing, believes the dingo contributed 'the spirit, the grit and the ability to handle heat' to the character of the kelpie. I think most of us who love collies would be reluctant to credit the dingo with the spirit and the grit, as we see plenty of those qualities in our dogs, but the ability to handle heat is a vital addition to working dogs in Australia. If, as most experts believe, the first kelpies were collies brought over from Scotland (the word 'kelpie' means water spirit in Gaelic), the searing Australian heat would be something they needed to adapt to, and a dash of dingo blood almost certainly helped.

Bob had plenty of grit, but even he rebelled against the heat at times, retreating to the shade under the ute (utility vehicle) whenever he got the chance. As it was regularly 35 to 40 degrees as we worked together, I couldn't blame him.

The sheep I was drenching were Merinos, which have very valuable wool. Over in the UK, the fleece is generally a by-product of sheep farming and we earn very little from the wool. Our wool is coarser, because of the climate, and we farm sheep to produce lambs for meat, rather than specialising in wool, but Merinos produce wonderful white fleeces, the best in the world.

Merinos are stocky, strong sheep, with claims to be one of the oldest domesticated breeds of sheep around today, coming originally from Spain but thriving in the Australian climate (other breeds brought in during the early years of colonisation simply couldn't survive the conditions). They proved to be very good foragers, finding food in the scrubbiest, most parched landscape where the grass is brittle and doesn't look as if it has any nutritional value. The rams have big, spiralled horns, and are tough old characters, as I learnt from experience. The sheer size of the Australian landscape means that these sheep are left to their own devices most of the year. They grow so much dense, close, fine, valuable fleece that it has become a major export for Australian agriculture. As a farmer working with livestock you often get covered in manure and interestingly it was noticeable how Australian sheep smelt differently from our sheep back home. Their dung is dryer due to the parched pastures that they graze on, and it is a smell that still sits in my memory.

Pete Dewar, the farmer's son, took me out on the first day of my mammoth task to show me the ropes. Back home in those days when we wanted to drench the sheep we gathered them and brought them to our permanent handling pens in order to treat them. So it was a novelty for me to see the mobile handling pen that Pete towed behind the old Suzuki ute, a pick-up with a flat-bed back, and I made a mental note to tell Dad in my next postcard home how useful it was. We used to walk the sheep miles across fields to our permanent pens, which was stressful for the sheep, time consuming, and knackering for the dogs. This more efficient way of doing it was made necessary by the vast acreage of the sheep station, but I could see it would also be very helpful even on our English farm.

Pete and I drove out to one of the paddocks, set up the pen in a corner of the field and started to round up a mob of sheep. I was accustomed to paddocks of ten or twenty acres, but out there they were more like a thousand acres.

We circled the paddock in the ute, zig-zagging to gather the sheep together, Bob on the back of the ute barking. Because of the noise he made the sheep would draw together. We skirted the perimeter to make sure there were no dead or injured ones and then Bob, who was a lovely red colour with a thick coat, took over. He jumped off the vehicle and worked behind them very naturally, moving them along without any commands from me, doing his job. He didn't need the standard sheepdog commands for 'left', 'right', 'lie down', and there were no whistle commands like we use with our collies, but if a sheep or two broke away the command 'Go back' sent Bob off to round them all up again. To the postcard I was mentally writing for Dad I added, 'We really need one of these amazing dogs.'

Bob's next job was to get the sheep into the pen, and then he leapt on their backs to the command 'Get up on them', packing them in tight, and funnelled them through into a narrow race, where I could drench them one by one. On the command 'speak up' he would bark, which underpinned his control of the sheep, and 'That'll do', told him to stop immediately. It was a very efficient system: without him I would have been running up and down in the baking heat trying to push them through by myself (which is why it was a job that one man would not be able to do on his own).

Occasionally, if the sheep were too far apart, Bob would fall into the race and instead of leaping from back to back towards me, he would end up having to weave under their legs as the sheep leapt forward to avoid him and often ran over him. He would let out a whimper as he made his way through them, but still managed to pack the sheep in tight. As soon as they were in I shut the back gate. Bob would clamber out and flop in the shade under the ute until I called him out to help me fill the race again. It was easy to drench them when they were so tightly packed as they couldn't move away from the drench gun. This made it easier to put the gun into their mouths and helped stop them leaping about, which could have caused damage to their throats. It is a very labour-intensive job but needs to be done carefully and accurately for the welfare of the sheep.

After the first day with Pete showing me what I was expected to do, I was on my own. I had a map, and Pete told me which paddocks I'd find the sheep in, I had the ute and I had Bob. It was exhausting work in that interminable heat, and with flies hovering around the sheep and me. Flicking away flies is known as the Aussie salute, also known as the Barcoo salute (after the Barcoo River) or the Bush salute. It's an automatic gesture to keep bush flies away from the nose or mouth – or at least, that's what you hope.

I had to wear long sleeves and trousers tucked into my boots. I also wore an Akubra, the traditional wide-brimmed hat made of rabbit fur felt, named after the aboriginal word for 'head covering'. I needed to protect myself carefully from sunburn, not just the flies.

Driving out to the paddocks where Bob and I worked was an incredible experience. In the throbbing heat of the day – and it was hot from dawn onwards – the hard, dry ground shimmered, the noise of the parrots was a raucous din, and the sight of them was blinding in the harsh light. There were flocks of galah cockatoos with their vivid pink faces and breasts and soft grey back plumage chattering constantly and calling to each other, and smaller flocks of sulphur-crested cockatoos.

These are white with soft yellow feathers under their wings and on their tail and a flash of acid yellow on the crest of their head, and every bit as noisy as the galahs. They flocked on to the ground pecking around for seeds and insects, or perched on the silvery eucalyptus trees. As we bumped along in the ute I'd see grey kangaroos, hopping along beside or in front of us. For a young man in his early twenties alone in this landscape this was all amazing, and made even better by the constant presence of my mate, Bob.

If the noise from the birds was deafening, the din was increased by Bob's excited barking. He loved working and he couldn't wait to get started. His racket drove me mad every morning, but by the time we returned after a hard, hot day working, he would simply lie down and keep quiet behind me on the flat bed of the ute.

On my first day I drank the whole of my water supply from its big polystyrene container by midday: this was a mistake I didn't repeat, as I was a couple of hours' drive away from my base and couldn't pop back for more. I made sure from then on to fill more of the huge plastic containers to sling on to the ute every day. When I took a break of any sort, even to just have a swig of water, Bob made his way to the shade of the ute and in the hottest part of the day I had to coax him out to carry on working.

Most of the sheep were ewes, like a flock here, but there were also mobs of wethers, which are large, castrated males who were kept solely for the huge, valuable fleeces they produced each year. Castrating them was supposed to make them calmer and easier to handle, but they were still big beasts with minds of their own. At least they and the ewes did not have sharp horns like the rams, who really were my toughest customers.

One day I was drenching a hundred enormous rams in forty-degree heat, and I literally found it impossible to touch their backs, the fleece was so hot. They did not want to move and Bob was more stubborn than usual, refusing to come out from the shade of the vehicle. The flies were driving me mad and I genuinely feared I would die of heat stroke.

That was when I realised that perhaps Bob was trying to tell me something. The old Noël Coward song (which no doubt my famous grandfather, the actor and comedian Leslie Henson, sang sometimes) about mad dogs and Englishmen being the only creatures foolish enough to go out in the midday sun was clearly true, and Bob was certainly not happy being cast in the role of a mad dog, however bonkers the Englishman was. I loaded him back into the ute, bumped across the rough paddock back to the shack where Duncan and I were living and settled in the shade until about 5pm, when the heat was abating. At this time of day Bob jumped willingly on to the back of the pick-up, and off we went again, working late until the job was done.

I never asked the Dewars whether without me they would have done the job in the cooler evenings; perhaps they laughed at me attempting it earlier. From then on, I was on the late shift.

Dotted around the massive station were deep man-made ponds, which were called dams. At over 30 yards long by 15 yards wide they were more like small reservoirs and were built to provide water, a very precious commodity, for cattle and sheep. Despite the fact that the water was pretty dirty and slimy, it was very tempting. At the end of a long day in the heat I often plunged into the cool, if filthy, dam that was closest to our home. It was big enough to have a good swim, as long as you weren't too particular about the colour of the water. At the end of a long, dusty day, it felt great.

The dams were full of crayfish, or 'yabbies' as the locals called them. They were regarded as a pest because if they burrowed into the walls of the dams the water would leak away. But they were a treat for Duncan and me. Pete Dewar taught us how to catch them. The yabbies were meat eaters with a great sense of smell and so were attracted to lumps of meat wrapped in a net. When this was thrown into the dam on the end of a rope and weighted down the yabbies would try their best to get to the meat, getting their claws tangled in the netting, so all you had to do was leave it for an hour and then haul them out. We would catch them, cook them and eat them with relish.

Our home was a shack, about the same size as a mobile home but raised on stilts, at the side of the farmhouse. There's an established tradition in the outback for building raised homes because they are better ventilated and cooler, as well as deterring some of the snakes and spiders (although not all ...) There were fly screens at the windows and door, and we soon learned to keep these closed. We had two bedrooms and more or less all we needed. We cooked our own food, which meant a fairly basic repertoire of chilli and spaghetti Bolognese, so the yabbies were a welcome change. We had to do our own shopping, but the nearest town was a good drive away, so the farmer's wife would sometimes take a list of what we needed and bring it back when she fetched her own supplies.

Bob slept in the yard with the other dogs: there were a couple of other kelpies and a couple of border collies. They were kept on long chains, and had barrels to sleep in out of the heat and trees to give them shade. Dog pellets were thrown to them, and sometimes they got raw meat – chopped up sheep or kangaroo meat.

For the month I worked with Bob, I came to adore him. He wasn't a demonstrative animal, but I think I earned his respect. He worked devotedly for me and I realised how impossible it would have been without him. Our weeks at Katanning passed very quickly, as Duncan and I were both working long and hard, and the time to move on came quickly.

Back home from our adventures, Dad was very receptive to my new ideas. He was always very open to new advances in farming and, besides, I think he wanted to encourage me, as he relished the idea that I would one day take over Bemborough Farm. He could see that I loved the place as much as he did, and that my travels may have broadened my farming experience but they had also cemented my conviction that this was the place I wanted to live and work.

We bought a quad bike and the mobile handling pen system. Next on the list was the kelpie, and that was down to me. If it was to be my dog I had to research and find it. At that time, in 1989, there were not too many kelpie breeders in England, but I saw an advertisement for a new litter in Hampshire. I drove down and instantly fell in love with a little red bitch, choosing red because she reminded me of Bob. The mother of the litter had been imported from Australia, so this little one was a first generation English kelpie.

I called her Bundy, naming her after the famous Australian Bundaberg rum – I'd enjoyed a few rums while I was out there, and she was a lovely dark rum colour. She was a smashing dog from the first day I had her. I taught her to 'speak', and she was an excellent yard dog, and great at getting the sheep into the pens. She was not so good out in the fields: some kelpies are on a par with collies in the paddocks, but it's rare to get one that does both jobs equally well.

By the time I bought Bundy I had moved out of the farmhouse and into a bungalow on the farm. It had been previously used by the stock manager, but when he left there was no need to replace him, as I was now working full time and Mum and Dad wanted to give me some more independence.

Bundy moved into the loo. Just like Nita had spent many happy hours sleeping in the downstairs toilet at the farm, Bundy accepted that her bed was next to the plumbing in the bungalow. Unlike the kelpies in Australia and the sheepdogs on our farm, she slept inside, but she never ventured into the living rooms. She was half-house dog, half-outside dog: house-trained and great company, but definitely a working dog, who liked nothing better than joining me at the crack of dawn to get on with my farm chores.

She was very good natured and quickly got on with the other dogs on the farm, Raven and Bill, working well alongside Bill. Dad and I both thought she was a real success and I was keen to breed from her. There were not too many kelpies in Britain at the time, but I found a kelpie dog living not too far away and he served her. I didn't take her to be scanned: I realised she was pregnant because she was getting bigger and coming in to milk. When I knew she was near her time I didn't take her out to work with me, but left her curled up on her bed.

When I got home she wasn't there, and I realised I had left the door from the kitchen into the rest of the bungalow open. Normally, Bundy would not have gone through, but on this occasion she had found her way into my bedroom and was under my bed. I'd left a book I was reading on the floor next to the bed and

Bundy had ripped it up and made a nest for herself under the bed, where I found her proudly licking one, really large, puppy.

I searched around all the other bedrooms and the living room to see if there were any others. Then I sat with her waiting for more puppies to come, although she was showing no signs of still being in labour. After a couple of hours I rang the vet and he told me that it was possible for a bitch to have one large pup, although it's not common. It's a great credit to Bundy as a mother that she raised her pup really well: I now know that singleton puppies can have a hard time, not having the warmth of their litter mates and sometimes gorging themselves because there are no others competing for the mother's milk. Apparently, there is a risk of such a large puppy getting stuck during the birth and a Caesarean being the only answer. But Bundy had delivered him on her own, showed no signs of having had a bad time, and was looking after him devotedly. What a star.

We called him Red because he had the same colouring as Bundy, and when he was old enough to leave her I gave him to Duncan. Duncan, like me, really liked the kelpies we met in Australia. At this time, he had a farm tenancy on Bryher, the smallest of the inhabited Scilly islands, with his wife Becky. Red took to his new life with enthusiasm: the island is only one and a half miles long by a mile wide, and Red regarded it all as his territory. He was a lovely, friendly dog, and everyone on the island knew him. He would go down to the quay to greet the boatloads of tourists when they arrived and stood proudly on the bow of Duncan's launch when they went to St Mary's to go shopping.

Red eventually moved back to Bemborough Farm when Duncan and I took over from my Dad and his partner, John Neave (who was known to me and my sisters as our lovely 'Uncle' John throughout our childhood). By this time the farm had expanded, after I'd convinced the landowners that I was serious about remaining at Bemborough. My private life had also changed: the bungalow had gone from being a scruffy pad that I shared with two mates in which I often had late-night parties, to the first home for me and my girl-friend Charlie.

With Dad and John both looking forward to retiring and with Cotswold Farm Park rare breeds centre to run as well, I needed help. Rather than employ someone, I knew that the best move was to go into partnership with Duncan, who was not only a great mate but also had all the skills needed to complement mine. Before Duncan moved to the Scilly Isles he had worked for an agricultural mortgaging corporation and got a really good grounding in business management and financial budgets, something I have to admit is not my strength. He was also happy to take on the arable side of the farm while I ran the livestock and Cotswold Farm Park. After spending a year travelling with him, living in each other's pockets, I knew we would work together well, an instinct that proved to be completely right.

He and Becky and their two children were happy to move back to the mainland, and Red came with them. He did not spend too much time on the farm (the usual problems of a dog among bitches ...) but I was surprised that when he and Bundy met, neither of them showed signs of recognising the other – or perhaps I was just not tuned in enough to see it.

By the time she met Red again, Bundy had had another two litters. Again, when I decided to breed from her, there was the problem of finding a suitable father. Wherever I went, if I met anyone who was interested in or had kelpies I discussed it, and one day I met a chap from Northumberland who agreed with me that the best way forward was to import kelpie semen from Australia and to get our bitches pregnant by artificial insemination. As a farmer I'm familiar with artificial insemination in animals, and I wasn't worried about it. We contacted an Australian breeders' association and we both bought some straws of semen (narrow PVC tubes into which semen is sucked, and then frozen in liquid nitrogen). We chose semen from a dog called Bonang Tommy, a black and tan dog from Bonang, Victoria, with a list of trialling wins to his credit. His CV said he was good at backing (jumping on the sheeps' backs) and at barking on command, and that he had a good breeding history.

The straws of semen were flown to Edinburgh, where they were stored at a laboratory that has the facilities and specialises in artificial insemination, waiting for Bundy to come into season.

When she did I was about to contact the lab to supply me with my straws and the vet to book in the insemination. In the meantime, I took all the sensible precautions, locking her in the bungalow when she was not by my side, but I underestimated the determination of a testosterone-driven dog. They can scent a bitch in season from as far away as three miles in the countryside, and one whiff and they are transformed from obedient, gentle dogs into crazed, lustful creatures who will stop at nothing to get to the object of their desire. In this case, a wooden back door was no deterrent to a black and white collie belonging to one of our neighbours: he simply gnawed his way through it until he had a hole big enough to get through to Bundy.

I was really annoyed, but I didn't rush her to the vet for a scan and an injection to end the pregnancy: I let nature take its course, crossing my fingers and hoping the marauding dog had not scored a bullseye. Of course he had, and nine weeks later Bundy gave birth to a litter of ten kelpie–collie crosses. I was relieved that it was a large litter (kelpies normally have between four and seven pups), as it meant the one single pup she had first time was not a pattern. They were delightful, Bundy coped very well with them all, and I didn't have any trouble finding homes for them. Nowadays, kelpie–collie crosses are sought after by shepherds and farmers, but back then the kelpie was still a little-known element. I let my neighbour know what I thought of his dog, the father of this litter, but the truth is that I understand how hard it is to physically restrain a dog when there is a bitch in heat in the area. It underlined to me why I prefer bitches.

As a responsible owner, I couldn't breed from Bundy again until the following year: bitches should be given at least one season rest between litters, and only irresponsible owners (and dreadful puppy farms) would put a bitch through birthing again in less than a year. When the time came, I kept her very safe until I could get her to the vet for insemination. I'm used to seeing it done with cattle, when the insemination takes place vaginally, but the vet explained that with smaller animals like dogs the best way was to anaesthetise her, cut her open and put the semen straight into her fallopian tube. She said it was more efficient, and it certainly worked.

Bundy gave birth, this time to 12 pups. A really big litter; some red, some black and two yellow ones. I hadn't seen yellow ones in Australia, and I wondered if somewhere in the past either Bundy or the father had some yellow Labrador genes. I rang Pete Dewar in Australia and he put me straight. Apparently yellow is a perfectly normal colour for kelpies, but they are not popular in Australia because their skin is pinker, more susceptible to sunburn, and their pale pads and noses can get sore in the sand and dry ground. Yellow ones, as a result, are usually not kept.

But the heat wasn't a problem in England and I so liked the look of my little yellow pups that I decided I would keep one of them. I called her Ronnie, full name Ronnie Barker, even though she was a girl.

Then I faced a dilemma. Twelve was a lot of puppies to feed, and Bundy only had the usual eight teats. How would she cope? I rang the vet and he said the best option would be to keep six or eight, and to be fair on Bundy I should get rid of some.

So I got two washing baskets, put all the puppies on the kitchen table, and started to sort them out. The ones I was keeping would go into one basket; the others, who were going to be put down, would be consigned to the other. I favour bitches, naturally, so they had a good start. Clearly the bigger ones had a better chance of survival, and so the small runty ones had to go. It was agony, as I debated their futures, changing my mind over and over again.

In the end, I had four 'rejects', all boys, and I found myself muttering my apologies to them. 'Sorry, little one, I wish I didn't have to do this.' They were tiny, blind, nuzzling each other as they squirmed around looking for their mother's teats.

It seemed so wrong, and I hated being the one who decided their fate. Although I am used to dealing with the deaths of animals, it doesn't come without senti-ment, and I had a lump in my throat as I looked at the little ones whose life was going to be over so soon.

'I can't do this to you,' I finally said to one little black fellow, lifting him up and putting him in the other basket. Then, when I looked down at the last three, I said: 'D'you know what? I'm putting you all back with your mum. It's survival of the fittest, and you are going to have to take your chances …'

They all snuggled up to Bundy straight away, and she was delighted to have her brood back, licking them enthusiastically.

'It's up to you now, old girl,' I said to her and I went off to bed, leaving her to it. I expected that some would not survive, but at least it would not be my choice.

Why did I doubt her? Bundy was a natural mother, and when I came into the kitchen the next morning she had her pups neatly sorted into two groups, six of them feeding from her and the other six asleep. She must have been exhausted, because no sooner was one shift of pups full of milk and drowsy than the other lot were waking up and demanding food.

I told the vet what was happening, and he advised me to start feeding some of them with a pipette, as he was afraid Bundy would not have enough milk to keep this up. She hardly had time to feed herself, let alone rest. So I bought a pipette normally used for feeding kittens, and some powdered puppy milk replacer. Now I was also part of the feeding production line, on duty every four hours to top up those hungry little pups.

At this time Charlie and I were serious about each other, but she was still living and working in London, coming down to stay with me at weekends. It was hardly a lovely romantic time, as she was also roped into the feeding rota. On the vet's advice, as soon as the pups could lap from a bowl we weaned them. Every single one grew into a healthy, good-sized dog, and I was able to sell them all – apart, of course, from Ronnie Barker.

One of the pups, Sledge, went on to be a renowned sheepdog locally, and I would bump into him and his owner at various times. I shudder at the thought that he may have been one of the boys I put into the 'wrong' basket ... Another one I kept in close touch with was a little bitch called Tui, named after a kiwi beer, who went to the stockman who was working on the farm. Some of the others went to nearby homes, so I saw them from time to time. The other little yellow one went to a guy who eventually bred from her, so Bundy's line definitely lives on.

A little time afterwards it occurred to me that I was paying to store the rest of the imported semen at the laboratory in Edinburgh. I did not intend to breed from Bundy again: she'd had three litters, which I feel is enough for a bitch. Nowadays the limit imposed by the Kennel Club is four litters over a lifetime, but at the time I was breeding with Bundy it was six, which most reputable breeders felt was too many. I was never into breeding as a living: I breed from my dogs because I feel it is good for the bitches to have a litter, and because I like the idea of keeping the genes of these wonderful dogs going, for myself and to share them with others. Of course, I do sell them as it covers the cost of breeding.

I would never be able to use the semen on my next kelpie, Ronnie, as it wouldn't be sensible to get her in pup to her own father. So I put an advert with my phone number in *Farmers Weekly*: For sale, kelpie semen. Two or three evenings later the phone rang and Charlie answered it.

'It's for you. It's about the kelpie semen,' she said, handing the phone to me.

'Oh, great,' I said. In my usual way I launched into an enthusiastic description of the semen.

'It's from a really good dog in Australia, Bonang Tommy. He's won lots of trials, he's got a great breeding record. We've had a wonderful litter from the semen, twelve healthy pups ...'

The man on the other end of the phone tried to interrupt, but I babbled on. Finally, I said, 'Tell me about your bitch. What colour is she?'

He spoke flatly, finally able to get a word in edgeways: 'I don't have a dog. I don't want to breed dogs. I've been trying to tell you. I'm your Dell PC man, I'm coming to install your computer ...'

Kelpie semen / Dell PC man ... It was an easy mistake to make. But it must have sounded very bizarre to the computer expert, and he gave us a couple of odd looks when he eventually came to install the new PC.

Bundy lived to a good age of 12, but eventually, following numerous operations to have lumps removed from her mammary tissue, she became seriously ill and passed away. I grieved for her: she'd been a great mate, a good worker, all I have ever wanted in a dog.

Ronnie was a smashing little pup, and she, too, grew into a great dog. She was not quite as good as her mother when it came to working the sheep, but handy enough, and a good companion. She and I bonded well, and I still feel emotional when I remember that we nearly lost her when she was two years old.

Ronnie went to the vet for her annual injections, and in retrospect it's clear she had an infection and was running a temperature at the time. The injections then caused a complete breakdown of her immune system: Vaccine Induced Autoimmune Disease is recognised by vets, with the symptoms being triggered or exacerbated by the vaccines. It happened very quickly after her vaccination and she went into a major decline the following day.

Our vet referred her immediately to the Bristol School of Veterinary Science, where they have state-of-the-art facilities and all the most up-to-date treatments. They had seen cases like hers before, but I was told it was rare. I was also warned that her survival was touch and go, and it was with a very heavy heart that I drove back home after leaving her there. She looked so weak and helpless. She spent two weeks there, on steroids, and all the time I was expecting the phone to ring with bad news. The house felt so empty without her.

At last, thank goodness, I was able to bring her home. She was skin and bone; she'd lost all her weight and muscle tone. I had to tempt her to eat, and I tried different foods: cooked chicken, beef mince, eggs and milk, rice, anything of which I could to get her to take more than a mouthful or two. It was a slow, steady recovery, and I very gradually weaned her off steroids, reducing the dose incrementally.

It was while we had Ronnie that Charlie and I had our two children, Ella and Alfie. Alfie, in particular, bonded with Ronnie; they were like two little mates. I loved seeing Alfie toddling around the farmyard with his faithful yellow shadow by his side. Ronnie, in the tradition of my dogs, also slept in the loo, and like Bundy she was half house dog and half farm dog; a pet but one who worked. I don't remember teaching either of them to be house-trained – they were both naturally clean and it happened without much effort on my part.

Ronnie lived until she was ten, but she had a sad ending. She was coughing and wheezing, and was given a course of antibiotics by the vet. Then, to my dismay, she started passing blood, so I took her to the vet where an X-ray showed she had swallowed a needle which was causing internal bleeding. The vet wanted to operate immediately, but admitted there was no guarantee that the needle would be located.

I was reluctant to rush her into having a general anaesthetic and so decided to get a second opinion from the senior vet, who I knew well. He ordered a scan which included her chest and it revealed a large tumour, which was obviously the reason for her breathing problems. He told me that there was really no hope: she had four or five months left at the most, and that she would be increasingly uncomfortable and in pain. I didn't vacillate. It was a very tough decision, but I knew it was the right one: I asked him to put her down. As with every dog I have had put down, the procedure is simple and they die painlessly. I held her in my arms, muttering goodbyes to a faithful, kind, hard-working dog, everything any owner could ask for. Then I carefully drove her back to the farm, for burial among all those other wonderful dogs at Buttington Clump. I cherish the fact that the dogs are buried on the farm: it feels right. This was their home in life and it is where they remain.

Alfie, who was four at the time, was very upset, and he really missed her. But farm children learn the cycle of life early, seeing animals breed, and then, eventually, seeing them die. For Alfie it was his first experience of grieving for a dog to whom he was very close, and I felt for him. But I also knew it is something we all have to learn to accept. I loved Ronnie, and missed her cheerful little snout pushing its way into my hand. But she had a comfortable end, and the alternative was not good.

CHAPTER 5

Three Wonderful Dogs

S ix months after I bought Bundy I acquired another sheepdog, this time a traditional border collie. I have now had a succession of border collies, but that doesn't mean I have turned my back on kelpies. One day, when I am doing less television work and have more time on the farm, I'd like to have another of those wonderful dogs. Our livestock manager has a kelpie-collie cross, which is another great option, with some shepherds classing them as the best of both breeds.

I bought Fenn from a great friend of mine, Dick Roper, who manages a farm not far from mine. He's an acclaimed sheepdog trialler, winning the *Countryfile* One Man and His Dog competition for England in 2016. The competition involves teams of a senior handler and a junior handler from Scotland, Wales, Ireland and England, and for many years has been a huge TV hit, now having its own slot on *Countryfile*.

I'm going to describe Dick as the doyen of sheepdog trainers, because he'll enjoy the joke. When he first heard the word 'doyen' he went home and looked it up in the dictionary, to find it means 'outstanding in his field'. So he reckons it is a description that fits him (and all shepherds) because he spends his days out, standing in a field.

'Outstanding' is a good description of him, especially as he won the championship despite having lost the sight in one of his eyes, which is a real handicap in trialling. But he's a cheerful person whose attitude to life is, 'Yes, I'm sad to have lost the sight of an eye, but on the other hand, at least it's not a red wine allergy …'

I first met Dick when I joined Dad and Uncle John on the farm and I went on a sheepdog training course organised by the Agricultural Training Board. I took Bundy, and that was the occasion when Dick made his unforgettable judgment on kelpies, something along the lines of: 'Sell her and get yourself a border collie …' He stands by that opinion.

'Collies are accurate in the way they work. They stare at anything that is moving, which is why puppies who live on a farm will chase vans and bikes before they get near to sheep. They don't run around like headless chickens, they run with purpose and balance, and that's what makes them so good at their job. The amount of "eye" they have governs how close they can work the sheep, how they can make the sheep go in the direction they want.' (As I've explained, eye is the ability of a dog to fix its stare on a moving object, essential when working sheep at a high level.)

I'm afraid Bundy had no eye; she was scatty. She wanted to work, but she never had an accurate point of balance. She was just as happy chasing the sheep away as rounding them up and bringing them to you, but with no style or accuracy.

'And that's the difference between collies and nearly all other types of working dogs. They have eye, and they'll work anything moving – they'll work the water coming out of a hose pipe,' said Dick.

Clearly, I defer to Dick in all things to do with collies. But I think he was a bit harsh on poor Bundy: she wasn't great by his standards out in the paddock, but she was a wonderful yard dog. Dick particularly loves border collies, but, despite his criticisms of kelpies, he recognises the abilities of other strains of collies. Bearded collies have less eye, but are still very good with sheep. One of our assistant stockmen bred beardies and he handled sheep well with them, but they would never reach trialling standard. They are lovely strong dogs, though, which is sometimes a great advantage.

Welsh collies have no eye, but they can still work sheep and are more versatile because they are also good at moving cattle. Dick admits he was very impressed when he was judging trialling in Brazil and he found the same dogs being used in the sheep classes and the cattle classes.

'It was very exciting watching them moving half-broken Aberdeen Angus steers around, and then seeing them working a flock of sheep. But you cannot use a good border, with real "sticky eye", with cattle because they are too stationary and will get kicked or trodden on, so you need a free-flowing dog like a Welsh collie.'

Dick has trained all sorts of dogs: Labradors, spaniels, German shepherd dogs among others. He believes that collies have brains that are wired differently, almost completely controlled by their eyes.

'The whole thought process of a collie is different. Other breeds are great at other tasks, but for working a flock of sheep, give me a collie every time. There's something about the German shepherds that makes me think they have a bit of collie in their breeding, but not enough ...'

Dick is often asked to help out with dogs that are not behaving well, and he says the first thing to consider is their circumstances. I know, because I've seen it myself several times, that the very best of dogs can be ruined by owners who don't understand the animal and it becomes unruly and even nips people. Dick cites the example of a serviceman based at a nearby RAF station who was worried about the behaviour of his collie.

'It never takes its eyes off the budgie,' Dick was told. The owner and his wife had a new baby, and they were worried that the collie now seemed to be watching the baby with the same fervent attention as it focussed on the budgie.

'I told them that the dog was 99 per cent guaranteed to be the best protector their baby could ever have, but there was a 1 per cent chance it would nip, especially if it was bottled up all day without enough exercise or mental stimulation. They gave the dog to me and I rehomed him with a shepherd who found him to be a really great worker.'

One reason for the problem of collies going to the wrong homes, which I've talked about, is that people see Dick and all the other great sheepdog trainers on television, they read that collies are so intelligent, and they think they would like to own one, without any consideration of what they can offer the dog. Some collies thrive as pets, particularly if they are taken to agility classes, especially flyball competitions. Flyball is a sport where competing teams of dogs race across hurdles, then release a tennis ball which they have to carry back before the next dog in the relay team can set off. It's fun to watch – they have competitions at Crufts – but it is also stimulating enough to keep a collie's brain and limbs busy. But so many get nothing more than a half-hour walk in the park and spend the rest of their day confined inside.

So it is from Dick that I have learned most of my sheepdog training – and unlearned the bad habits I developed growing up!

When he expressed his disdain for Bundy, I was, at first, determined to defy him, and prove that I could train Bundy to round up sheep the way I wanted her to do it. I still had the image of Bob, the kelpie in Australia, in my mind. But after a while I realised that my best plan was for Bundy to work the sheep in the pens and to get another dog for out in the fields, because rounding up sheep was not her greatest talent. Dick, I was forced to admit, was right.

I rang him up and he told me of a litter of puppies, bred from one of his own trialling dogs and a mother who was kept as a pet. The sire was Dick's dog Cap, who was a national champion sheepdog four times, so I was keen to see the puppies. We looked at the litter together and Dick helped me choose the right one for me. His rule of thumb for choosing a good pup is to look for a brave and curious one, with good 'eye'. Dick likes to get a broom and see which ones in the litter chase it as he moves it around, showing that they have a natural inbred herding instinct and a fascination with anything in motion. He also drops an empty metal feeding dish, making a loud clatter. Any dog that doesn't run away may well be deaf or stupid, so he ignores that one. Then he looks for the pups who come back to the source of the noise quite quickly, with curiosity, not too frightened but naturally wary.

I knelt down on the floor with the puppies. There were two bitches I liked, but one of them came up to me, taking more interest in me than the others, jumping to try and get on my knees. As Dick says:

'A puppy chooses you, not the other way round. It's an old adage, but it's true: a puppy will choose the right owner if it has the chance. You can't hide your character from a dog, they can judge you in a few seconds. It's part of their history, from when they lived in packs and had to understand the hierarchy very rapidly. They learn, as puppies, which ones to get on with, which to back off from, which to scrap with. You rarely see a major fight in a pack, because they each understand their position. And that's how they quickly judge humans, knowing instinctively who they will get on with.

'It's because they make instant judgments that they are also good guard dogs, sensing which human beings are friends and which are foes.'

Predictably, like everything people like Dick and me know instinctively, there has now been a university study to confirm it: scientists in Japan have demonstrated that dogs are good at working out who their masters' friends are, and similarly they remember anyone who has not shown kindness to their owner. The scientists' conclusion is the same as Dick's, that dogs are very quick to sort out who is who in a pack, and will be ready to protect the animals (or people) who look after them. It demonstrates, they concluded, that dogs show sophisticated intelligence and make use of their observations 'to reach a decision about which individuals to interact with or to avoid'.

As Dick says: 'Puppies will go to a person they like, automatically, and a confident dog will go to a confident person. A subservient puppy can still flourish, but will be much happier with a gentler owner.'

If Dick is interested in a litter, he tries wherever possible to make his choice when the pups are seven weeks old, which he believes is the right time to assess their characters.

'There are lots of odd myths around choosing a sheepdog, but one that is true is that at seven weeks a dog's eventual character is established. They may go through a mad teenage period between seven months and up to 12 or 14 months, but then they will revert to the personality they had at seven weeks.

'Many police forces also make their selection from litters at seven weeks, choosing the dogs best suited to police work and rehoming the ones whose personalities don't measure up to the criteria they need. At one time, far more puppies went forward for training only to fail at a later date, which was expensive. By choosing well at seven weeks the failure rate is cut back, and the other puppies go on to work that suits them better, perhaps security work, or simply to be pets.'

Dick also judges pups by the position of their tails. He doesn't like dogs who keep their tails up – another strike against Bundy, who always worked with her tail up.

'In a collie if the tail is up it is a sign that they are tense, under pressure, or even that they are simply thick. I like a tidy tail. If it is rammed under their body that is just as bad, as it means they are wound up or scared. What I look for in a border collie is a nice relaxed tail, because that signals a relaxed dog. Other signs of tension are when they eat sheep droppings, or when they yawn.'

The little pup I chose was beautifully marked, even at ten weeks old, which was when I saw her for the first time. She was adorable and seemed to like me too, and I was very happy to take her home with me. Of course the first thing you need to do when you have a new puppy is choose a name. With a dog I am a strong believer that it needs to be something short and snappy, ideally with one syllable. That's why many sheepdogs are called names like Fly, Pat, Meg or Ben, so that they can be said quickly and clearly with no chance of misunderstanding. For my little puppy I wanted something a little bit different to the ordinary and went for the name Fenn.

It didn't take Bundy long to accept her, which was probably easier because Fenn was kept outside in a kennel, as working sheepdogs are, and Bundy slept in the loo. At first Fenn had a lamp in there to keep her warm. Our kennels are large, with a comfortable bed for the dogs. Working sheepdogs housetrain themselves very quickly: a young pup will mess in its kennel but it soon learns to keep its own home clean.

Fenn was a beautiful black and white bitch. If you asked a child to draw a sheepdog, the result would be Fenn. She looked exactly the way everyone thinks a sheepdog should look, and her behaviour didn't let the side down, either.

The first thing any dog of any breed needs to learn is its own name, and to come to its owner. It needs to come not in answer to a polite request, but on command, obeying an order. If it doesn't come at once, don't shout at it or punish it. You can do this with a disobedient older dog, but a puppy has to feel that being by your feet is the safest and best place. Teaching a dog to come to you is the most essential, but also one of the hardest, lessons. When the dog obeys, even if not straightaway, it should be rewarded with a stroke and some words of approval. The dog will know from the tone of your voice that you are pleased with him. Dick's advice is to ration stroking and fussing over a dog, so that when you do it really knows that it has earned your praise. Much harder said than done! I'm nowhere near as strict, and I'm happy to stroke and fondle the ears of my sheepdogs on greeting them every morning. I treat them a bit like when you see a pack of wolves on a natural history programme, when they wake in the morning and they all fuss around one another, whimpering, wagging their tails and saying hello. This is all over in a matter of minutes and then it is off for the hunt. I do the same with my dogs, a lot of fuss to say good morning and then it is off to work.

The importance of having control of your dog and being able to get it to come or stop on a sharp command is obviously fundamental. Every parent knows that a child who doesn't obey first time can end up in danger, touching something hot or walking into a road. So it's something that every dog owner, even if the dog is a pet who will never work, needs to be able to do.

Fenn was easy to train. At six months old she met the sheep for the first time, and she instantly took to them and the job. I knew she would: I'd seen her trying to round up the chickens in the yard. It always amazes me how the instinct is there in sheepdogs, thanks to selective breeding down the centuries. The herding instinct is part of natural hunting behaviour, but these dogs have learnt not to follow through and kill their prey, but to try and please their owners by bringing the prey, in this case sheep, to them.

If a dog is really difficult to teach to come (or any other behaviour problem) Dick told me his method of bringing it into line: 'Dogs are pack animals, and even if you only have one dog it feels part of a pack with you. So the worst thing that can happen is to be excluded from the pack. You do this by ignoring them, making it clear you don't want anything to do with them. If you are in a field, simply walk away and shut the gate. When the dog attempts to follow you, ignore it, leave it there. If you speak to them at all, tell it to clear off. It sounds harsh, but you'll find that it quickly picks up on the fact that it has to come when it is called.'

Of course, Dick is training sheepdogs, and it is much easier to enforce rules when the dog lives outside, which explains why most working sheepdogs are kennelled (plus the fact that they are often covered in mud and muck). The same rules apply to family pets, although it is much harder to enforce them within a family. I may be trying to ignore the puppy, but that doesn't mean that Charlie, Ella and Alfie will ignore her ... puppies get mixed messages, especially if they are living inside with several family members.

I am a strong believer that the family should decide what the rules are for the dog in the house and everybody should make their best efforts at sticking to them. At home we don't allow the dog to have titbits from the table as this leads to begging when you are trying to eat, which drives me mad. Our dogs are never allowed upstairs, so even one paw on the bottom step is out of bounds. Many people let their dogs upstairs, even sleeping on their beds, but when you live in a muddy farmyard it really doesn't work. I also think that a dog should have its own bed and as it views you as the alpha male/female, it does not have the right to sleep on yours. A bit of dog psychology, which I am sure is right. For a similar reason, our dogs aren't allowed on the furniture. It is always important to scold a dog at the moment it breaks the rules so that it can identify with what it has done wrong. We all use the same commands so there is no confusion, and simply say the word 'No'.

Trialling dogs like Dick's, of course, have to learn so much more even than a working dog on a farm, like Fenn, and the amount of time given over to training them has to be so much greater. I never took up trialling when I was younger. Partly because trials take place at weekends, and, back then, weekends were for playing rugby ...!

Also, if I am honest, I don't think I would ever have been good enough. But I love watching sheepdog trials, and I'm full of admiration for the experts like Dick, just as I'm full of admiration for hill shepherds who control

My sister Libby with Chemmers, the first dog in my life, and her puppies

Nita was the only dog allowed upstairs – Mum and Dad turned a blind eye

My kelpie, Bundy

Red, Bundy's first pup

Grown up Red enjoying life on Bryher, where he lived with my friend Duncan and his family

Bundy was a natural mother, rearing this huge litter

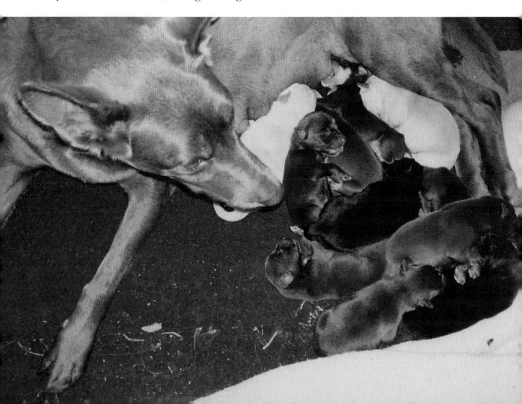

Fen, a great sheepdog
and a great companion

Ella with a loving guardian, Fen

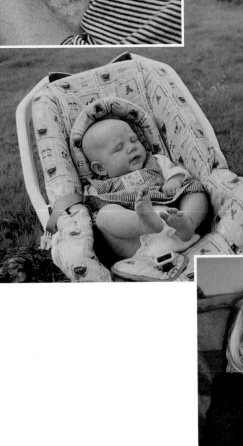

Little together: Ella with
one of Fen's puppies

Three friends in the sunshine: Ronnie, Dolly and Maud

'The cold doesn't worry us, we've got fur coats.' Maud and Pearl love romping in the snow

Two lovely mates, Maud and Pearl

Ronnie Barker, my lovely kelpie

A boy's best friend: Alfie with Ronnie

Dolly as a pup

On top of the world: Me, Alfie, Dolly and Boo

a dog in a howling gale from one and a half miles away. It's awe inspiring to watch them.

I started training Fenn with the sheep by walking her along the edge of the field and then taking her into the corner with a small group of sheep (I used Bundy to round them up). Then, because her instinct was to be on the other side of the sheep, I made her sit before giving her the command to go to the right of the sheep – 'Away'. When she mastered it we went to another corner to learn the 'left' command – 'come by'.

We practised for 15 to 20 minutes every morning and every evening. I learnt from Dick that if she got it wrong the worst thing I could do was to show anger. I had to walk away, put the dog back in the kennel, let my steam out, have a cup of tea then go back later. Different dogs take different amounts of time: sometimes weeks, sometimes months. Fenn was very good, and she learnt the voice commands and whistles within days.

After mastering right and left, I moved the training to the middle of the field, where I erected a circular pen out of hurdles and stakes. (It's interesting that dogs, like humans, have a natural preference for left or right. They'll obey the commands, but if simply sent out to round up some sheep they'll tend to choose their own favoured way.) I used Bundy to round up some sheep and pen them, and then I walked around the pen with Fenn. I didn't let Fenn run with Bundy all the time, although that is a method used by some farmers and shepherds. There's always the risk that the puppy will learn bad habits from the older dog and will end up watching the other dog instead of listening to you and watching the sheep. And besides, Bundy wasn't the best model for the kind of work I wanted Fenn to do.

I took Fenn back to Dick after I had been training her for a few months to refine some of my techniques and sort out a particular problem I had. I probably started working her with sheep too soon, before I had perfected a strong 'stop' command with her. Dick stresses that you need to be able to stop your dog before it works with sheep 'otherwise you end up chasing behind it, ranting and raving, in a bad temper, and the dog recognises your temper but it doesn't understand what you want it to do.'

Dick sometimes introduces a puppy to sheep before he teaches 'stop', but he does it in an enclosed space with a few sheep, so that they cannot scatter and run away. He taught me that when you have a particular problem with a dog, as I did, you go right back to basics, and start teaching 'stop' in the yard, until she has it.

'Do it at five yards away, fifty yards, a hundred yards, and bring it back if it doesn't obey. You are going to have to control your dog from a long distance away, so you need to be sure and confident in what you are doing. A dog quickly senses when you are not confident.'

If you ask Dick how he knows he can stop his dog at a thousand yards distance he simply says: 'Because I know it's going to stop and therefore it will stop.' Confidence is the key.

A general tip that Dick gave me about training dogs, and which I always remember, is never to overdo it.

'Sometimes a dog seems to have mastered a command, then it loses the plot and goes backwards. My advice is to stop training for a few days,' he says. 'Dogs, especially those being trained at a high level, sometimes need a bit of thinking time to absorb what they've learnt. If you are trying to teach too much at once, it can all go to pieces.' It helps having their own kennel, their own space, in which to reflect and not be distracted by everything going on in a busy house full of people.

Dick says the warning sign that a dog is worried and overstretched by training is that it will begin to act out of character, perhaps chasing its tail, carrying things in its mouth, eating sheep poo. Obviously, lots of dogs carry sticks all the time; it is only a sign of stress if it is outside their normal behaviour.

Fenn developed into a really useful working dog and was happy to work for our stockman, John King, as well as for me. John had his own border collie, and they worked well together. This was really important for me, because although the idea of 'one man and his dog' is very appealing, on a working farm a dog should respond to other masters. This doesn't mean she wasn't first and foremost my dog, but I could happily go away and leave John to it, knowing she would do everything he wanted her to do.

When I have a good dog like Fenn, it is natural for me to want to breed from her, to keep her genes going. I arranged for her to be served by one of Dick's dogs, and she had a litter of six puppies.

It's easy to know when a bitch is ready to conceive: it happens three or four days after they finish menstruating. They start to get overexcited. Generally, the bitch is taken to the dog, and usually they have a bit of fun running around together. When he eventually mounts her they get 'dog tied', because he swells inside her and for up to about 20 minutes they are tied together, until he deflates and it's all over. Often it's wise to follow up with a second visit to the dog a couple of days later, just to be sure.

The owner of the bitch pays for the service, either in money or by giving the owner of the dog the pick of the litter. Our sheepdogs have their litters in the stables and it is really fantastic fun: there's nothing better than seeing those adorable little bundles of fur finding their way about, playing roly-poly with each other. It's especially nice if a litter is born in spring, because they will be with their mother for ten to twelve weeks and if the weather is good they can have more freedom running around in the garden and exploring.

We kept one of Fenn's pups, another little black and white bitch called Maud. Charlie and I chose the name for no particular reason except that we both liked it. Maud worked out very well, but I didn't put as much time into her training as I did with her mother, so she never quite lived up to Fenn's standards.

Fenn lived a long and active life, but eventually, when she was really old and in semi-retirement from work, her back legs gave out. I took her to the vet who told me her spine had prolapsed, and there was nothing we could do. I made the decision there and then, and he put her down. I took her body back for the usual burial at Buttington Clump, driving with tears filling my eyes. I was very sad to say goodbye to her, but I knew her time had come and she had lived a great life, doing what she loved best. If I can, I always bring the vet to the farm to put down an animal so that they feel at home, away from the alien smells of the surgery and in familiar surroundings with a familiar, loving hand to hold them. It's hard to suppress tears, but I never let them flow until the dog is dead: I never want to unnerve them in those last few minutes by showing my own sadness.

With Fenn gone, Maud became my top dog and she was proving really useful. I had started working for *Countryfile* but was still very busy with the livestock on the farm, and my loyal, hardworking sheepdog was invaluable. During foot and mouth when we couldn't have any cloven-footed animals on Cotswold Farm Park – i.e. sheep, cows, pigs or goats – I started to give sheepdog demonstrations using ducks and taking them around a course to entertain the public. Maud was brilliant at this and the skill came into its own for

Countryfile, as you will read in Chapter Seven, Other Kinds of Sheepdog.

With Maud doing so well I was keen to breed from her, too. I took her to a friend of Dick Roper's and she successfully conceived and gave birth to a lovely litter of six puppies: three bitches and three dogs. We chose one bitch that we called Pearl, John our stockman had another and the rest were sold to local farms.

When Pearl was still quite young, about a year old, I made a stupid mistake that I will never make again. I allowed Pearl to ride on the back of the quad bike with her mother, Maud. She was too young, and I should have been more sensible and only had one dog on the bike. As I went round a corner, Maud slipped and Pearl fell off the side going straight under the wheel of the mobile handling system I was towing. Thankfully she wasn't killed but her leg was badly damaged. It is not uncommon to hear about dogs getting run over on farms, usually due to the farmers rushing around in their very busy lives. Our daughter Ella was particularly close to Pearl and I knew she would be devastated if she couldn't be saved, so we invested quite a lot of money having the vet pin her leg back together with a Meccano-like structure. I was under strict instructions for her to be rested in her kennel, with only gentle exercise on a lead. The accident occurred just at the peak of her training, and the long layoff, coupled with what turned out to be a permanent limp, meant she was only ever half trained – a useful dog to have as an extra but I rarely used her on her own, or for anything difficult. She has lived to a ripe old age, over 13, quite deaf and a little bit stiff, but still game for pottering around the farmyard. She sleeps in the stable and is always there, ready for a walk, when Charlie takes our family dogs out.

Maud also lived a long life, reaching 13, which is above the 12-year average lifespan of a border collie. She spent all those years as my constant companion in the field, and it is hard to think of a better life for a dog bred to love working.

CHAPTER 6

Finding Peg

With Maud gone and Pearl becoming older, slower
and more deaf, it became apparent that I really
needed a fit, young replacement. So I went in search of
a new border collie. I knew that my requirements were
going to be tough to satisfy. As I was now away from
home quite regularly working on *Countryfile* I knew I
would not have time to train a puppy, which would be
my usual method of taking on a new dog, and is something I have always enjoyed in the past. I was looking
for a middle-aged bitch – so about five or six years old –
who was well trained, but who would also work for other
members of my team when I was away. As we run
Cotswold Farm Park and have lots of visitors, it was
very important that she would be kind natured, good
with children and definitely didn't nip like old Carlo. I
also wanted to be able to take her away filming with me
when the opportunity arose, so I wanted a dog that was
happy to travel and stay away overnight, and who would
not be fazed by a variety of different situations. Yes, I
know, this was a big ask.

The first time I saw Peg was in photographs and I have
to say she was quite an unusually marked border collie,

and I was unsure about her. But if you are a working farmer like me, you don't judge a sheepdog on its looks, and when I met her, I realised what a beautiful dog she is.

Peg was a highly trained, successful trialling dog whose life had been overtaken by tragedy. Her owner, a dedicated sheepdog trialler called Steve Barry, had died of a sudden, unexpected heart attack while he was out walking his dogs. He was living alone and nobody in his family wanted to take on a sheepdog, so a very good friend of Steve's, Meryl Fox, became temporary custodian of his two dogs, a puppy and a trained trialling bitch, Peg, who was just beginning to win prizes. Meryl set about finding permanent homes for them.

This was in 2014, and at roughly the same time, I asked my great friend and the expert I always turn to, Dick Roper, if he knew of any sheepdogs that matched my difficult requirements. I knew it was a long shot, as fully trained dogs rarely come up for sale – if they are good the farmer or shepherd wants to keep them, and if they are getting rid of them there may well be a problem with them.

Of course, top breeders do sell trained dogs, and at the sheepdog auctions really good dogs can command high prices. The record is just under £15,000, but that's exceptional, with a good dog costing £2,000–£3,000. I wasn't in the market at those kind of prices and, besides, I wanted a working dog to help on my farm, not a top trialling dog. Although that's exactly what I now have in Peg ...

Dick looked at a couple of collies for me but felt they weren't right. Then he heard about the plight of Peg. He suggested we might be a perfect match, but first of all I had to be carefully vetted by Meryl. She was very keen to make sure that Peg went to a really good home, and so she wanted to see me with Peg, to see how we reacted to each other. She brought Peg to the farm to meet me, and we immediately hit it off. There was something in the set of her head, the intelligent, inquisitive eyes and the good nature that brought her straight up to me, even though I was a stranger. Dogs, as I have said, have a sense that tells them which human beings are going to be their friends and which to be wary about: I always find when I'm visiting someone's house that their dog will make a beeline for me and settle down pressed against my leg. But there was something a bit extra about Peg, as if she recognised a kindred spirit in me. I knew without hesitation that I wanted her, and I crossed my fingers that Meryl, who took the vetting process very seriously, would think I was a suitable new owner for her.

With Meryl's agreement, and after a two-week probation, I bought Peg and she came to live at Bemborough. She and Steve had been very close; apparently she sat on his lap while he was driving his quad bike. She would also run towards him and then jump up into his arms for a cuddle when he asked her to. When she lived with Meryl she slept inside the house, but as she is a working dog I wanted to kennel her outside. So I bought a new, roomy kennel from Timberbuild and installed it by the farm back door, so that I could let her out and spend time with her with ease. The right kennel is very important: it needs to have a good-size run to give plenty of fresh air and a warm, dry area to sleep in at night. At the end of Peg's kennel there is an insulated boxed area where she can curl up in the straw, snug against frosty nights. On a hot summer's day she can sit on the top of it, in the shade, to keep cool.

I spent quite a bit of time for the first few days sitting with her in her kennel, letting her build confidence and trust in me. I was aware that she'd been through major changes in her life, losing Steve and then settling with Meryl before coming to me, so I gave her extra attention to help her settle in.

She's now very happy in her kennel – collies love having their own space. She also likes to wander into our kitchen, which most sheepdogs don't do, but which she was allowed to do when she lived with Steve and so we let her continue (there's an old saying that when a sheepdog is brought into the house to lie in front of the fire, it knows its days are numbered). She gets on with our house dogs, and the kids and Charlie love her.

There was only one big problem with Peg when she first arrived. Every sheepdog is trained to the voice commands and whistles of its owner, and although there are some standard ones, with perhaps a few variations on each, the whistles in particular are very individual. Although plenty of people had seen Steve running Peg at trials, there wasn't any video of him and nobody could be exactly sure of Steve's whistles and commands. Steve was a very good whistler, with his fingers not a metal whistle, and I'm OK at whistling, but I'm not in his league. As for voice commands, Steve had a loud, booming Welsh voice, and I admit I have tried to imitate it when I'm out with her in a field far away from anyone hearing me ...

Meryl had discovered how to make Peg go left, right and stop, but she wasn't performing as well as she could, because she clearly was a bit hazy about the commands. We tried out the standard ones, with mixed success.

OK, so here are the basics. Stop, walk-on, left and right. For stop you can use the verbal command 'sit' or 'lie down' or 'down', or even 'stop'. After a few goes, I discovered 'lie down' was what she reacted to best and for the whistle a straight blast and she would drop to the ground. For walk-on she responded well to what I have used with my other dogs; simply saying 'on' or two short, sharp whistles. Run to the left was the standard 'come by'. My other dogs just go on 'by'. Right is usually 'away', and an extra command when you want to pick up some sheep that have been left behind is 'look back'. These were my usual verbal commands, and Peg generally reacted well to them.

But the trouble is, when a dog is working at the far side of a field and there's a wind blowing, you need the whistle command because they won't hear you shouting. With my sheepdogs I've trained from puppyhood, like Fenn, Maud and Pearl, I have simply made up my own whistles, and all three worked to the same ones. But these improvised whistles didn't work with Peg.

Apparently Steve had a very strong whistle, using his teeth rather than the plastic mouth whistle that many shepherds use. I can whistle with my mouth but my whistle is not that strong. What I had to do was try and work out the whistles that Peg understood for 'come by' and 'away'. Despite standing in the field with her trying various different pitches and tones, I wasn't really getting anywhere.

So Meryl and I took Peg to see Dick.

Dick whistles brilliantly with his mouth, like Steve did. He claims it is due to his slightly crooked front tooth that got knocked about when he played rugby. Dick experimented with various whistles until he found the ones that worked for her. They are fairly standard whistles, although not ones that Dick himself normally uses. As soon as she heard whistles she recognised, you could almost see her relief, and she was very keen to get out in the field, working the sheep.

When Dick had her running well, I took out my phone and recorded him whistling. He and Meryl thought it was very funny that it took me a few minutes to work out how to use my phone to record: they teased me that, as I make TV programmes, I really ought to under-stand the technology better. But in the end I had a good recording, which I played to myself in the car and prac-tised as I was driving for several weeks until I knew them. Duncan, my business partner, thought it was really bizarre when he rang me one day and after we finished chatting I somehow left the phone line open, and all he could hear at the other end was me whistling the commands ...

I got there in the end but it hasn't been easy. Under pressure, when something dramatic is happening with the sheep, I sometimes automatically revert to the whistles I used for the other dogs. For instance, to send them right my usual whistle is low and up, with a tail, but for Peg it has to be low and high. So in a crisis I make matters worse by giving a whistle she doesn't understand.

Dick's advice to me, and the problems of taking on a ready-trained dog, made a good feature for *Countryfile*, and we filmed Dick putting me though my paces with Peg. He told me off for gesticulating so much: sheepdogs should not be looking at the shepherd, but using their ear to hear the commands. So me flapping my arms about was at best pointless, and at worst a distraction. I'm a person who naturally uses my arms when I am talking, and I have also been taught to use my arms to give commands to gundogs. So it went against nature for me to stick my hands in my pockets while controlling Peg, but that's what Dick made me do.

Luckily for me, my dogs have always obeyed the voice and whistle commands and taken no notice of my arms. But there's a danger that a dog can become 'hand trained' rather than voice trained. Dick had one young lad who came to him for training and every time he told the dog what to do, the dog did a full pirouette before setting off. Dick realised that he was taking no notice of the voice command and was watching for the hand signal. When Dick told the lad to put his hands in his pockets the dog could not perform at all. As he was a mature dog, it was probably too late to retrain him, and he worked well enough if he got a clear hand signal. But that limits the distance at which he could work, as he always had to have a clear sight of his master, and meant there was inevitably a delay while he twizzled round, plus he wouldn't be able to work for anyone else.

Dick also taught me that the strength of my whistle or my voice command is another way of communicating with the dog. A strong command or whistle means 'Do it now, fast'. A softer one means 'Let it happen more moderately'. For example, the 'stop' command can change from a flat out 'drop down NOW' to 'slow down, canter, trot, then down'. I had been struggling to get Peg to go down quickly, and that was because my command was too weak.

I haven't got these new whistles off to perfection: sometimes my right hand whistle makes Peg look back over her shoulder, as if to make sure of what I meant. She doesn't ping off immediately, as she would have to in trialling, but that's not what I'm trying to achieve, and we are working well enough together.

Dick can fine tune the commands he uses with his own dogs. For instance, if the dog is going wide he can put an accent into his whistle which tells it to go wider. He has so many little additions, and seeing him work his dogs is like watching a masterclass, which is why he's the best in the country.

You need a very good, brainy dog to be able to work at that level. It's also a question of personality. A schoolboy who hates exams will go into a funk in the exam room and fail the exam even though he has done all the revision and knows all the answers. In the same way, some dogs are sensitive and can't cope with too many commands. They have done all the training, know all the commands, but they will only ever be good working dogs, not top level trial dogs, because they can't cope with working in different environments and with strange sheep. Like the rest of us, dogs have their limits. Dick knows dogs that have been brilliant in training, learnt all the commands well, have the speed, the fitness and everything a great trialling dog needs, but their temperament is just not quite right, and they blow up under pressure.

'Another dog will seem at first to be a very basic sort of character, but he'll train and train and turn out to be a top dog. I'm always wary of dogs who are too brilliant too soon,' he says. 'There's a fine line between brilliance and madness in a collie.'

I know that Peg is good enough to get back to trial-ling, which she did with her first owner Steve. If she spent three or four weeks with Dick she'd be up to that standard again; she's a brilliant dog. But I'm not that skilful and my understanding of dog psychology is not at that level. I recognise my own abilities and limitations. I was a good rugby player and always managed to get into the first team for the local clubs wherever I was in the country, but at the same time I always knew I was not international standard. It's the same with dog training: I know my limits, and I also know what I want and need my dogs to do.

Peg is very happy working on the farm. She gets enough stimulation and satisfaction from what she has to do, and she loves doing it. If there is a day when no work with the sheep is needed, she'll happily go out for a walk with Charlie and the other dogs. She's got her own eccentric little habit: she loves jumping into the water trough. She has a very thick coat, and she clearly loves cooling down in the water, but she'll do it even on a day when the weather is bitterly cold, and you would think a soggy wet coat is the last thing you'd want. If there isn't a water trough around, she'll lie down in a puddle, and when there's ice on the ground she pulls herself along on her tummy, like a seal. She clearly doesn't feel the cold at all, but you need to stand clear when she leaps out of the trough, if you don't want an icy cold shower when she shakes herself.

Many of the jobs for a dog on a farm like ours are routine, rounding up the ewes and their lambs, bringing them to me. But Peg is well up to doing anything out of the ordinary, and when she's working, the sheep know who's in command. It's the slightly unusual tasks that test a working dog, and often result in the shepherd shouting 'Damned dog, stupid sheep!'

When you are working a sheepdog you have to be in the dog's head, but also in the head of the sheep. You have to be able to look at a sheep and understand why she has stopped. Is she ill? Is she being awkward? Or is there an obstacle she doesn't like, like a puddle of water? Water will always stop sheep. If there is a puddle at a gateway they won't go through, or an obstacle they won't go past, or you are trying to load them into a lorry when they don't want to go, the best way to deal with it is catch one and pull it in front of the rest of the flock and they will usually follow. Shepherds have always found it very useful that they follow each other – just like sheep in fact ...

Dad always said: 'A farmer who calls a sheep stupid is a farmer who has been outwitted by a sheep.' Sheep are definitely not brainless, and they have their own personalities. As a dog handler, I have to be aware which sheep is the leader, which one is likely to break away. A really good collie shares the ability to suss out where the problems are without help, but the shepherd should never rely solely on the dog, instead anticipating the problem and giving the right command.

I was lucky enough to go to Australia with *Countryfile*, and I was asked to help round up some cattle on horseback, which isn't my favourite mode of transport, and I was quite nervous about the prospect. I don't regard myself as a good rider and this horse was a spirited animal, so I wasn't completely confident. The farmer agreed to take the horse round the cattle to 'knock the sting out of her', as he put it. He galloped flat out downhill with the kelpies barking, cracking his whip, and the noise was enough to keep the herd of cattle running in front of him, with dust everywhere. It was an amazing sight, like something out of the movies. I always fancied being a cowboy as a child and now was my chance. The farmer pulled the horse up next to me, jumped off and said: 'Right, it's your turn.'

I replied: 'Crikey, what if she bolts under me?'

He said, 'Just head for the fence and hopefully she'll stop.'

The fence was huge and topped with barbed wire, which didn't make me feel any happier ...

I managed reasonably well and the horse was surprisingly well behaved. As we moved the cattle to the corner of the field, trying to get them into the pens, I could see that one of the calves was going to make a break for it. I could tell from the way she was moving and looking to the side, which is a sense you acquire after years of working with stock. A good dog would have acted to head the calf off as soon as I gave the command, and a very good dog would have spotted it before me. In the seconds that I was thinking about the problem, the horse took off, heading in exactly the right direction to turn the calf back to the herd. I've wondered about it since: did the horse feel the slight pressure of my knees as I looked at the breaking calf? Or did it have the same instinct as a good dog– did it understand the cattle in the same way a collie understands sheep? A horse isn't a natural predator of cattle, with the instinct to chase that a dog has. But having worked with cattle for years, perhaps it had simply assimilated a deep knowledge of what they do, and how to recognise the signs. Just as I, as a stockman, could see what was going to happen, perhaps the horse also recognised it. Thankfully I was ready for the sudden move, otherwise I could have ended up in a heap on the floor and looked a right buffoon, especially with the cameras running.

Importantly, Peg works for anyone else on the farm who needs a sheepdog. I'm away a lot, so I don't get to work her as much as I would like to, but she still gets out to the sheep most days.

She's also a brilliant dog to take on location for *Countryfile*. She's happy being filmed, and when we have to repeat the same scene over and over again, she's up for it and never complains.

I'm hoping to breed from Peg soon. She's got a good pedigree, and she's such a great worker that I'd really like to keep her genes going. I'll take her to one of Dick's dogs when the time is right. Peg is now not only part of the farm workforce, but also part of the family, and I love her to bits. I feel hugely grateful to Meryl for having trusted me to take her on and also to Dick for recommending me and for helping me out with her. I can certainly reassure Steve's family that Peg is well cared for and very happy, and I like to think that Steve would approve of her new owner. She has become well known due to her appearances on *Countryfile*, and has pride of place on the front cover of this book.

CHAPTER 7

Other Kinds of Sheepdog

D ad sparked my interest in farming, but he also sparked something much deeper in me. It was his work, pioneering the Rare Breeds Trust and setting up Cotswold Farm Park that started my lifelong fascination with the history of the animals we see around us every day as we drive through the countryside, or even as we walk in city parks.

Dad loved animals of all sorts, and he cared particularly about preserving the breeds that are in danger of extinction. In his early farming days, when he and his partner were running a mainly arable farm because they didn't have much money and arable was the most cost-effective way to establish themselves, Dad bought a couple of Gloucester Old Spot sows and two Gloucester cows, more or less as a hobby. He loved the idea of breeding pedigree livestock.

In 1969, when I was a lively little three-year-old, Dad was asked to join a working party set up by the Royal Agricultural Society and the Zoological Society of London to find a home for a collection of rare breed farm animals that had been kept at Whipsnade Zoo. The zoo needed the space for more exotic animals.

When he saw them, Dad knew he had to save them. That's when he had the idea for Cotswold Farm Park, a safe place for the animals to live. By opening the park to the public he hoped to fund the cost of keeping the animals, but, more importantly, he wanted to educate people about the need to conserve these wonderful breeds.

Two years later, the first rare breeds farm park in Britain (possibly in the world) received its new residents: a small flock of Jacob, Soay and Portland sheep, with one lone Norfolk ram, plus five different breeds of cattle: Highland, longhorn, White Park, Belted Galloway and Dexter.

Cotswold Farm Park was, from the day it opened, a great success. As well as educating the public about the precarious survival of these beautiful animals, Dad always made time to talk about them to me and my sisters. We all had animals that we had to look after: mine were a couple of Exmoor ponies. We were in charge of buying and selling the stock for our breed, with half the profit going into our piggy banks. It was a brilliant way to motivate us, and I loved going to market with him to buy new animals.

A couple of years after Cotswold Farm Park opened its doors, Dad helped to found the Rare Breeds Survival Trust, and became its first chairman. The members of the Trust wanted to stop rare breeds disappearing: between 1900 and 1973, 26 native breeds of farm animals became extinct. Now they publish an annual watchlist of endangered breeds and encourage farmers and other enthusiasts to keep these heritage animals going. Today the Trust has 10,000 members, and Prince Charles is its patron.

At about the same time as he took on his work with the Trust, Dad's TV career was launched properly, with a guest appearance on the very popular *Animal Magic* show on children's television, presented by Johnny Morris. Dad was a natural, and from then on he appeared regularly on a variety of animal programmes. I was very proud, never dreaming that he was also sowing the seeds of my other career (I already knew I wanted to be a farmer – well, I quite liked the idea of being a cowboy in the Wild West, too ...)

So, because of Dad's work on Bemborough Farm and the farm park, from a very early age I developed a strong interest in the history of domesticated animals. It fascinates me how breeds have evolved – and how some have been completely discarded – to fit with modern farming methods.

For many animals you can easily see the origins: the wild boar is clearly recognisable in today's pigs, even though wild boar became extinct in Britain by the twelfth century. Way back in time it originated in North Africa and Eurasia, and it was probably humans who spread it further, domesticating it more than three thousand years ago. A couple of efforts were made to reintroduce it, but it was not until the 1980s that boar were re-established here. At the farm park we have Iron

Age pigs, the only animals we have which are not pure bred, but rather are a reconstruction of the type of pigs our ancestors first herded from the wild during the Iron Age. They were created for a BBC television programme where the producers wanted to see how people coped living like Iron Age people, with the same clothing, houses and livestock. We mated a Tamworth sow (the oldest of the existing British breeds) with a wild boar.

We also have Highland cattle, which are the closest descendants of the massive Auroch cattle that appear in Neolithic cave paintings. Attempts have been made, and are being made, to re-establish Aurochs by breeding for their characteristics, or by sequencing their DNA from remains and comparing the genome with existing breeds. As well as Highland cattle, we also have White Parks at the farm park – another breed that have these ancient genes.

Goats have claims to be the earliest animal to have been domesticated as there is evidence that Neolithic men had herds of primitive goats. The first evidence of them in Britain is 5,000 years ago, and there are still pockets of feral goats dotted around the country who are descended from these early goats. Among the breeds we have at the farm park is the Bagot, which legend says was brought to Britain when Richard the Lionheart returned from the Crusades.

Naturally we have rare breed sheep: 14 different old breeds, with at least a couple who still have the genes of the earliest known sheep in the world, the wild mouflon.

Sheep are in contention with goats for the position of oldest domesticated animals, and their value was recognised more than 10,000 years ago in Asia as producers of meat, milk and wool – all valuable commodities. When I look at our small herd of Castlemilk Moorits or our Soays, which are unchanged from Viking times, the history of sheep is right there in front of me: I can see the way our modern breeds are descended from these hardy pioneers. The Merino sheep I became so familiar with in Australia are another breed with genes from the wild mouflon, although there have been centuries of refining the breed since.

But the animal whose history intrigues me even more, and who is not represented in our rare breeds park, is the animal I work with every day: the sheepdog.

Experts are agreed that dogs are descended from wolves, and the process of domestication was more the choice of the dog than of the humans who took them into their camps. Towards the end of the last Ice Age, men survived by hunting and gathering. They had no domesticated animals and they grew no crops. The wolves who learnt to forage around the human camps for bones and left-over food became useful as guard dogs, warning of predators and enemy incursions, and there soon developed a symbiotic relationship: the wolves/dogs stayed around for food and warmth at the fires, the men encouraged them for protection and also, after some time, to help with hunting. I expect, by taking in young wolf cubs, they managed to befriend them even more. The wolf gradually evolved physically but, more importantly, in its characteristics, to accept that hunting with a pack included a human pack.

Eventually, individual dogs became attached to families or groups of humans, even to one specific man. The 'ownership' of dogs by man had begun and has continued down the millennia. With the domestication of other animals – goats and sheep mainly – the dogs had another vital function, to guard and preserve the flock on which their human masters relied for food and skins. I've heard it argued that, given that man is the most successful animal on the planet, the dog is the second most successful, because it has learnt to have all its needs catered for simply by being useful to its masters.

As we all know, dogs have evolved into all sorts of different shapes and sizes, and have now been subdivided into breeds. There are dogs to sit on laps, dogs to race round tracks, dogs to guard our homes and premises, dogs to help us in specific ways, and even more dogs whose sole role in life is to be a good companion to its human owners. Despite how different they look – a St Bernard is one hundred times bigger than a Chihuahua, for example – they have a lot more in common than their appearance sometimes suggests.

All the different breeds of dog we know today evolved over centuries of selective breeding from the dogs who did the kind of work I still do with my dogs. If dogs had not become 'sheep' dogs, it is possible that no other domesticated breeds would exist. When I look at Peg or Pearl, I can see the history of all dogs before me, as they are where it all began. Their body shape may have changed, but the job they do is still principally the same as it was when Bronze Age men ran flocks of sheep, goats and pigs to feed their communities, using dogs to herd, guard and drive their livestock. Although today's sheepdogs do look different in some ways from the remains that have been found of their ancient predecessors, they are much closer in appearance to their forebears than any of the ornamental breeds. Farmers and shepherds have always wanted functional dogs: we don't judge them on their looks but on how well they can do the job. So there have been no excesses of interbreeding, and a sheepdog is about as close as we can get today to an ancient breed.

There are, though, different types of livestock working dogs that have evolved. As we've seen, there are sheepdogs like Peg, who work rounding up and moving sheep, using all the attributes I described in the last chapter, and will tell you more about in the next. There are droving dogs, like the Welsh collie, who were used to take cattle and other livestock long distances. And there are pastoral dogs, who lived with the herd to guard it from predators and are still used in some parts of the world.

First, let's look at droving dogs.

For centuries, before railways and long-distance travel became normal, the people who moved around the countryside for miles and miles at a time were mainly drovers, taking cattle, pigs and sheep to market. Great cavalcades of drovers with their flocks would block the routes of the stagecoaches and horseback travellers for hours on end – not too different to being stuck in a motorway jam today.

To farmers like me, used to loading our livestock onto trailers and lorries, it's difficult to imagine how important drovers were. But in days gone by I wouldn't have been able to leave my farm for weeks at a time and so would have relied on a drover to take my flock to market and bring the money he got for selling my livestock back to me. It was a vital job, and every drover had at least one dog. Flocks of sheep as big as 6,000 strong, collected from different farms, would be taken to markets all over the country, even making journeys from the Pennines to the famous Smithfield market in London. The drovers would team up on the road, working together and using their dogs as a pack. For days, weeks and occasionally even months, the drovers, who were sometimes mounted on hardy horses used to rough terrain, but would often travel on foot, would steadily move their charges onwards, settling them at night in fields specially reserved for them. The dogs were vital for keeping the sheep together, keeping them going, and separating the different flocks when they got to market. Usually the flock or herd would wait for a few days before making the final few miles to market, to allow the sheep or cattle to rest and fatten up. At this point the drover's dog turned into a guard dog, fighting off any predators, including thieves and village dogs. Sometimes the enormous trains of animals in a drove would be accompanied by hunting dogs, which were used by the drovers to provide hares and rabbits for food on the journey: these dogs are the ancestors of today's lurchers. The droving dogs were fed on anything left over when the men had been fed.

A description from a book published in 1800, *Cynographia Britannica* (a very early description of different dog breeds), says about these remarkable droving dogs:

'He is sagacious, fond of employment and active; if a drove is huddled together so as to retard their progress, he dashes amongst and separates them till they form a line and travel more commodiously; if a sheep is refractory and runs wild, he soon overtakes and seizes him by the foreleg or ear, pulls him to the ground. The bull or ox he forces into obedience by keen bites on the heels or tail, and most dexterously avoids their kicks. He knows his master's grounds and is a rigid sentinel on duty, never suffering them to break their bounds, or strangers to enter. He shakes the intruding hog by the ear, and obliges him to quit the territories. He bears blows and kicks with much philosophy.'

What a dog! He was loyal and hard-working, and when he and his master finally delivered their charges to the market he was often turned loose to find his own way home, even if this was a journey of a hundred miles or more. He would scavenge for his own food on the way, saving the drover from having to feed him. If he never made it, the drover would simply acquire another dog, or use one from the small pack he bred especially for the job.

The drovers (like shepherds) were not concerned with how their dogs looked; they were breeding them for working qualities, not to win beauty contests. As Iris Combe, a renowned historian of herding dogs, wrote:

'To define a droving dog would be impossible, for they were a collection of canines of every shape and size, make and colour, each selected by the drover for its natural instincts and to deal with the specific type of livestock to be transported. The requirements for a drover's dog were a stout heart, good lungs, rock-hard feet, great physical courage and a strongly-developed instinct for self-preservation. The framework which housed these qualities was of relatively little importance.'

Sadly, not all the drovers were kind to their dogs, which usually lived short lives, due to exhaustion, accidents, ill-treatment and neglect. If a bitch gave birth to pups on the journey, the pups were often left to die, although there are heartening stories of bitch and pups being left at the nearest farmhouse and collected when the drover returned.

The routes the drovers used formed a criss-cross network across the countryside, which can still be seen today as the old droving roads are rediscovered and preserved as routes for walkers. They did not necessarily go in a straight line: the main roads had toll gates, and the cost of taking a whole herd through was too high for the drover who was paid a flat amount by the farmer. So routes were devised that bypassed the tolls.

Even when railways spread across the country in the mid-nineteenth century, droving dogs were still in demand. They no longer had to make the weeks-long droves all the way to the markets, but they were still needed to get livestock from the farms to the holding sheds at the railway stations, which could be journeys of many miles.

It wasn't only sheep and cattle who were escorted across the country by the drovers: flocks of geese and turkeys were also driven, with dogs urging them on and keeping them in line, often for several days at a time, to get to market. Just as cattle were usually shod like horses to protect their feet on long journeys, turkeys wore leather boots and geese were first herded through wet tar, followed by sand, to give their feet a protective coating. The dogs had to drive them through the tar – not something the geese were very willing to do – and the dogs hated the job because they ended up with tar on their own feet.

To illustrate the hard life the drovers led, I followed an old drover's road for three long days for *Countryfile*, taking 40 geese across the Brecon Beacons to the market town of Llandovery. We couldn't use sheep because of the strict movement licences that are now in place when you transport these animals from farm to farm, but geese are free from these restrictions. Nor could we walk them through tar – the RSPCA would not have approved. Before we set off, and at regular intervals along the route, my little flock were checked out by Peter Laing, a vet who caught up with me whenever we stopped for long.

My adventure was shown over three episodes of *Countryfile*, leading up to Christmas: geese were very popular in the Christmas markets in Victorian times. I dressed for the part, in a long drover's coat and a wide-brimmed hat, which I was very glad of when the rain swept across the open heathland.

We weighed a sample three geese before I set off, because, as a good drover, my employers would expect me to get the geese to market in good condition. An important part of my job, as well as covering the distance, was to take care that my charges were well fed, got plenty of rest, and plenty of access to water. Every couple of miles we stopped for 20 minutes, which was all the geese seemed to need to feel refreshed and ready to go.

My sheepdog at the time was Maud, and she was very happy to switch her attention from sheep to geese, having already herded geese and ducks in front of visitors at Cotswold Farm Park. She wasn't fazed by them, and understood the slow pace they needed to waddle along at. I was nervous that one of my flock would get lost or hurt, but Maud was vigilant.

As well as Peter the vet, I was also joined along my route by Richard Moore Colyer, a historian who has studied the ancient droving routes and the men who travelled along them.

'There is evidence of drovers moving animals in Saxon times, and probably earlier,' he told me. 'But the heyday was from the sixteenth century to the end of the nineteenth century. Wales had poor quality pasture, so the cattle the farmers bred were taken to lusher pasture in England. Lots of animals, including geese, were taken to the markets at Llandovery.'

The whole area I was walking was honeycombed with drovers' roads, and in days gone by I would have met up with many other men in charge of flocks and herds of animals, but I'm pretty sure I was the first drover to walk this way in the past hundred years or so. Halfway through the first day the rain came down, the geese looked muddy and bedraggled, and I could feel trickles of cold water running down my neck. But if I was feeling sorry for myself I only had to remember that at least my coat and hat were made of waterproof material: the old drovers, with their heavy woollen coats, would have been a lot wetter than I was.

The first night we stopped at the village of Caio, which was an important droving centre in the eighteenth and nineteenth centuries, when the population was three times larger than it is today. Richard told me about a famous drover, Dafydd Jones of Caio, who lived between 1711 and 1777, who didn't fit the usual image of drovers, who were known as hard-drinking, hard-womanising, wild men. Dafydd Jones spent his hours on the road composing hymns and translating English hymns into Welsh. In one of his hymns, Richard said, he compares souls going to heaven with all the cattle and sheep converging on Caio.

Our first night was spent in a tent, while the geese were corralled in a sheep pen lined with a generous amount of straw. Because of the rain, we built a tarpaulin shelter to keep them dry. I was exhausted and also worried about the safety of the geese, as there were foxes about. We'd travelled across some difficult open country, and it was a bit disappointing at the end of a hard day to find that my drover's rations were a hunk of bread, a piece of cheese and a raw onion. The geese, on the other hand, got a generous helping of barley for their supper. I tried not to think about the luxury of a warm dry bed as I settled down for the night, cold and wet.

Maud loved the luxury of sleeping in my tent with me and I was glad of her company, but I know the original droving dogs would have been expected to live in the pen with the geese. The drovers in fact would not have had tents – they slept in barns and haylofts, and, if the weather was reasonable, underneath hedges, with nothing more than blankets to protect them. The drovers faced many dangers. On their way to market there were rustlers intent on stealing their livestock, and on the way back the risks were even higher, because they were now carrying money, often gold sovereigns, for the farmers whose stock they had transported. Highwaymen, sometimes operating in armed gangs, would target them, which was another reason that the best drovers did not release their dogs but kept them alongside to alert to danger and to attack human predators just as enthusiastically as they saw off foxes.

The next morning I was relieved to count all my 40 geese present and correct, and almost all looking fit and healthy. There was one goose I was worried about. She was struggling a bit the day before, always lagging behind. This morning, while the others had preened their feathers and were now pure white again, Jemima (I called her after Jemima Puddleduck, the Beatrix Potter character) was still muddy and wet. I caught her and dried her with a towel. Peter had a good look at her, because I was worried about whether she could continue.

'She's not got such good feathers as the others, but she's healthy, her eyes are bright,' he said.

Thankfully, the weather was dry, so I was able to light a fire, brew some tea, and have a good breakfast of fatty bacon cooked over the fire. I'd hoped for some eggs from my flock, but Peter explained that they would not lay in the bad weather we had overnight.

We set off again over open moorland and I asked Richard why the drovers didn't follow the roads.

'Most of the roads had turnpikes, which meant that you had to pay twopence for every animal that went through. If you had a large herd or flock, that represented a lot of money. The drovers had to balance the cost against getting the animals to market quicker and probably in better condition.

'The drovers also had to avoid mixing their sheep, cattle and geese with other animals also being driven to market. If a drover had a very large number of animals he may have had to hire other men to help him.'

As I strode out, I carried poor old Jemima for some of the way. She was so valliant, trying to keep up with the others when it was obviously hard work for her. Without Peter or Richard to accompany me I felt isolated on the big wide open hillside. But I didn't feel lonely: hundreds of drovers and millions of animals had trodden this path, and somehow their spirits felt alive to me.

Maud really came into her own as she had to drive the geese down some hazardous, narrow hill tracks. She was ducking and darting, keeping them safe. I was worried one would disappear over the edge, but I should have had more faith in her: she brought them all through brilliantly.

It was late when we stopped for a lunch break, because we had to keep moving down the dangerous track. We were all exhausted, and once again I was on bread, cheese and raw onion, and beginning to fantasise about a good hot meal. The geese enjoyed a swim on the next leg of the route, with only Jemima needing a helping hand to get in and out of the river.

We stopped that night in the village of Cilycwm, another droving centre in the old days. There used to be five pubs catering for these wild men who drove their animals through, but today there is only one left. Luckily, I was staying there, so a warm bed, a pint and a hot meal were in sight.

Lots of villagers came out to see me and my flock arrive – I'm sure they thought I was a harmless eccentric. But Richard explained that in times past when the drovers came through, locals would 'lock up their daughters, their mistresses, their sisters and everybody else. They definitely had an eye for the ladies.'

While we were happy to relax over a pint, the drovers were known for kicking up a fuss, with records of them appearing at Quarter Sessions and being bound over to keep the peace, or fined for being drunk and disorderly.

Still worried about foxes, I arranged for my geese to spend the night in a stable. When he checked them the next morning Peter said they looked so fit and relaxed 'they could be on a holiday cruise'.

On our final day we covered most of the distance by road, and I admit we cheated a little bit by loading the geese into a trailer because we were causing such a tailback of traffic. But only for a short distance: we faithfully walked the rest. Richard broke the journey for me by walking with me to explain that geese were not just a valuable foodstuff, they also provided feathers for pillows and mattresses, goose grease for mothers to rub on their children's chests to ward off the cold, and even fuel for lamplighting.

When we arrived in Llandovery I was fascinated to see a plaque outside Lloyds Bank, commemorating one of the first banks established in Wales. Not only did the drovers have money on them from selling animals, they were also used to transport deeds and documents. For example, on the journey from Wales to London with the cattle and sheep, they often carried rents from Welsh farmers for their English landlords and taxes levied by the government. So in both directions they were targets for villains. If, instead of gold, they were given credit by banks, they were no longer such a target, and that's why the banks were established.

Enterprising men like David Jones, a farmer's son who worked as a drover, set up the Black Ox Bank in Llandovery in 1799, using his own savings and the substantial sum of £10,000 (£800,000 in today's money) which he acquired when he married his wealthy wife. The name 'Black Ox' came from the depiction of the Welsh Black cattle, the local breed, on the bank notes. In one year, 1800, the Black Ox bank lent over £6,000 without any security for the purchase of cattle, sheep and geese. That's about half a million in today's money. In 1909 Lloyds Bank acquired all the branches of the Black Ox bank, ending the existence of the last and largest of the independent banks in Wales, and one that made life so much safer for so many drovers.

We were given a great reception as we arrived in the town, and, to keep up the spirit of droving, I delivered a letter from the satchel I was wearing to the mayor, a scroll commemorating our historical trip and thanking the town for welcoming us. Despite the crowd that turned out to greet us, and all the cameras being aimed at them, my geese remained calm and dignified and Maud kept them in check. When we retired to a quiet field to feed and rest them, Peter reweighed the same three we weighed at the beginning, and to my astonishment they had all put on weight, one of them even putting on three pounds.

It was an amazing three days for me. I felt I had stepped back in time, and got a real taste of what it was like to be a drover centuries ago. My life today, and the life of all farmers and shepherds, is very different from the life they lived. But one role hasn't changed in all that time: the job of the sheepdog. Maud worked brilliantly, doing exactly what her predecessors would have done. During the filming, as we went from farm to farm, one shepherd who saw her working was so impressed he wanted to buy her. Of course, it didn't matter how much money he offered, she was definitely not for sale ...

Now to another type of sheepdog, the ones who lived with the herd to protect the livestock from predators. They're sometimes called pastoral dogs, although that definition strictly means all breeds working with animals, so it is more accurate to refer to them as guardian dogs. There are many different breeds, developed in different countries, and with different names – sheepdogs, mountain dogs, mastiffs – but all with the same job.

When I was little we had, for a short time, a lovely Old English sheepdog called Guinevere. She was huge, especially to me as I was only five or six at the time, and I still remember her massive paws and the density of her thick coat. Because of Dad's interest in old breeds, he liked the idea of having an Old English sheepdog and so he bought one for Mum as a present, getting her from a local breeder at Rissington. She was a beautiful puppy, just like the one in the Dulux adverts, but in a muddy farmyard she was constantly filthy. When she was fully grown we clipped her a few times to keep her cool in summer and cleaner in winter. Unfortunately, she hated being separated from Mum, and whenever Mum was down at the farm park, Guinevere, who was left behind in the farmhouse, became a brilliant escapologist, nipping out of the back door at any opportunity. Then she would bound a quarter of a mile over the fields to be reunited with Mum. The problem was solved eventually when the breeder lost her own dog and offered to have Guinevere back, giving her a lovely home where she lived to a ripe old age.

The thing is, although her name includes 'sheepdog', Guinevere no longer had a working role on a farm like ours. Back in time, she and all the other huge breeds were vital to farmers and shepherds. They lived outside with the sheep, and any predators who turned up during the night were given short shrift by these large, tough dogs. In some parts of the world, close relatives of the Old English sheepdog are still working as flock guardians, sleeping and eating alongside the livestock, spending all their time guarding them, but it's a dwindling number.

The flock-guarding dogs developed alongside their smaller, more agile cousins, the collies, who could herd and move animals. The guardians needed to be big and fierce, as thousands of years ago and in different parts of the world they had to be prepared to fight lynx, lions, wolves, jackals, tigers, leopards, cheetahs, foxes and huge eagles. They needed to be brave and strong, and they had to have a well-developed instinct to protect. They did not need to be able to hunt, or to herd. Their sole job was to live with the flock of sheep or goats and see off any predators. Often they simply needed to bark, from the centre of a flock, for a predator to turn tail; a bit like a pet dog's barking can make a burglar go elsewhere. Their size also meant that they could carry large fat reserves, which helped them survive the worst weather and protected them from bitter cold, which a smaller dog couldn't survive.

Although we no longer use them – in England today there are few natural predators of sheep – there are times when I feel they could still be useful, especially when I hear of rogue dogs worrying sheep, or even of rustlers stealing them. Luckily I farm in an area of the country that has not been badly affected by rustling, but I really feel for the farmers and shepherds in the north of the country and in Northern Ireland, where rustling offences are up by nearly 200 per cent in the last five years, with about 90,000 animals stolen each year, probably to be illegally butchered and eaten. The word 'rustling' can sound amusing and even romantic, with connotations of the Wild West, but for a farmer who has spent decades building up the bloodlines in his flock and investing money and time in his animals, it is devastating to lose them.

Unlike my working dogs, the collies, these flock guardians did not work to commands, and often did not have or know their own name. In some parts of the world they lived with the flock from birth: pups were put among the sheep before their eyes were open. Charles Darwin, the most famous naturalist ever, noted when he was in South America that shepherds would teach pups to be suckled by ewes and the dogs slept in a bed of sheep's wool. They were trained to go to a set place every day for meat, but the rest of their life was spent exclusively with the flock, and when sheep were sold it was usual for the dog to be sold with them.

The breeds of dog developed differently according to the parts of the world where they were used, so in the harsh climate of northern Europe, where they often worked on mountainsides and open steppes, they developed thick, waterproof coats. In more temperate areas they had smoother coats. But common to all was the thickset body and powerful legs that Guinevere had. They lived tough lives, sleeping outside in snow and icy winds, giving birth to pups in a hole in the ground.

Many different breeds still exist, but many more have sadly been allowed to become extinct. Some have found other uses, like the St Bernards used in mountain rescue and the German shepherd dogs and related breeds which have become excellent guard dogs in a completely different context, working with police and security firms.

Nowadays, some of these ancient breeds are reared for their appearance and for showing. Old English sheepdogs are endearing to look at and in personality, and as a result they have their own niche in books, films and, famously, advertising the Dulux brand of paint. Nana, the dog who looks after the children in the story of Peter Pan, is sometimes depicted as an Old English Sheepdog, as is the Colonel in the film and book *One Hundred and One Dalmatians*. Yet a couple of years ago these magnificent animals were on the endangered list, but now I'm happy to say there has been a surge in popularity, and they have been taken off the list.

Several breeds of guardian dog are white, selectively bred over centuries to camouflage them in a flock of sheep. One of these is the Maremma sheepdog, originally bred in central Italy, and still used to this day to protect the dwindling number of sheep that are over-wintered by shepherds in the Maremma marshlands.

They've spread across the globe, having been used as livestock guardians in the USA, Canada and Australia.

I've been lucky enough to meet some of these huge, friendly dogs, which from a distance look like small polar bears. A group of owners arranged to meet up at Cotswold Farm Park for a most unusual fund raiser, which really fascinated me. So with Charlie, Ella and Alfie I took a stroll across to the farm park to chat to them, and we were enthusiastically greeted by about 12 boisterous, adorable dogs, probably averaging about 40 kilos in weight each (for comparison, Boo, our wire-haired Vizsla, is probably about 20 kilos, and Peg the border collie only about 14).

The Maremma Sheepdog Club of Great Britain had organised the money raiser to give support to a touching initiative in Australia, where these woolly giants of dogs have been protecting an endangered species – a subject close to my heart, of course.

The smallest penguin breed, known originally as the Fairy penguin and now as the Little penguin, colonises an uninhabited island, Middle Island, off the coast near the town of Warrnambool, in South Victoria. The penguins are only 30 to 40 centimetres tall, so definitely little.

There used to be hundreds of them on Middle Island, until an enterprising fox discovered that at low tide it was possible to cross to the island, only a matter of a 150 metres off the mainland, without even needing to swim, just getting his paws a bit wet. He told all his mates and in a very short space of time the population of penguins was almost completely wiped out. The problem started in about 2000, when the sea's natural current shifted and there was an increased build-up of sand, and it rapidly got worse as the fox population escalated with this free and easy source of food. Foxes also kill for the thrill of it, not necessarily just to eat, and in the space of two nights in 2005 around 360 corpses were found on the island by the Penguin Preservation Project monitors.

Patrols were set up to shoot the foxes and poisoned bait was laid for them. Sadly nothing was very effective, and it looked as though these delightful little birds were not going to survive in this spot. It wasn't going to be the end of the Little penguin species, as there are other colonies around the coast of Australia and New Zealand, but it was desperately sad for local conservationists. Finally, only four Little penguins were surviving on the island.

Step forward local free range chicken farmer Alan 'Swampy' Marsh. Alan was using a Maremma to protect his chickens, having successfully trained her to regard them as her 'flock'. He suggested his dog, Oddball, might be able to see off the foxes on Middle Island. There was a lot of scepticism, and even downright opposition (some people suggested the dog would attack the penguins), but as nobody had a better idea and the penguins were almost wiped out, Oddball was dispatched to the island.

She stayed there for three weeks before swimming back to the mainland to be reunited with her master. But her presence had done the trick: the foxes had been scared off by her barking and her scent. The Preservation Project monitors saw no more fox paw-prints on the island.

Two more Maremmas were trained up to take over from Oddball, and since 2006 there have been a succession of dogs. They stay on the island during the warmer months when the sandbar appears, and volunteers feed and check on them each day. They are trained to regard the penguins as their friends and the island as their own territory, barking if anything suspicious happens. They have never had to kill a fox because, since their arrival on Middle Island, the foxes have beaten a hasty retreat. But their trainers have no doubt they could and would kill a fox if they had to, just as their ancestors did to protect sheep. The population of penguins has increased to 200, and not one has been killed by a fox since the project began.

Oddball sadly died recently, but she'd reached the grand old age of 15, well above normal life expectancy for such a large breed. A children's film was even made about her and Swampy, her owner: it was called *Oddball* and was popular in Australia, sparking an influx of tourists to the area. They go to meet the Maremmas that are in training and to do a tour of the island.

Buying and training dogs is expensive, and that was why the Maremma owners who met at Cotswold Farm

Park were raising money. I'm pleased to say they were able to send £200 to the project as a result. It was a lovely day, with the sun shining, and the dogs and owners were able to go on the farm wildlife trail, which is where we caught up with them. A sudden shower drove us all into the café where these lovable dogs, who seemed mischievous while we were outside, settled down obediently.

I know that guardian dogs like Maremmas are used not just for sheep and goats, but for turkeys, chickens, deer and even alpacas in areas of the world where there are still predators, but I had never heard of them being used to protect penguins before. The local council, which had to be convinced reluctantly to give Oddball a chance to protect the penguins, is now talking about erecting a statue in her memory.

So that's two types of sheepdog: the droving dogs and the guardian dogs. In the next chapter I will look at the history of the ones I am very familiar with, herding dogs.

CHAPTER 8

My Kind of Dogs

I never imagined I had much in common with Queen Victoria but it turns out I do: collies. She loved them too. This was, naturally, very influential, because before she became devoted to them, collies were a Cinderella dog in the fashionable world. They weren't lap dogs or sporting dogs, they were dogs who worked for a living and were treasured by their owners – shepherds and farmers – for their great skills, not for their looks. Their history stretches back to the beginning of civilisation.

So does mine: I'm very proud to call myself a shepherd. It's one of the oldest professions in the world – yes, I've heard all the terrible jokes – but herding sheep and goats really does go back to primitive times. Hunters came first, of course, but it was the shepherds who tended livestock and the farmers who planted crops who moved civilisation on, and made it possible for men to put down roots, build permanent homes, and feed their families in safer, better conditions than their nomadic forefathers.

The men who rounded animals up, domesticated them, moved them from pasture to pasture, bred them to provide even more meat and better wool, are the men who laid the foundations of life as we live it today. As I go about my livestock work on the farm, or meet other shepherds through filming for *Countryfile*, I know that I have a connection that extends all the way back to the beginnings of domestication, about 15,000 years ago. I am part of a very long tradition, and by my side my dog Peg, and all the other sheepdogs I have known, are just as much a part of that tradition.

There are shelves full of old books about spaniels, setters, pointers, beagles, foxhounds and gundogs, but relatively few books about herding dogs. The men who owned them were rarely even literate, and so not likely to go into flights of fancy about their wonderful dogs. A shepherd will describe a dog as great if it can round up sheep, divide them, pen them. He doesn't care about its colouring, the colour of its eyes, whether its ears are a perfect match. When they win prizes today, it is for their agility and intelligence, both of which they have in spades, and both of which are reasons they are so vital to me and all others who depend on them daily. A working shepherd in the market for a new dog is keen to know how well its parents were able to work, not how many rosettes they won at dog shows, and the dogs that sell for huge sums at sheepdog sales are bought for the working history of their forebears and the signs of ability they show.

The history of sheepdogs, as I have said, is as old as the story of domesticated animals, but it came relatively late to Britain. Domestication of animals began in western Asia, and that's where dogs are first believed to have been used to herd animals. It was another 10,000 years, during the Bronze Age, that farming really began in Britain, with dogs guarding and then herding the flocks.

Herding dogs worked alongside the guardian dogs, the ones who lived with the flock, and then really came into their own after the need for protection dogs receded as wild predators disappeared and flocks could be moved around for better grazing. Now shepherds could turn their flocks loose and allow them to wander, but they needed to be able to round them up again. Dogs with an instinct to herd were highly prized, and breeding for the purpose began. Herding dogs are smaller than the guardian dogs, more agile, and, most important, they are able to be trained to respond to their master's commands, whether it's voice or whistle. They are not directly descended from the large protection dogs who would have been difficult to train for this job, and would have caused havoc if they had tried to move a flock by herding.

The ability to herd – to cast wide and round up a flock of sheep – developed when great swathes of the country were covered in forest, and sheep and goats would be left to crop the vegetation among the trees. The shepherd needed a dog that worked silently, out-flanked the animals and nudged them together simply by his presence, but did not chase or attack the animals.

Most importantly, the dog had to be able to respond to its master's commands when it could not see him, because of the trees. It also needed, at times, to work on its own initiative when it spotted a problem – a sheep making a break, say – that its master could not see. Over generations this specific, gifted sheepdog evolved. The hills and forests of Scotland and the border country was a good breeding ground, but all across the country sheepdogs with traits peculiar to their particular area were being bred, all of them for the same purpose.

Agriculture in Britain developed massively in Roman times, when many independent farms were established with shepherds tending their flocks in different terrains and weather conditions across the country, including on remote hill farms, where even today the living is still bleak, tough, and essentially unchanged over the centuries. The farmers supplied the Roman forts and camps with meat and wool, and as the soldiers were often stationed in forts for years at a time, many of them, too, became part-time shepherds, with their own flocks and their own dogs. Sheep and goats were imported to Britain by the Romans from Spain and North Africa, where herding was well established, and dogs and herdsmen often came with the flocks. As the climate and terrain here proved to be good for sheep, the wool trade became a very important part of the Anglo–Roman economy, so the flocks grew, and so did the role of herding dogs.

The value of sheepdogs was recognised by the Roman writer Marcus Terentius Varro, who wrote: 'Be careful not to buy dogs from hunters or butchers, for the dogs of butchers are too idle to follow the flock, and hunting dogs, if they see a stag or a hare, will chase after it instead of after the sheep. Thus the best is one that has been bought from a shepherd, and has been trained to follow sheep ...'

The wool trade became the backbone of the economy of this country until the late fifteenth century, and to this day the Speaker in the House of Lords sits on 'the woolsack' – now a large wool-stuffed seat but originally a bale of wool – a reminder of the huge importance of wool to the nation's wealth. The very name of my area, the Cotswolds, comes from the word 'cot', an enclosure for sheep, and 'wold' for hill, so it literally means sheep enclosure on the hills. It was well known throughout Europe in the Middle Ages for the quality of its wool, from sheep known as Cotswolds Lions which have long lustrous coats and a faintly golden hue to their wool. They remained very popular until after the First World War, when their numbers declined so much that they became a rare breed. Of course, we have a flock at Cotswold Farm Park, and their numbers are now building up well. I am proud to continue breeding these wonderful historic animals that have called this area home for many centuries.

Wealth from the sheep trade largely went to the church in the Middle Ages, which owned vast flocks of sheep, and to rich merchants. These merchants made enormous contributions towards the building and expansion of fine churches, known now as 'wool churches'. (They are spread across East Anglia, another prosperous sheep area, as well as the Cotswolds.) The story is that they believed that endowing churches would help buy them an easy journey to paradise after their deaths. The legacy for those of us who live in the area is wonderful, architecturally important, church buildings around us.

Of course, wherever there were sheep in large numbers, there were also dogs in large numbers. A good working dog was a precious commodity. The word 'collie' for a working sheepdog has been around for many years, and there are arguments as to where it originated: it could come from a Gaelic word meaning 'useful', which these dogs certainly are, or, as I've mentioned before, it could be a version of 'coaley', a Scottish word possibly referring to dogs working with the black (or coal) faced sheep of Scotland and the border countries, which is still the most common sheep breed in Britain. These Scottish collies spread across the country, especially in the second half of the nineteenth century when Scottish sheep farmers and shepherds moved to East Anglia, bringing some livestock and, more importantly, the dogs used to handle the flocks.

The word 'cur' became a derogatory description of an ill-behaved mongrel of very mixed parentage, and in years gone by an insulting word for a scoundrel. But the name derives from the word 'curtail', which means to cut short. In the seventeenth century, taxes were imposed on dog owners. The only exemptions were for shepherds and others who needed working dogs for ratting or other jobs. To claim the exemption the dog must have a docked tail, or 'curtul'. This led to all working dogs becoming known as 'curs'.

Although shepherds and farmers were not normally the sort of educated people with time on their hands to wax lyrical in print about their wonderful dogs, there are exceptions, the most notable being a man called James Hogg, who became known as the Ettrick Shepherd, and who, in the early 1800s, published poems and magazine articles about his amazing sheepdogs. He was a shepherd in the border countries from an early age and educated himself through reading, eventually becoming a well-respected writer and friend of the literati of the day, including Sir Walter Scott and William Wordsworth. But it is his stories about his real-life dogs which endure, and which any shepherd today will recognise.

He had a dog called Sirrah, who he bought from a drover who was starving him and treating him badly. Sirrah had not been trained as a sheepdog, 'and he knew so little of herding that he had never turned a sheep in his life; but as soon as he discovered that it was his duty to do so I can never forget with what anxiety and eagerness he learned his different evolutions. He would try every way deliberately till he found out what

I wanted him to do, and when I once made him understand a direction he never forgot it again ... He often
astonished me for, when hard-pressed in accomplishing
the task that he was put to, he had expedients of the
moment that bespoke a great share of the reasoning
faculty.'

Hogg told the story of 700 sheep which escaped their
pens in the middle of the night, scattering in three different directions, and could not be found in the dark.
Eventually he and his assistant gave up, but Sirrah did
not return when called. The next day they found Sirrah
holding the entire flock in a deep ravine, not one injured
or missing. He had been there for several hours.

The status of collies shot up when Queen Victoria
adopted them as her all-time favourite dogs – quite an
accolade, because she was a renowned dog lover. When
she and her husband Prince Albert built Balmoral
Castle in the Scottish Highlands in the 1850s it triggered
a fashion for all things Scottish, and that included collie
dogs. The queen already had kennels at Windsor Castle
with several dogs, but it was in Scotland she met and
fell in love with collies. Many dogs were given to her –
what do you give to a queen who has everything? Well,
another dog never goes amiss, and with so many
children, she could hand them all on.

The queen herself especially loved smooth-coated
collies, and as a result these became the fashionable
choice for carriage dogs for aristocratic ladies (not a
job an active, intelligent collie would relish, but I guess

they had servants to make sure the dogs got plenty of exercise before being taken out for stately trips in a carriage!) The queen's favourite, called Sharp, lived until he was 15, and there is a statue of him on his grave in Windsor Home Park. After Sharp, she had Noble who lived for 16 years, and in his final illness was attended by the queen's own physician, who also had to give her a sedative because she was so distressed. He, too, has a statue on his grave. Next came Roy, who was with her until she died. Although she had many other dogs these three were special: they lived inside her palaces with her, and from pictures and the statues, I'd definitely describe them as border collies, although that name was not used until later, in the early years of the twentieth century (border collies were not recognised as a breed by the Kennel Club until 1976).

Partly influenced by the royal patronage, wealthy Americans were also impressed by the cleverness of these dogs and breeding for commercial purposes began, with canny Scots farmers and shepherds selling their best-looking dogs (but never their best working dogs). Scouts went around country markets buying up dogs, purely for their looks.

Two things happened at roughly the same time. Although local farmers and shepherds had for a long time held competitions among themselves, properly organised sheepdog trials began to spring up across the country. The first was held in Bala, North Wales in

1873, with ten dogs competing. The following year there was a trial in Scotland, and they quickly spread.

Today, I'm really pleased to be involved in the *Countryfile* coverage of One Man and His Dog, a competition between England, Scotland, Ireland and Wales, with a junior and senior member in each team. I've always loved watching trials, and I'm constantly amazed by the highly refined skills of these super dogs. So it's terrific to get to meet the competitors, both two-legged and four-legged.

Coincidentally, showing dogs became popular at much the same time as trialling began to emerge, and breeders started to turn their attention to how the dogs looked. The first Crufts dog show was held in 1891, with 2,000 dogs competing. Nowadays, Crufts is a four-day event with classes not simply for the appearance of competitors, but for obedience, agility, flyball and heeling to music. Nonetheless, the overall champion is awarded for the dog which best conforms to its breed standards. In the 104 shows held since 1905, it's interesting to see that collies have only won three times, the first being a 'Scotch' collie in 1906, probably as a result of them still being popular with the royal family. (Queen Victoria's daughter-in-law, Queen Alexandra, was very keen on rough-coated collies, and bred them at Sandringham House.) Despite their few years in the fashion sun, they have resolutely remained as working dogs, proving themselves in agility and flyball rather than parading round the ring being assessed for their looks.

In the early days of dog shows an interesting challenge was issued to the show fanciers from working dog owners: a competition to demonstrate that show dogs very quickly lost their ability to work, by setting them a task of rounding up sheep. That's exactly how it turned out: the show collies barked, yelped and lost control of the sheep. The winner of the sheep herding was a working collie called Maddie, who may not have had the looks but certainly had the ability to move sheep around. I'm not sure it meant the show dogs had 'lost' the ability to work – they had never been allowed to work, and had no training. What a shame for them: as you know by now, I personally believe dogs are happier if they work, and literally thousands of years of breeding by shepherds and farmers have made sheepdogs what they are today, finely tuned to the demands of the job, without so much as a thought for how they look.

Today there are many different types of herding sheepdog: Welsh collies, rough-haired collies, Shetlands, smooth-haired collies, border collies, kelpies and Huntaways, plus lots of continental breeds. Some breeds are no longer used for their original purpose, but they all have their origins in the proud tradition of the working dogs of farmers and itinerant shepherds, who relied on them for a living.

When I look at Peg, and at any of the sheepdogs I meet as I go about my work as a farmer or filming for *Countryfile*, I know I am looking at hundreds, even thousands of years of history, and it's a history I love being part of.

I enjoy all the stories we feature on *Countryfile*, but naturally the ones that speak to me most are the ones where I meet shepherds and farmers who are doing the same job as me, but in wildly different terrains and climates. I love watching them work sheep, and I am full of admiration for what they achieve. The way some of them live and work makes life at Bemborough Farm look like a walk in the park ...

Perhaps the most spectacular was when I joined the shepherds of the high Alps in Switzerland to bring a huge flock of black-nosed sheep down from their summer grazing near the Aletsch glacier, a journey which involved herding them along a precarious mountain path and across a narrow bridge over a thundering, icy river. I had to travel up to the village where the sheep belong, Belalp, by cable car, as there are no roads. The annual movement of the sheep is spectacular, and it was a privilege to see it, but, boy, did those shepherds earn my respect as they clambered across this rugged territory to bring their livestock more than a thousand metres down the steep mountain to winter in kinder pastures.

I helped out with similar challenging missions to round up and move animals in difficult terrain here in Britain when I visited Devon for the annual check-up carried out on the feral goats of the Valley of the Rocks, near Lynton. They lived up to the name 'mountain goat' by running away from us up near-impossible rocky inclines. Then again, I helped introduce sheep to the magical island of Tintagel in Cornwall for the first time since 1896. With some difficulty I assisted the Tintagel property manager, Matt Ward, and assorted helpers get a small herd of Soays along a wooden path, across a bridge and up 148 steps, so that they could graze the land around the ruins of the castle built on what legend says was the home of King Arthur and his knights of the Round Table.

In all of these cases it was decided not to use dogs as they may have chased the animals too close to the cliff where either dog or livestock may have fallen to their death, so the herding was all done on foot by humans. This can prove very tricky, particularly as the animals you are trying to round up are far more agile and quicker than you.

The reason the Soays, a hardy Scottish breed of sheep which I know well because we have them at Cotswold Farm Park, were introduced to Tintagel is to help manage the land and preserve rare species of plants. The sheep graze on the coarse grasses which, left untended, would out-compete and eliminate the valuable, diverse plant life. Matt told me that he was hoping the sheep would increase the number of wild flowers from hundreds to thousands of different species.

The use of sheep and other animals to manage and preserve the landscape is a common theme in the shepherding programmes I've made for *Countryfile*. It makes so much sense. But I was taken by surprise when I filmed a flock of sheep on a beach at Ainsdale, because I had no idea that sheep could live on sand dunes.

Ainsdale is a 13-mile stretch of beach and dunes between Southport and Formby, on the north-west coast. It's a wide, sandy beach area that was once used by locals to run rabbit warrens, when rabbit was an essential animal for the family pot. Sadly, the rabbits were wiped out by myxomatosis in the 1950s, and it was only some time later that ecologists and other experts realised what a good job they had been doing of managing the dunes, chomping away at the vegetation to keep it in check and allow different species to thrive.

Now the 253-acre site is maintained by Natural England as a National Nature Reserve. There are way-marked paths for the public to use, but because of the diversity of rare animals and plants, people are not allowed to wander all over.

But one creature that is allowed to wander in the winter months is a flock of 250 Herdwick sheep. I'm a great fan of Herdwicks: they are tough little animals who live on the Lakeland fells, so they are accustomed to rain, snow, sleet and anything else mother nature throws at them. They stand as solid as rocks, unde-terred by howling gales and blinding rain. Flocks from remote and difficult hill farms are often sent to kinder pastures to over-winter, so I wasn't surprised by the fact that these fell dwellers go away for a holiday each year. But a holiday to the beach?

I took Peg to Ainsdale, hoping she could help out rounding up the flock. Peg was new to me at the time and this was the first long journey we'd done together. She was great, travelling peacefully and sleeping in the back of the truck outside the hotel where I and the film crew were staying. She was such an easy companion, and I couldn't believe my luck in having her. Because I don't know much about her early years, I had no idea if she had ever been to a beach or seen the sea before. So prior to linking up with Dave Mercer, the senior reserves manager for Natural England who is overall head of the conservation project on the dunes, I took her across the sand to the sea. She went in up to her waist when I threw a stick, but she never went out of her depth and she seemed a little bit nervous of the waves. Collies are not renowned as water dogs, so I wasn't surprised that she jumped a bit when the waves swept in, but I already knew she was a brave little dog and she didn't seem at all fazed by it.

It was a beautiful day, with a wintry sun taking the edge off a chill breeze, and the view of the dunes was impressive. What surprised me was the amount of vegetation.

Dave explained: 'If left alone this area would be a birch forest, or even an oak forest. But a forest is not as rare as an open dune landscape, so we're halting the degradation of the dunes with our four-legged lawn-mowers, the sheep. This area has a European designation as a special area of conservation, and if we want to keep the diversity of the plant and animal life here, we have to hold the dominant vegetation at bay.'

The dunes are a natural sea defence that prevent flooding and maintaining them means keeping the right sort of grass, the type that binds the dunes together. Dave told me that the dunes are home to a really large population of Natterjack toads, with as many as 50 per cent of the British population living on this coastline in some years. They are so noisy that they are known as 'the Birkdale chorus', Birkdale being the neighbouring stretch of the sand dunes. As well as the toads there are great crested newts and sand lizards.

There are also 473 different species of plant, including the heath dog violet, which is the food source for the very picky caterpillar of the Dark Green Fritillary butterfly. Other rare flowers include dune helleborine, seaside centaury, yellow bartsia and sticky stork's-bill. The plants encourage all sorts of insects to live and thrive on the dunes: it's an inter-connected web of life, and I can appreciate how tricky it is managing the area for the benefit of so many different creatures.

That's where the sheep come in. They've been grazing here for over ten years, starting with a small group to see how well they survived and whether or not they had the right impact on the vegetation, which had been uncontrolled since the rabbit population disappeared. The flock is contained in a wide parcel of land, and when they have exhausted the grazing there they are moved on to a different area. And moving sheep is a job for sheepdogs, so I hoped Peg was going to be useful. It was going to be a real test for her, as she would be operating among the dunes and for much of the time not able to see me, just responding to my whistles and shouts. Dave gave me a tip: climb to the top of a high dune so that I could keep an eye on her as much as possible.

Easier said than done: the sheep were roaming happily among the dunes, but Peg and I made heavier weather of it, unused to walking on sand and constantly sticking our feet into hidden rabbit holes and tripping over the rough scrub. Peg was, as ever, very eager to work, and she shot off like a bullet when we sighted some sheep, going round them and encouraging them to flock together. They disappeared from my sight behind a sand dune and so did she, but I knew she was still working, using her own brain. Sheep have an amazing instinct to collect together whenever they see or hear a dog, or hear a shepherd's whistle, and they were soon running in from all around, funnelling through tight gaps in the dunes, and heading down to the gate we were trying to get them through.

Peg wasn't the only dog rounding up the sheep. Tony Meadow, the reserve warden, and his assistant Sophie Bray, were also there with Molly, a five-year-old collie, and Tato, another collie who was retired from his working life, but more than happy to help out. They worked together as a team and we drove the flock on to fresh grazing.

The sheep are on the dunes from October to April, and they thrive, returning to the Lake District well fed and with none of the foot problems sheep can get in winter, because the sand is so dry. Herdwicks have proved to be the best breed for the job: when some Icelandic sheep were brought in they were a lot less successful, not being used to being moved by dogs and not thriving in the damp of the north west of England.

While I was there I saw another animal that has been brought in to crop the dunes. Seeing sheep was a big enough surprise, but it was even more bizarre to see five rare breed Shetland cattle, which were being trialled as another way of managing the vegetation. Since my visit a couple of years ago the breed of cow has changed and the dunes are now host to a small herd of Red Poll cattle, who, like the sheep, come to the dunes to spend the winter months keeping the vegetation in check. It's a win-win situation: the dunes are maintained, and the farmer gets his sheep or cattle looked after without having to provide any winter fodder.

It was a similar conservation project that took me to Snowdonia a few months later, real hill-farming countryside. But there are special habitats for wildlife and plants here, too, and it's a juggling act getting farming and conservation to work hand in hand, in a way that benefits both.

The farm I visited, Hafod y Llan, was bought by the National Trust in 2000 with the aim of preserving the mountainous area that was being overgrazed by the sheep. After reducing the number of sheep from 4,000 to just under 2,000, it was clear there were still problems. The Trust did not want to reduce sheep numbers further, but after looking at the conservation work of hill farmers in the Alps and the Pyrenees, they decided the way forward was to actively manage the sheep with a shepherd on the mountain with them all the time between May and September, moving them away from sensitive places where overgrazing was damaging the plant life.

It is a five-year project, and the aim is to have flower-rich mountain tops with grazed valleys below. The problem is that the sheep that live on this land are, like most sheep on hill farms, hefted. This means they have a particular area of the mountainside which belongs to them and their own small group of sheep. The lambs are taught by their mothers that this is their patch, and the ewes teach them the terrain, where to find shade, where to find water and all the pitfalls to avoid. To move them to different 'hefts' or 'heafs' (the word changes depending on which part of the country you are in; the Welsh word is 'cynefin') is going to take a long time and careful management.

I went up there when the project had been going for a year, and when the farm had just appointed a second shepherd to help cover the long hours that have to be spent up on the mountainside with the sheep. It's a lonely job, but very fulfilling for the right person who loves sheep, has a good four-legged companion and doesn't mind his own company.

I met Arwyn Owen who manages the farm for the National Trust and I asked him why the sheep needed this special, full-time attention. He explained that the sheep need more management.

'They are not always eating what we want them to eat, and without intervention they linger in some areas and graze the vegetation too closely. These are areas where the wildflowers and plants need to be safe-guarded. So we've gone back to the way things used to be, with a shepherd actually on the hill with them all the time in daylight hours. He leads the sheep to the areas that need to be grazed.'

With Peg by my side I climbed up the mountain to where the latest recruit to the shepherding project, Daniel Jones, was going about his job of checking where the sheep were cropping. There were about 800 Welsh mountain sheep. They're a lively little breed whose thick, coarse wool protects them from the harsh Snowdonia weather. In different parts of Wales there are derivatives of the same breed with various Welsh names: as well as white Welsh mountains, there are Torddu, or Badger Face, with a white body and black belly. Torwen are the reverse – a black body and white belly. Black Welsh are, as the names suggests, black all over, and the little Balwen have black with white socks and a white tip to the tail and are the only one of all the Welsh sheep considered a rare breed.

The flock were dotted around us and I realised how difficult Daniel's job is. It's not like moving a flock: he has to monitor individual sheep and move each one when it's in the wrong place. I commented that he must be fit; Peg had romped up the hill but I was breathless by the time I reached him. He described his job as 'awesome', and said he had learned a lot in the six weeks he had been there.

'There's a lot of walking, and without dogs we'd be pretty useless up here. They're an essential tool, and we couldn't work the sheep without them.'

I noticed a small box attached to the collar of Dan's dog, which I recognised as a GPS tracker. Dan explained that it records where they have been working and how many miles they have covered. There are also fixed cameras dotted around the hillside which monitor the movement of the sheep. Combining both technologies shows where the sheep are grazing the most.

Dan was happy for me to let Peg have a go bringing a few sheep down from an area above us where they were not supposed to be. Working individual sheep on steep slopes was not something either she or I are used to, and I'm afraid Peg in her eagerness did move the sheep a little bit faster than Dan wanted, the ewes charging down the mountain at a bit of a lick. Unlike me moving a flock, when speed helps, the art here is to be able to move individual sheep so gently that they don't realise they are being nudged. I reckon Peg and I would get the hang of it if we practised ...

I was amused when Dan told me he knows by sight several sheep that are persistent offenders, always grazing in the wrong places. He even puts a blue mark on the naughty ones so that he can pick them out more easily.

Although it is clearly an idyllic and ancient way of life (if you don't count the trackers and cameras), I wondered how the project was going in terms of saving rare plants, so I met up with Sabine Nouvet, who is the National Trust conservation ranger for Snowdonia, and who is monitoring the project.

'It's very encouraging. We have plants like heather and bilberries that are starting to recover, and we're hoping that the new shoots that are appearing now will survive.'

She led me further up the mountain, to show me the little green bilberry fruits, and heather with new shoots.

'Bilberries respond very quickly to a change in grazing,' she told me. 'We had some heather flowers last year and we are hoping for more this year.'

She also explained that it wasn't simply a matter of saving the plant life: the sheep are also benefitting, because the diversification is bringing back plants that are more palatable and nutritious for them. The sheep and the ecology of the mountain are both gaining from the project.

For me, the most satisfying thing was seeing a shepherd working in the old-fashioned way, alone with nothing but his dog and his sheep, upholding a very ancient tradition.

Another very traditional shepherd I met for *Countryfile* is a young woman called Ashley Stamper, who works on the Cheviot Hills of Northumbria in the harshest of conditions. The work she does very much follows the old, largely unchanged, routines of centuries of shepherding, with her dogs by her side and only a quad bike and some good waterproof clothing to distinguish her from the men and women who ran flocks on this land for generations past.

Yet in some ways, Ashley is very different from those shepherds of yore. For a start, she's not from a farming family. In fact, quite how she has ended up living in the lee of the Kielder Forest and working a flock of north of England Blackface sheep on the Otterburn ranges, where the landowner is the Ministry of Defence, is, to me, a surprising story, and hearing it made me think of my dad, who also had no family background in farming. I recognised in Ashley something that he must have had: an urge to work outdoors, close to nature, at one with the land. Something that they both intuitively knew, without having any experience of the life, as I was lucky enough to have as a child.

Ashley's mother and father both work in different branches of the beauty business, her mum as a beauty therapist and her dad running a company that has developed and sells tanning machines. As a child, the only connection Ashley had with the great outdoors was her love of horses.

At her school near Edinburgh, Ashley was studying for her Highers (the Scottish equivalent to GCSEs) when her parents bought her a beauty salon. She was 15 at the time, going to school in the morning, and rushing out to run the salon at lunchtimes and after school in the afternoons, putting herself through courses in accountancy, beauty therapy, massage, reflexology and holistic therapy, managing staff who were many years older than her. She even opened a wedding dress shop at the rear of the salon.

So far, so very girlie, and clearly Ashley had a good career laid out for her when she finished school. But she wasn't happy. She'd sold her pony to a farmer and to keep in touch she spent a few school holidays helping out on the farm, and she realised that these were the happiest times of her life.

So, despite having won accolades as one of Scotland's youngest entrepreneurs, and as the world's youngest salon owner with a good wage coming in from the salon, at the age of 17 Ashley decided she would never be happy working inside all day, and beauty therapy wasn't what she wanted to do for the rest of her life.

'Dad said I was mad, and told me I needed to knuckle down and get on with the business. But I was adamant: I wanted to go to university to study horses. When I looked into it, though, horses wouldn't take me far enough, and I realised what I needed to do was take a degree in agriculture.'

Without enough qualifications to get on to a degree course, Ashley went to college for two years to get Scottish Vocational Qualifications, combining her time studying with working on the farm where she had spent school holidays. She'd gone from having money in her pocket every week to working on the farm free in return for board and lodging, staying with her grandparents while at college, and relying on her mum for subsidies.

'But I was so happy, I knew this was what I wanted to do for the rest of my life. The people I was working for, Pam and Paul, taught me lots, including how to train a sheepdog. I also found some local contracting work to help out financially.'

The first year of her four-year degree course was in Dumfries, and the following three years in Edinburgh. She had a beaten-up £300 car, she didn't go out socialising and she got stuck into her studies, getting excellent results.

When I met her she was still in the final year of her degree, attending uni only a couple of days a month and studying at home, with the rest of her time spent working on a large farm up in the hills looking after sheep. It's clear she loves her job, and when I watched her loading sheep onto a lorry for market, I could see she has the calm personality that you need around animals.

Where she works on the Ministry of Defence ranges where the army test heavy artillery and rockets, the landscape is constantly changing because of the explosions and there is only so much work she can do with a quad bike. 'Thank goodness for the dogs, I couldn't manage without them,' she said. Because nobody is allowed on the ranges when firing is in progress, she often has to get up there at 4.30am to check on the sheep, and be off by 9am.

It struck me as a very tough life, but Ash told me she prefers being up on the hills to having the sheep down in the valley.

'It changes all the time. You think you've learnt the hills and then one morning the fog is down in front of your face and all of a sudden you've no idea where you are. When you are on the hills by yourself and the mist is in and it's just you and your dogs, it feels very special.'

Ashley rents a small cottage from another local farm, where she lives with her three border collies, Dot, who is a quarter kelpie, Jim and puppy Mo.

'I'm very lucky, everyone helps me out,' she says.

'When I could no longer stay at the farm where I was working for nothing, because I needed to earn money, Mum said "Come home". It was tempting, it would have been very easy. But I knew I couldn't leave this valley, the people here, the sheep. At the same time I was homeless with three dogs and two horses. Luckily by then I had a boyfriend, James, and his family let me stay for a while, then I was offered the cottage. Another friend had a garage full of furniture she did not need, two friends took my horses and one horse now has a loan home. It was a real community effort.'

One chunk of very welcome help came from the Prince's Countryside Fund, a charity set up in 2010 by the Prince of Wales to improve the prospects of family farm businesses and the quality of rural life. One of the major worries for the future of farming in this country is that the average age of farmers is 59, so in conjunction with the car manufacturer Land Rover the Countryside Fund launched an initiative in 2016 to give five young people under the age of 35 the chance to drive a Land Rover Discovery Sport for a whole year to help them in the difficult early years of their career. It was the head of agriculture at her university who told Ash to apply.

'I had to put in a one minute video of why I needed the Discovery to help with my work. I was in Edinburgh, without my dogs, and I was up against the deadline to apply. So I borrowed a collie from Mum's next door neighbour, a pet dog who has probably never seen a sheep, and I had a couple of feedbags and medicine bottles in the back of my old car. We filmed it pretending it was 5am and I was hauling myself out of bed for work. I'm really surprised I got through the first round, because the dog was so fat I had to lift her in and out of the car ...'

Luckily, after interviewing Ashley over the phone and visiting her on the farm where she works, the team from the Countryside Fund and Land Rover could see how she would make great use of the car, especially commuting from Northumbria to Edinburgh.

'I put the two people who came to assess me on the quad bike and took them up on the hills where I work. I think they were impressed by the vastness and hardness of it all, and the long hours we work. They could see my little car was overflowing with feedbags, medicine and dogs.

'The only sad thing is that I only get to keep the Land Rover for a year. Then it will be back to another old banger, I guess. I've been a bit spoilt, having such an amazing car.'

One of the things about Ashley that intrigues me is that she has chosen, for her university honours project, to study sheepdogs. As she told me: 'There's not much data that shows how much work these dogs do, so I'm looking at energy consumption, comparing working dogs with non-working dogs.'

It will be useful to have some scientific data – although, I must say, I don't need any stats to tell me that my dogs, and dogs like Ashley's, are burning a lot more energy than the average family pet. Her project has two other parts; one on how dogs gather sheep, to assess whether they could ever be replaced by drones (like me, Ashley thinks this will never happen, but she's carried out an impartial study). The other part is an attempt to analyse the behaviour of dogs competing at sheepdog trials.

Ashley told me she was nervous about meeting me, because my dogs look so well behaved when they feature on *Countryfile*. She was worried hers would let her down. But I reassured her that mine are not perfect and sometimes the same scene is shot over and over until they do it right. I must say, working with her, I think she is doing really well with her dogs, and they are lovely animals.

Does she ever wish she'd stuck with the beauty business? 'When it's 4am and howling with wind and rain outside, it takes a bit of strength to get out of my bed. But I never seriously think about changing my job. I've never wanted to go back. Sometimes when Mum has to attend a big beauty show in London, I'll go with her to help her out – I owe her for all the support she has given me. So I wear a dress and makeup, do my hair. I like being girlie sometimes, and I sometimes give friends a massage, or do waxing, but I don't miss doing it every day, and I do miss the farm whenever I'm away from it.

'People tell me that with a degree I should go after a graduate job, earn a lot more than I do as a shepherd. But it's the part of the job I love most, and find constantly challenging: it's a lot trickier for me starting a tractor and picking up a bale of hay than it is writing 3,000 words on the protein requirements of ruminants. I know that if I took an inside job, after a couple of days I would crave the hills, the farm, the dogs.'

As I met Ashley and her dogs just before Christmas, filming for a *Countryfile* Christmas special, she and I popped in to hear the choir at a local chapel, Bowden Kirk, practising for their Christmas service. Lay minister Pam Walker explained to me why dogs are welcome in the church.

'It's a tradition in the borders, especially at times of festivals like Christmas, for sheepdogs to come to church. Dogs are part of the family as well as working companions, so shepherds would naturally bring them along to church.

'It was a bit strange for travelling priests, not used to the area, who were puzzled as to why their congregation was not standing up at the appropriate times in the service. But if they did stand, the dogs would get up, assuming they were off home. So it was easier, and kept the atmosphere more holy, if everyone stayed sitting down.'

As the choir sang, appropriately, 'While Shepherds Watched Their Flocks by Night', Ashley's three dogs settled down very contentedly and never stirred. It's wonderful to think of those old shepherds whose bond with their dogs was so strong that they went everywhere with them, even to church. And it's wonderful, too, that the church welcomed them.

Ashley is a fine example of a young person who has been attracted into shepherding, and I'm passionate about enthusing other young people to take on the job. If the average age of a farmer in Britain is 59, we need as much young blood as possible.

So I was very happy to travel with Peg up to Cumbria, to visit Newton Rigg college, which is a few miles from Penrith in the rugged, high fells of north Lakeland, where an exciting new course has been launched, the only one in the country dedicated to sheepdog handling.

The course, which has attracted 15 enthusiastic young students, is run by Derek Scrimgeour, a top dog trialler and sheep farmer. When I caught up with him he was impressing on the students how important it is for a shepherd or dog handler to stay calm.

'The dog buys into your mood. If you are loud, excited and rushing about, the dog will be the same. It's a technique you learn. I'm not a naturally calm person,' he confessed, 'but I can act calm.'

Derek enjoys passing on tips and skills to the young-sters, particularly the things he had to learn through making mistakes when he was their age.

Matt Bagley, from the college, was instrumental in getting the 20-week course off the ground and he believes as passionately as I do that we need to encourage the shepherds and farmers of the future in any way we can.

'It is fundamentally important because the bond between a dog and a handler is so special, and if we don't harness it in young people we may lose these skills. In this terrain a quad bike is of little or no use. You need a dog to do the job quickly and efficiently. When you buy a tractor, you get a manual, but not when you get a dog. All dogs and all handlers are different.'

The youngsters I met that day all seemed to be enjoying themselves, and knuckling down to learning their whistles.

One student at Newton Rigg college who doesn't need to do a sheepdog-handling course is 16-year-old Tom Blease. Tom was partnered with my old friend and mentor Dick Roper in the 2016 One Man and His Dog competition, and they were the winning team.

Tom now combines his studies at the college with an apprenticeship on a sheep farm near Ullswater, and he's intending to do more trialling. He says, 'I am earning a bit of money to pay for my own sheep and for when I can start driving, and I'm doing something I really enjoy,' he told me.

That's the key thing: enjoying the work. It's what gets us all, me included, out of bed on cold, wet mornings and outside into the fields. I'm thrilled that at *Countryfile* we've established a Young Farmer of the Year Award, for under-25 year olds, because these youngsters are the future of farming in this country.

I can't leave the subject of herding dogs without looking at New Zealand Huntaways. I've been to New Zealand twice, but on my first visit, when Duncan and I were making our way around Australia, New Zealand and North America on next-to-no money, I didn't get much chance to see Huntaways at work. Then, we spent a month pruning kiwi vines and the rest of our time driving around enjoying the breath-taking scenery. I'd heard of this special breed of New Zealand dog, and after working with Bob the kelpie in Australia, I was interested to see them. But I was slightly put off because I was told they barked from the moment they were let out of their kennels in the morning until they went back at night. I now know that this is not the case; although barking is an important part of their skill set, they are taught to do it on command, not incessantly.

The farmer who generously gave me and Duncan somewhere to stay did have a Huntaway, a remarkable three-legged dog that brought the cows in for milking in the morning, but because I was not working with livestock I didn't see a Huntaway working sheep.

I went back to New Zealand to make four programmes for *Countryfile* at the end of 2016, and this time I saw Huntaways working. They are beautiful black and tan dogs – they look like great big Labradors with a dash of hound in the mix. Nobody knows their exact heritage; they were first mentioned by the 'huntaway' name in the late nineteenth century. They were developed in response to farming in the hilly countryside. The vast sheep stations needed dogs that could work for days on end on steep, rough terrain, covering great distances. The sheepdogs brought by the settlers from Britain worked silently, but occasionally one would bark, and this was seen as useful, because the dogs had to work out of sight of the shepherd. So barking traits were deliberately bred for, as well as the agility, stamina and the intelligence needed for a dog that can work to some extent independently of his master.

A Huntaway does exactly what its name says: they hunt away, and they are not used for rounding up sheep. Their job is to take the huge flocks of sheep that are farmed out there up the mountains or along the valleys. In New Zealand it is normal for one man to handle a flock of 2,500 to 3,000 sheep, compared to here where it's usually one man to at the most a thousand. The dogs are therefore vital, each one doing the work of a couple of men.

The sheep in New Zealand are very hardy Romney sheep, which originated on the Romney marshes in Kent. They have been toughened up out there by natural selection: if a ewe can't lamb on her own or rear her lambs, they and she will die. Only the fittest live, so the surviving flock is naturally strong. Also, through careful genetic selection, the New Zealand farmers have bred sheep with worm resistance, foot-rot resistance, good growth rates and other desirable traits. So the sheep may have originated back here in Britain, but now we import them from New Zealand. At Bemborough Farm we buy New Zealand rams to put on our Romney ewes.

People sometimes ask why New Zealand lamb is so cheap: they have the advantages of very low overheads, with vast flocks and limited manpower, plus their grass grows all year round, not seasonally like ours. And much of that low production cost is down to these fantastic dogs. A collie wiggling about at the back of such a large flock would not be seen by the hundreds of sheep at the front, but the booming bark of the huntaway tells all 2,000 of them that there is a dog around, and the shepherd can work them from as far away as two miles. It's really impressive, watching one of these Huntaways zigzagging at the back of a huge mob of sheep, barking and controlling them.

During the *Countryfile* trip I also saw Huntaways driving a herd of Welsh black cattle, which were owned by an 83-year-old farmer who was as tough as his dogs. He lived in an old, very remote farm bungalow, two hours' drive down a forest track. I genuinely thought I was lost and was considering turning back, when at last I came to the farm. He works with his two grandsons, two collies for rounding up sheep, and two Huntaways, which get up behind the cattle and push them in the direction he wants them to go. I could see how responsive they were, and how quick to avoid getting too close to the cows. The farmer used whistle commands, and he had a whistle that told them to 'speak up', or bark.

He also had a remarkable little black and white Jack Russell, called Rhondda, who would travel about on the quad bike and hang out with the working dogs, occasionally dashing away to catch a rabbit. He lived outside the bungalow in a box he shared with a cat, and they curled up together. If the men went away for a few days they left food and water and both the cat and Rhondda fended for themselves outside. I asked one of the grandsons: 'What does the dog do when you're not here?'

'I don't know – I'm not here,' he replied, pragmatically.

Much as I admired Huntaways, because they are really lovely looking dogs, and I thrilled to the sight of them working, I wouldn't want a Huntaway back here. I simply wouldn't be able to use it to its full potential. We have small fields, and we don't need to drive enormous flocks over long distances.

While I was out in New Zealand, I heard about Pig dogs. They are cross-breeds with some qualities of herding dogs and border collies, with a touch of hound so they bark and have a good sense of smell, and genes from pit bull terriers so that they are brave and have strong jaws. The end result is a dog that barks when it smells pigs and will hunt them, but rather than chase them away it rounds them up back towards the dog's owner. Once the pig stands its ground the dog will grab hold of it. I recognise the skill of the dog but I'm rather glad I never witnessed it. Hunting wild pigs is a popular pastime, especially in the more remote areas. It is talked about as a great night out at the weekend in the same way that people here talk about a night down the pub. Whole generations of families – fathers, sons and grandsons – turn out together with their dogs. Pig hunting for sport also happens in America and Australia. The New Zealanders still have a bit of a frontier attitude, but sports like this in the UK were banned centuries ago.

CHAPTER 9

Have You Thought About Hungarian Wire-haired Vizslas?

After Ronnie died, our house felt very empty. Charlie and I both believe that a house needs a dog living in it, but for a few months all we had were the sheep-dogs kennelled outside. There was no welcoming snuffle when you came through the back door and nearly tripped over Ronnie on her bed in the passageway. There was no feeling of the comforting, unquestioning, non-judgmental presence of a dog to rush up to you with a wagging tail, delighted to see you even after the worst of days. There is nothing more relaxing than a dog pressing itself against your knee while you absent-mindedly stroke its head.

And there was no furry companion for Ella and Alfie, who were nine and five when Ronnie died. I'm a great believer that children thrive when they have a dog to love and be loved by. Of course, Ella had Pearl, but Pearl, despite her tricky start, was a working sheepdog and had always lived outside. We all felt the loss of Ronnie acutely, because the house felt strangely empty.

So there was no question: Bemborough farmhouse needed a dog. We'd also had a couple of break-ins on the farm, and we know that a barking dog is the best protection you can have against thieves, especially as we live in a fairly isolated place. When you go to sleep at night, it's reassuring to know there is a dog downstairs that will make all the right noises and make sure a burglar thinks twice about trying to get in, but neither Charlie nor I wanted a proper guard dog, like a German shepherd or a Rottweiler. We wanted a dog with a good bark, to alert us if necessary, but we also wanted a gentle family pet, and, for me, the bonus would be if it was also a gundog. So the big question was: which breed of dog should we go for?

I have fond memories of the Labradors I grew up with, but I know how gluttonous they can be, and how it's always necessary to check there is nothing within their reach that they may decide to devour, which can be tiresome. I also vividly remember the death of Raven after eating rat poison, and I don't want to experience something like that again.

Of course, after Nita, I'm a fan of springer spaniels, but Charlie is not so keen on them. They can be neurotic and non-stop, which can get irritating in a busy household. I considered German pointers, which are good gundogs, but I was told they are highly strung – like spaniels only with longer legs – so I crossed them off the list. So we faced a blank canvas, with all the many dog breeds – the Kennel Club recognises over 200 – to consider. We discussed it endlessly, and somehow no dog that we came up with completely suited all our needs, or appealed to us. There was a lot of talk of various small breeds but I like a larger dog that you don't have to bend too far down to pat, so the search went on.

Until, that is, the day I was filming for *Countryfile* in Norfolk and I was interviewing a gamekeeper, Tracie Rickman, about the way warreners used to keep rabbits in enclosures. The rabbits were such a valuable commodity that the warreners had fortified buildings in which to butcher them for meat and for their pelts. We were filming ferrets being used to catch rabbits in an area where the soil is sandy and riddled with rabbit warrens.

When we were on a break I talked to Tracie about our dilemma, explaining our reservations about the obvious candidates, Labradors and spaniels.

'Have you thought about Hungarian wire-haired Vizslas?' she asked.

I had literally never heard of Vizslas and had no idea what they looked like or what temperament they had.

'Come and see mine,' she said, after filming was over. So I went back to her home and was met by four big, gingery, long-haired dogs, who barked loudly when I first arrived but settled down when she told them to. She explained that they were good gundogs, easily trained, and excellent house dogs, guard dogs and companions.

They ticked all our boxes and I fell for them straight away. Friends later joked that I chose a Vizsla to match my own hair colour, but the main attraction for me was that they had the right combination of attributes that we were looking for.

Charlie's birthday was coming up later in the month, and as this dog was to be mainly hers, a house dog, I emailed her a link to a Hungarian wire-haired Vizsla website and asked if she liked the look of them. She replied enthusiastically. Like me she had never heard of them: there weren't that many around back then, although in the years since I have seen more and more at agricultural shows, both smooth coated and wire haired.

Before I left, I asked the gamekeeper if she knew anyone who was breeding wire-haired Vizslas and who might have puppies. She told me about Clint Coventry, who lives in West Sussex with his partner Anita Scott. They are renowned and well-established owners of Hungarian wire-haired Vizslas.

Before I committed to buying one, I read up about them. The wire-haired Vizsla is now recognised as a different breed from the Hungarian Vizsla, which has a smooth coat. But the wire-haired ones are actually close descendants of the smooth-coated ones: they were bred from traditional smooth-coated Vizslas crossed with German pointers. They were only recognised as a distinct breed in Hungary in 1966. So much of their heritage and history is intertwined with their smooth-haired cousins.

The cross-breeding, which began in the 1930s, was done by two Hungarians, one a breeder of Vizslas and the other of German wire-haired pointers, with the express intention of creating a dog the same colour as the Vizsla but with a bigger, stronger frame, with a wiry double coat, better suited for working in cold weather and retrieving from icy water, which they get from the German wire-haired pointers. The undercoat is dense and water repellent and the outer coat is long, harsh and wiry. They also have thicker hair on their tails and ears than the original Vizslas. They are a very fast breed, running at a top speed of 40mph (the fastest dog is a greyhound, with a maximum speed of 43mph, so not too far adrift ...)

During the Second World War, there was more inter-breeding and it's possible there is some Bloodhound, some Irish setter, some English pointer and even some standard poodle mixed in there, all contributing more assets to the eventual Hungarian wired-haired Vizsla that is now the breed standard.

So that's a relatively short history. But the original Vizsla, the smooth-coated one, goes back a very long way. Yellow hunting dogs arrived in Hungary with the first settlers in the country, the Magyars, who came from Asia in around AD 900. The Magyars had two types of dog: one for guarding their flocks and another for hunting and water fowling, and this second one was the ancestor of the Vizsla. The name comes from a tiny hamlet in Hungary, and has been in use since AD 1100. Traditionally the dogs were used for boar hunting and hunting with falcons, and later, after firearms were invented, for retrieving game and flushing out birds.

These were the dogs of barons and warlords, owned only by the land-holding aristocracy, who jealously protected their breeding. There's a story that during the Second World War, both the British and the Americans made plans to capture the Crown of St Stephen, the historical symbol of power in Hungary, as a major psychological blow to the Nazi regime, which was ruling the country. The Brits got there first, with an MI5 officer, Derek Peters, parachuted into Hungary with plans to get into the castle in Budapest, shoot the two guards who he believed were keeping vigil, and escape with the crown. Unfortunately for him the two guards were Vizslas, who hurled themselves at him and pinioned him to the floor.

Peters was imprisoned by the Nazis, and saw more of the reddish-coloured dogs, which were being used to guard the prison. Despite the way they had foiled his plans, he became a great admirer of them, and when he finally got back to England after the war he made his mind up to import the breed. By this time Hungary was behind the Iron Curtain, and Peters could not legally bring dogs out. Clearly not frightened of risk, he smuggled himself into the country again, but this time was dealt with ruthlessly when he reached the border on his way back home: his body was found riddled with bullets, and beside him, shot through the head, a handsome male Vizsla. Such is the pull of these beautiful dogs.

To me, the extra assets of the wire-haired breed make them a better choice than their smooth cousins. They are generally confident dogs – not aggressive but they'll take a stand if they have to. They have an easy nature, they're good company and easy to train (apart from housetraining, as I was to find out ...) One of the facts I read, that really endeared them to me, is their nickname 'Velcro dogs', earned because they have great loyalty to their owners and love to stick close to them. They've also been described as 'a dog for all reasons', because of their multi-purpose skills. There's been quite a discussion about the correct description of the colour of their coats: 'yellow'; 'golden rust'; 'amber'; 'brownish amber'; 'the golden colour of bread crust'; 'russet gold'; 'copper'; and 'dark sandy gold' have all been suggested.

Anyway, with Charlie as keen as I was about these interesting dogs, I made contact with Clint, who had a litter of puppies just weaned and ready to leave their mother. We had a long chat over the phone and arranged to meet up in a layby on the Warwick bypass as he was attending an event near there. He brought the bitch and one of her female puppies, so that I could see them together.

Meeting in a layby, or a car park, or at a motorway service station, is something dog owners are advised never to do. It's the way ruthless puppy-farm owners get round showing their puppies in the terrible conditions on the farms where they were born. But this was very different. I knew that Clint was a responsible and very well-respected Vizsla breeder, who runs a very good set-up. He is not a professional breeder, only having a litter when he wants a puppy for himself, and he laid down strict rules about me not breeding from our puppy until she was at least two. I signed a contract that said that if we decided we did not want her, he would have first refusal on having her back. So I was satisfied with him, and he knew enough about me from the many questions he'd asked me on the phone to be sure I would be a good owner for her. He brought all the paperwork that I needed, including her vet certificates to show she'd been wormed, her pedigree, insurance documents and a certificate of microchipping.

Puppy farms often sell dogs that are cross-breeds (especially tiny handbag-type dogs) to avoid having to give pedigree details, and they either don't have, or even forge, veterinary certificates, and they are frequently reluctant to give receipts. Bowled over by the cuteness of the doe-eyed pup, new owners either forget to insist, or don't even know what paperwork they should have. Often the consequences are dire, with puppies that are really sickly being passed on to unsuspecting owners who end up with vast veterinary bills or, worse, a puppy that is not healthy enough to survive. A reputable breeder like Clint will provide a record of the dog's first visit to the vet, of the first of his two vaccinations and the flea and worm treatment he has had. Since 2016, all puppies are required by law to be microchipped by the time they are eight weeks old. However, good breeders like Clint were doing it years ago. Breeders like him also make sure they know what kind of home the dog is going to: obviously, I'm very experienced with dogs, but if I was new to owning puppies Clint would have wanted to inspect our home to make sure we had the right facilities and the right degree of knowledge for bringing up a puppy. It's an old adage, but it's true: a dog is for life, not just for Christmas.

I knew there was no risk with buying a puppy from him. And, of course, I fell for the wriggly little pup who was put into my hands. I don't claim to be a dog expert, but I have handled enough animals in my life to know a sickly one, and this little girl was as healthy as could be. The only surprising thing was that, next to her shaggy mother, she was remarkably smooth looking, more like the traditional Vizsla except for the flatter head and stronger build of a wire-haired. She didn't have a lot of hair, but what she had was smooth.

'Don't worry,' Clint assured me, 'the longer hair will come in as she gets older.'

It never did, and it became a standing joke between me and Clint. 'The hair's in the post,' he would say. And I used to reply that I was expecting a discount if I ever bought another one from him. But I know he was slightly embarrassed by having sold me a wire-haired who didn't have wire hair ...

In fact, there is a wide range of hairiness in wire-haired Vizslas. Some are quite smooth, others have a coat that is more woolly than wiry. And the wiry hair can come in for up to four years after birth. Dolly, as we decided to call her, appeared on TV with me quite a lot and I was always having to tell people that she was one of the wire-haired breed.

Clint is an interesting character. He uses his Vizlas for hunting. He goes to pheasant shoots like many people with gundogs do, but also has a more unusual hobby. Clint and his partner Anita hunt with eagles all over Britain and across Europe. He has two eagles, a young male and an older, mature female. He tells me the females are always larger and more aggressive and if his two were ever released together the older female, Galina (which means chicken in Latin and Italian), who weighs 9lbs 6ozs, would kill the 7lb 6oz boy. This eagle doesn't have a name – eagles apparently are not called by their names, and are frequently not given one. He's not fully grown yet, and may put on another half to one pound, but he'll never be as heavy as the female.

The eagles hunt hares and sometimes the dogs are used to flush out the quarry. But not always: an eagle could easily attack a Vizsla. There is a shortage of hares in the UK, and so most of Clint's hunting is in the Czech Republic, Hungary, Germany, Austria, Slovakia and Croatia. Every year he goes to a big meeting in Opočno, in the Orlicke mountains in the Czech Republic and meets up with eagle hunters from all over the world, some flying in from America and Canada. Some of the really big female eagles hunt and kill foxes and deer, and Clint even knows a Croatian falconer who uses his eagle to take jackals (there is a strain of jackal, the European jackal, that thrives across Eastern Europe). There are, Clint estimates, only 30 to 50 eagles in the UK that are being flown.

It's a passion Clint has had since he was a teenager; working up from flying a kestrel, then a buzzard and a falcon. It took him 20 years to get up to a golden eagle. It's a dangerous sport, but he loves it. He wears a heavy glove on his left hand and arm, but as he takes hold of the leather straps (jesses) dangling from the eagle's ankles with his right hand, he has on more than one occasion felt it sink its talons into his unprotected hand, once being manacled by an eagle for 30 minutes. He knew that struggling would make the bird aggressive, so he simply waited, in pain, until it released him.

'Luckily I've never had a talon in a joint, like an elbow, so I've never needed hospital treatment,' he says. 'But my right hand and arm have taken a lot of punishment over the 20 years I've been flying eagles. I've had a talon go right through a finger and out the other side.'

When I ask why he does it his answer is simple: 'There is nothing like watching these magnificent birds in flight. It's not about the kill, or any kind of blood lust: most eagles only catch prey once in ten flights, and they are the least productive birds in all falconry. What makes all the work worthwhile is watching a wonderful, graceful creature fly free. It's such a thrill.'

I've only ever caught glimpses of golden eagles in the distance when filming in Scotland, so to see these awesome creatures up close at Clint's home was great. Clint loves his birds deeply, and talks movingly of a bird that was poisoned (inadvertently, by another eagle hunter) and which lay with its head on his lap, and which he held tenderly when it had to be put to sleep, which reminded me of the final minutes of my dogs.

Clint discovered Vizslas by accident. He was using German wire-haired pointers to pick up at pheasant shoots and he bought a puppy he thought would work well with his eagles. But the eagle attacked the bitch and Clint discovered the dog had been stealing the bird's food. The relationship was never going to work, so the puppy went back to her original owner, who told Clint he could borrow a young Vizsla for a hunting trip he was making to Scotland.

At the time there were fewer than 150 wire-haired Vizslas in the country, and Clint had never heard of them. The one he borrowed, Lady, was a very withdrawn dog who had no energy, but gradually she came out of herself, and he found her to be loving, loyal and hard-working, a very special dog.

'I wish I'd discovered them 20 years earlier,' Clint says.

Lady had a litter, and one of her pups, Emmie, was the mother of our new little one, Dolly.

Charlie and the children were just as besotted with her as I was when they saw her and she quickly became Charlie's dog. If she was attached by Velcro to anyone in the family it was Charlie, and although I fed her and took her out around the farm with me she'd choose Charlie first every time. Dolly was the first house dog we had owned together, which made her extra special.

I soon realised that Vizslas as a breed are far more sensitive than the collies and spaniels I had previously trained, and that the main ingredient needed for their training is love, not discipline. It took longer to house-train Dolly than I expected, and I admit I was probably a bit too strong with her. With a spaniel you need to show them who is boss and you can be quite tough with them, yelling at them when they have done wrong and left a puddle in the house. Dolly would be broken for a whole day if she was spoken to harshly: if you raised your voice at her or went to grab her to carry her outside for a wee, she would whimper and cower away. Throughout her life she was a bit insecure and very sensitive.

Once, when she was still very young, she was lying near the Aga when I took a boiling saucepan of peas off the heat. As I moved it a tiny droplet of water fell onto her back and she yelped. It didn't burn her or cause a blister, but it obviously stung her. From then on, whenever anyone started cooking she would leave the room. She never forgot that tiny incident.

We wanted to breed from Dolly, so she went to stay with Clint and Anita to run with one of their dogs. It turned out Dolly was completely frigid: she wouldn't let the dog anywhere near her. She just wasn't having it. When a bitch refuses to breed there's not a lot you can do, but we were disappointed because we had planned to keep one of her litter. Most disappointed of all the family was Alfie because we told him that he could have the puppy we kept as his own dog. He was really excited when Dolly went off for her romantic assignation in Sussex and crushed when she came back resolutely not pregnant. He'd even chosen a name: his puppy was going to be called Boo.

We were thinking about what to do when I was chatting to a friend, Jon King, who used to be our livestock manager, one day shortly after Dolly's return and he mentioned that he had heard about a litter of wire-haired Vizslas that were ready to find new homes. The breeder lived in Gloucestershire, not too far from us, so Charlie, Ella and I headed off to see them. It was early May, and Alfie's tenth birthday was only a couple of weeks away, so we planned to get a puppy for him, although we didn't mention it to him because we didn't want him to be disappointed again. Some of the pups in the litter of six were already spoken for and they all wore a different-coloured collar to make sure the right ones went to the right new owners. We played with them in the garden, threw toys for them and I checked them over looking for any health problems. In the end, we settled for the one with the red collar.

On the day of Alfie's birthday, we had arranged for Charlie to pick up the puppy on her way back from her job in Bristol where she worked in television, as it was only a short diversion from the motorway for her. It meant that Alfie didn't get his main present until late in the afternoon. He had a few presents in the morning before we all raced off to work or went to school and Alfie was told he could open the others in the afternoon when we were all back, and then we'd cut his birthday cake.

It was a sunny day, spring was slipping into summer and the garden was looking green and lovely. Ella, Alfie and I were sitting outside, but it was late afternoon by the time I heard Charlie's car, and I know Alfie was beginning to fear his longed-for present wasn't going to materialise.

'I was sort of expecting it, because we'd talked about names for a puppy when Dolly tried to have puppies,' he says. 'But it was getting late and I began to think it wasn't going to happen.'

When I heard Charlie's footsteps approaching I cupped my hands over Alfie's eyes. As she walked into the garden with the little bundle nestled in her arms I uncovered his eyes and we all shouted: 'Boo!' And there she was, his very own Boo, a little bundle of joy.

Alfie's face beamed with the biggest smile you have ever seen, and for a few moments I relived that wonderful Christmas when I first set eyes on Nita, snuggled in the old tea chest. Alfie was, literally, speechless. He took the puppy in his arms, and that was the start of a deep relationship between the two of them. As Nita was my dog, as Dolly was Charlie's, as Pearl is Ella's, so Boo is Alfie's. If we are walking around the farm together and Alfie heads off in a different direction, Boo never hesitates: it is him she goes with, not me.

Boo has grown into an excellent gundog, with the softest of mouths. Gundogs need soft mouths because they must never bite into the game they are retrieving. No one wants to eat a pheasant or partridge that has been chomped into by an over-zealous dog. Boo's mouth is so soft that one day Charlie saw her in the garden with wings sticking out from either side of her mouth. There were loads of birds fussing round the bird table and clearly Boo had caught one. Charlie shouted to her to let go, and when Boo opened her mouth a blue tit flew out, completely undamaged.

A good gundog will carry an egg without breaking it, and Vizslas have proved to be every bit as good as the more traditional Labradors and retrievers. From childhood I have loved watching gundogs work. Before I went to agricultural college I spent a year working on the Chatsworth Estate of the Duchess of Devonshire, and although I missed Nita, who stayed at home, there were dogs all around and I was in awe of these highly trained gundogs. Ours at home were really good field dogs, but these were trained to an even higher level, and each gamekeeper would have his own – perhaps as many as four or five – mainly Labradors and spaniels. I was full of admiration for the control they had: a gamekeeper could send one of his dogs to fetch a pheasant and the others would sit and stay.

Of course, to a gamekeeper a well-trained dog is a tool of the trade, and must be kept in good condition like any other tool. The dogs on the Chatsworth Estate needed to be very well controlled because it was a very professionally run estate and there was no place for an unruly dog.

The head gamekeeper also had a German shepherd. It had been trained as a police dog and he used it to deter poachers. He had fantastic control over it. It was a lovely, soft dog, who would play with me and muck about – until he put its collar on. The minute the collar went on it was just like turning a switch and the dog was in work mode. It was a lesson to me in how well trained dogs can be, if you have time and effort to put into it.

I'm sure our Vizslas could work at that level: the breed is capable of it. But from my point of view, all that is required is that they are competent and willing retrievers of game, and the rest of the time are affectionate family pets.

We bred from Boo while she was still young, at three years old. I heard about a lady in Bristol, Rebecca Bye, who has a dog called Frost, and we arranged to get them together here at the farm. It was a bit of a palaver: Frost got over excited the first time and swelled up before he was inside Boo, but they had another go when he had calmed down and this time he hit the jackpot. Rebecca brought him back for a follow-up mating, just to be sure.

I took Boo to the vet a month later and she was scanned, which showed she was having six or eight puppies (it's hard to tell on a scan with so many of them wriggling around). The scanning was filmed for *Countryfile* to be included within one of the 'Adam's Farm' pieces, telling the story of everyday life on the farm.

We borrowed a whelping box from a friend, which is a box big enough for the bitch to lie down but designed so that she can't squash or smother her own puppies. Then we waited for it all to kick off, which it did a day or two later. I heard her whining, panting and padding around the kitchen at 4.30am so I went down to her, took her outside for a wee and settled her in the box. It was 6am when the first puppy showed its head, but I could see it was stuck and Boo was panting and distressed. I've helped lots of lambs being born and I've seen puppies being born, so I had no hesitation in helping her, by easing it out. She yelped a little bit as the first puppy popped out, but she was not at all aggressive towards me for helping, which some bitches are.

Her firstborn was a lovely little girl pup, and she instantly licked her all over. I knew at that moment that Boo was an instinctively good mother, even though the whole process must have felt alien to her this first time. After that, she gave birth to another puppy every half-hour to 45 minutes, and it took all morning for the full litter of six to be born. The vet had told me that if any of the pups took more than 45 minutes I should ring for help, but I didn't need to – although I was watching the clock with a couple of them.

Boo was brilliant. I helped them latch on, and they were happily suckling as soon as she had licked them clean. They were all the Vizsla reddish colour, but a bit stripy at birth, which is normal. Ella loves the theatre, so she gave them all Shakespearean names: Beatrice, Romeo, Rosalind, Desdemona, Gertrude and Ophelia, completely ignoring my preference for one syllable names! They had different lengths of hair, and as they got older it was clear that Romeo and two of the little bitches had shorter hair, more like Dolly, and the other three were as hairy as Boo herself.

We sold them all to local people: I think Dolly and Boo were good ambassadors for this special breed of dog and, having met them, there was no shortage of people wanting to take one. I copied Clint's example and gave them all similar contracts to the one he gave me. Because the new owners lived locally it was easy enough for me to ensure they all went to suitable homes.

We decided not to keep one as we fully intended to have another litter from Boo a couple of years later, and keep one of those puppies so that, as Dolly grew old, there was another little one in the house.

Tragically, our plans were overtaken by Dolly's death, which I will talk about in the next chapter. Now we regretted not keeping one of Boo's litter because we were down to one dog in the house, and we like to overlap them so that we have a little one growing up alongside the older ones. We could not breed from Boo again so soon, so we rang Clint on the off-chance he may have some pups. Clint told me his bitch was pregnant and he would, of course, save us a bitch pup if there was one.

By coincidence, I was filming down in Sussex, so when they were born I went to see the new litter of puppies, and in particular to see the parents. The dog was one that Clint had imported and was very hairy and really lively. Clint let him out and he bounced around full of beans and clearly adored Clint. We took him out into the field where Clint had his chickens – the dog stalked one and then went on point, freezing to the spot. Clint explained he was a brilliant working dog. I was slightly worried that his excitable temperament may be a bit too much for me to handle, though, if it was inherited by the pups. Next I met the bitch who had a shorter coat than the dad, with sweet, loving eyes and a gentle nature. Clint explained that she, too, was brilliant at working and very intelligent. I really hoped we could get one like her.

A couple of weeks later Charlie and I went down together to choose another little girl wire-haired Vizsla. There were six pups, two dogs and four bitches. Clint had chosen a little bitch pup for himself and that left us three to choose from. Clint was away in Hungary with his golden eagles when we visited, and so his partner Anita looked after us. We popped all those that weren't available into the kennel, leaving the three prospective pups running around. One immediately went to the corner of the run and sat there looking very shy and insecure. For me this meant that it wasn't the sort of character I was looking for. The other two bounded around and jumped up at us. The first one Charlie picked up nestled into her arms, holding its head back and pressing it under her chin. I could see in Charlie's eyes that she was quickly falling in love with this one. I picked up the other one and checked its teeth, feet and nipples to ensure they were even, in case we wanted to breed from her in the future – that's the farmer coming out in me. The one Charlie was cuddling was quite small with shorter hair. Charlie and I swapped pups and again the one she was holding nestled into her with as much love and affection as the first. What an impossible decision to make. Two gorgeous puppies, either would do us well. The final decision was made because we really wanted a reasonably sized dog with a similar coat to Boo, not too long but not too short. Out of the two puppies, the one I was originally holding was probably the best option for us. Anita confirmed to us that we had made a great choice and as she has seen dozens of puppies over the years, I trust her judgment. So we had our new puppy.

She wasn't ready to leave her mother, and I was just about to set off on an amazing three-week trip to Australia and New Zealand, filming for *Countryfile*. But as soon as I got back, Charlie drove down and collected her: the latest addition to our household, who we have called Olive.

At least, the rest of the family chose Olive. I'm all in favour of a dog having a one-syllable name, as a short, sharp name is easier for them to learn and better when you are training them. But I was outvoted, and now that she's here, very much part of the family, Olive seems very appropriate.

Alfie said he was going to train her: 'I was very young, just ten, when I got Boo, so I probably didn't work hard enough at her training. But I'll put in more time with Olive.'

Olive is certainly a very sweet-natured puppy, and she loves other dogs almost as much as she loves us. The first thing she does when I open the back door in the morning is to run over to Peg's kennel to say hello. Peg is very tolerant with her.

There are so many dangers on a farm that it is important to acclimatise her nice and slowly. I've been taking her around with me on certain routine jobs, getting her used to travelling in the back of the Polaris 4x4. When she was four months old I introduced her to sheep for the first time. They can be very flighty and it's important she learns to respect them. She has behaved very well with them so far: on that first meeting, which was filmed for *Countryfile*, I put her down near them. She was clearly a little bit nervous, but her reaction was perfect: not over-excited, backing off when the sheep approached her.

All dogs, not just those that live on a farm, should be taught to be respectful around sheep and kept on a lead at all times when they are being walked through fields with sheep, especially pregnant ewes and ewes with lambs. A dog that is loose can worry sheep, at worse attacking them or causing them to abort. It's every shepherd's nightmare: a rogue dog, following its instincts to prey on sheep, causing havoc with the well-being of the flock and the livelihood of the shepherd.

It's also important that Olive learns to be patient and quiet in the back of the trailer, so I left her in there for a while with the other dogs and she was very good. To introduce her to the cattle I put her on a lead – cattle can be inquisitive and aggressive around dogs, and as she's going to see a lot of them for the rest of her life, it's vital she knows how to react to them. The first time she met the cows she barked a bit, not very loudly, and I made sure I kept the encounter short. Gradually she has been introduced more and more to the animals and the routines of the farm.

Living on a farm is exciting and scary for a puppy, but one thing is certain: she'll never be bored. And I enjoy her company – having a puppy around always brightens up my day.

CHAPTER 10

Losing Dolly

D olly was the loveliest, gentlest dog you can imagine. Her own sensitivity meant that she was, in turn, very sensitive to the needs of those around her and she always seemed to know intuitively whenever one of us was low, or had problems.

For example, when Dad died in October 2015, the whole family was plunged into grief. It seemed impossible to imagine life at Bemborough going on without him, even though he and Mum no longer lived at the farm. After his death, in the days before his funeral, we all coped with our grief in our own ways, and Dolly was always there, with a comforting wet nose to push into your hand, a gentle pressure on your legs as she leaned into you. It was her way of telling us she understood, and wanted to give her support. If I was sitting, quietly, going through my memories of Dad, she'd put her head on my lap.

Grief rolls over people in waves and we were all up and down in our emotions. Dolly seemed to sense exactly which member of the family needed her most at any time. When my sister Libby, fighting back tears, took herself away for a contemplative walk through the

fields she had known since childhood, and which sym-
bolised Dad to all of us, without being summoned Dolly
rose from her bed in the kitchen and attached herself to
Libby's side – a comforting presence on a tear-stained
walk. She knew that Libby was, at that time, most in
need of a gentle, undemanding companion.

About eight months after Dad's death I was absent-
mindedly stroking Dolly when I felt a lump on her
ribcage. It was very small, but it grew rapidly until it
was about the size of a golf ball; a smooth lump raised
on her chest. She was only nine years old, so I hoped it
would be a lipoma, a benign fatty lump of the sort that
I was familiar with because Labradors are prone to
them (as are Doberman Pinschers, miniature schnau-
zers and larger mixed-breed dogs). But it's always
advisable to get a lump checked out, so I took Dolly to
the vet, which of course she hated because she associated it with sterile smells and needles.

The vet didn't seem to share my optimism about the
lump, which was harder than a lipoma, and he kept
Dolly in for a biopsy that involved taking quite a large
slice of the growth. She came home the next day, the
stitches came out and she seemed as happy and energetic
as ever. But the bad news was that the biopsy results
showed that Dolly had an aggressive soft-tissue
sarcoma. Cancer, and one that would progress fast
through her body if it wasn't checked.

She went back to stay at the vet's and this time had
major surgery: not only was the lump removed but an

area of tissue around it was also taken, including between the intercostal muscles of her chest. The vet warned us that, although he hoped he had got rid of the tumour and enough tissue around it to halt its spread, there was a chance that it could come back. Dolly came home with a large scar and a shaven chest but she was soon back to normal, ready to come out around the farm with me in the mornings, always up for a long walk with Charlie.

When I took her for a check-up about a month later, I could feel a few tiny nodules on her scar, but the vet was hopeful that these were just scar tissue. She seemed so well in herself that I optimistically believed he was right.

Charlie, the children and I were due to go on a fort-night's holiday to Italy a few days later, and we went without any worries about Dolly, as she was trotting around happily and did not seem to be even slightly off colour. Doris, a good friend of ours, stays at our house to look after our menagerie of animals while we are away, and Dolly adored her.

When we got back, though, we could see that the lump had returned, and I took her to the surgery again. Yes, the vet said, the cancer had returned. To operate again, and be sure it was all removed, he would have to take away two or three of her ribs, and rebuild her ribcage with a wire mesh. It was a difficult operation and she would need a long, slow recovery; she would almost certainly never get back to the level of exercise she enjoyed. On the other hand, he told me, it might stay the way it was (it was clearly not bothering her) and not get any worse.

She was nine years old, and although that is short of the life expectancy of a healthy dog (the Kennel Club lists the life expectancy of a wire-haired Vizsla as 'more than ten years') she was already approaching old age. So we decided to go for the second option: take her home, give her the life she so much enjoyed, and hope for the best.

Charlie was very upset. Dolly was almost like a third child to her. They adored each other. At first it seemed to be going well: Dolly was her usual self, charging around on the farm. A few days later Charlie went to see a friend and they took the dogs for a long walk, and Dolly was every bit as energetic as she normally was. We were beginning to be hopeful.

But that evening she was lying on an old easy chair in the living room. (Despite my edict that dogs don't go on furniture, we have an old chair, covered with a blanket, that they can lie on. So much for my strict rules ...) As she lay there the swelling on her chest suddenly blew up. You could virtually see it getting bigger. She could hardly move and was clearly in pain.

We let her sleep there overnight. I crept down in the small hours to check on her and thankfully she was sleeping peacefully. I got up even earlier than usual and was downstairs at 5.30am to find that the whole of her side had expanded and she struggled to walk. I managed to get her out into the garden to wee, but it was costing her a massive effort.

I broke the news to Charlie, then I rang the vet and asked him to come to the farm, and to be prepared to put her down. While we were waiting for her to arrive, Charlie stayed with Dolly and I walked up to Buttington Clump to dig another grave: I knew that her end had come. When the vet came, she told us the cancer was rampaging through her body. I sat with Dolly in the garden while Charlie took refuge in the house, and we were both grateful that Alfie and Ella were away with friends. I held Dolly in my arms, keeping my emotions in check so as not to alarm her. The vet gave her a large dose of anaesthetic and after a few seconds I felt her beautiful body go limp. I carried her reverentially to the clump and buried her.

It was a sad time, especially for Charlie. She and Dolly went everywhere together. A few months after her death, when I was at the Bath and West Show, I met a charming artist called Sophie, who had studied at the Royal Agricultural University in Cirencester before deciding to turn her hobby of drawing into a profession and starting up Sophie Cotton Limited. I was very impressed with Sophie's work and commissioned a portrait of Dolly for Charlie's birthday. Sophie works from photographs, using fine graphite to create intricate portraits, and Charlie was delighted with her present. The drawing now hangs on the wall outside the living room door, and we pass it every time we go into the living room or upstairs – it's a lovely reminder of the beautiful dog we still miss.

We had Boo, Pearl and Peg, but there was a Vizsla-shaped hole in our lives. After six months we knew we had to do something, so that's when we got Olive.

The story of Dolly's death was used on *Countryfile*, with archive film of her walking through the farmyard with me, to introduce an item I did about cancer in dogs, and the way new treatments are being developed. After the programme I received an amazing number of letters of sympathy and support, with many dog owners sharing their own similar experiences. As I said in the introduction to the programme, treating cancer in dogs has always been notoriously difficult, but technology is giving more and more dogs a chance of life, and as long as an animal is young enough and fit enough, some owners are prepared to give it a go.

I went to meet TV's 'Supervet', Professor Noel Fitzpatrick, who founded the Fitzpatrick Referrals hospital at Godalming, Surrey, in 2005. As anyone who has seen *The Supervet* programmes knows, Noel has pioneered an amazing array of treatments for animals, things that would not have been available even ten years ago. The hospital is at the forefront of cutting-edge technology, which is combined with genuine care for the sick patients. His team treats orthopaedic and neurological conditions in small animals, and the hospital is a world leader in joint replacements for animals, including, to my amazement, hip replacements for cats.

I can't imagine anyone being able to perform such a delicate operation, but it happens here. All spinal and neurological conditions are treated, and prosthetic limbs are fitted to any animal that needs one.

But, because of Dolly's recent death, what interested me was a new hospital, Fitzpatrick Referrals Oncology and Soft Tissue hospital, opened just a year earlier and dedicated to the cure of cancer in animals. In that year, more than 1,000 furry patients have received cancer treatment there. It was there I met Noel, as well as the hospital's clinical director, Professor Nick Bacon. The two hospitals employ over 200 staff, 40 of whom are vets, and the operating theatres are constantly busy.

Before I went to see the work they are doing, I met a dog and his owner who have both benefitted from being referred to this highly specialised unit. Anne Rogers, a farm manager from Hampshire, has a lovely collie cross called Monty. On Christmas Day Anne had a friend round for Christmas dinner, and when Monty sat on her lap for a stroke, Anne's friend noticed a small lump on his leg.

When Anne's local vet examined it and sent a sample away for testing, the diagnosis was cancer. The only option available to the vet was to remove Monty's leg, but Anne wanted to give him another chance, as he was a young dog. At this point she was told about Noel's hospital.

'Monty's a very important part of my life. I spend a lot of time on my own in the day and he is with me from dawn to dusk, checking round the farm. He's a pet and a work companion,' Anne said.

Monty was referred to the hospital at Guildford in the hope that he could be treated without a radical amputation. He was successfully operated on, recovered fully, and when I met him he was full of beans, a lovely, healthy dog: you'd find it hard to imagine he had been through such a tough time.

The hospital itself is a state-of-the-art building, and Noel is as charismatic in person as he appears on TV. I was not surprised when I learned later that, after training as a vet, Noel had a spell when he combined veterinary work with acting, appearing on TV in popular dramas like *Heartbeat* and *Casualty*. Thank goodness he didn't find acting stardom: thousands of animals owe their lives to his decision to give himself full time to his first love, being a vet. And not just any vet … But I'm guessing the acting gives him the confidence to appear in front of the TV cameras in an unselfconscious way, and adds just enough showmanship for him to be able to explain his work so clearly to those of us who don't have degrees in veterinary science.

Noel is passionate about his work. He loves cars but once sold an Aston Martin to pay for an extra vet, that's how dedicated he is. Some people are ready to criticise pet owners who spend thousands on their animals, but Noel understands the pure, unconditional love that owners have for their pets. He knows that for many people the value of a pet in their life is incalculable.

He points out that every advanced medical drug treatment used in humans has been tested first on animals before being declared safe for us, so why shouldn't we give something back to them, now that we have the technology and the skills?

My first question for Noel was, 'Is cancer more prevalent in animals than it used to be?' He explained that it has always been there, but with modern diagnostic techniques owners are hearing about it more.

He introduced me to Archie, a dog with a tumour in his jaw, which was bursting through his gums. It looked very nasty to me, but Noel explained that it was operable, and that Archie would soon be back to his old self.

Noel told me that the hard statistical fact is that half of all dogs over the age of ten will die of cancer. After accidents and trauma, cancer is the biggest single canine killer.

'People used to say that nothing can be done when an animal got cancer,' Noel said. 'But today that's not true. We can cure some cancers, and we can give good palliative care for most, so that the quality of their lives is good. Dogs can have all the treatments that humans can have. It's a game changer.'

The treatments the hospital provides include surgery, chemotherapy, immunotherapy, radiotherapy. Surgery alone cures more tumours than any other treatment, or combination of treatments. The same anaesthetic drugs, surgical equipment, instruments and suture (stitch) materials are used as in any human operating theatre.

The chemotherapy drugs are also the same as those given to humans, but in lower doses to keep life as normal as possible for an animal that can't understand what's happening. Anti-sickness drugs are used to make sure they keep their appetites.

'Our chemotherapy goal is for your pet to look so well that none of your family or friends would know they were on chemo,' I was told.

Having just had to make the heartbreaking decision to end Dolly's life, I said to Noel: 'It must be very difficult for the owner to make a decision on how much they want to put their dog through, and how much the vet thinks the dog can cope with.'

'In every case,' Noel said, 'all we can do is promise the family hope, but not in the absence of reality about their situation, and that includes the possible financial costs and the moral implications of what we will put the dog through. 'I feel very, very strongly that it's not enough to be able to do something, it has to be the right thing,' he said.

Every pet owner who comes to the hospital with a sick animal is given a copy of *The Little Book of Cancer*, which explains the nature of the disease, the different types of cancer and the treatments available. One section that struck me was the page headed 'What would you do if it was your pet?' This is a question often asked of Noel and the other vets – and is probably familiar to every vet in the country. Anxious owners, unable to make the decision themselves, turn it back on to the vet.

'Many factors come into the decision: the type of tumour, its growth rate, the tumour location, if it has spread, how far you live from the cancer centre, what your own personal experience of cancer is, your financial situation and your pet's character – to name but a few. What we promise is that we will carefully explain the pros and cons of various options and patiently work with you to find the one that feels right. We do not judge, we do not criticise and we do not coerce. We are on your team.'

I went through the door marked 'Dog Ward' to meet up with Nick Bacon and one of his patients, a gorgeous Labradoodle (a Labrador/poodle cross) called Fudge, who had come from Cardiff with his owner Andrew. Andrew wanted to know if the cancer in Fudge's leg had spread to other parts of his body, so the dog was gently sedated before being given a CT scan. As his limp body went into the scanner, Nick explained to me how it works, with a rapid series of X-rays being taken and then built into a 3D image, enabling the vet to look inside the dog's organs for traces of the cancer.

'It can find much smaller things, much faster,' said Nick.

I asked him if the future for Fudge would depend on whether or not more cancer was found, and where: 'If, say, you found tumours in the lungs, would that affect his treatment?'

'In that case,' Nick said, 'we would look at ways of making him feel good for as long as possible, but we probably wouldn't do surgery.'

For me, it was extraordinary seeing human technology used on dogs, and I think it is brilliant that a hospital like this can now give owners a real choice about the future of their animals based on scientific evidence of what is going on inside their pets. Before technology made this level of diagnosis available, most dogs with cancer would be given a very slim chance of survival.

Another dog I met while I was there was Lola, a Labrador and a working gundog. Lola is a success story: she was back at the hospital for a check-up after an operation to remove a tumour earlier in the year. Lola reminded me of the Labradors, also working gundogs, I grew up with at the farm. She was only three and a half when the cancer was diagnosed.

'She was such a young dog,' said Sharon, who explained that Lola had trained beautifully to work in the field with her husband, who works her three times a week. 'We felt we couldn't throw all that away, and we wanted to give her the best chance of survival. It would have been a different discussion if she was eight or ten years old. But she was very young, she'd done so well in training.'

I understand how close owners are to their working dogs: after all, that's my way of life, too. But Nick explained that it is not just owners of working dogs who will go the extra mile – and extra cheque, if they don't have pet insurance – to save the lives of their dogs and cats.

'For Sharon and Lola it's a working relationship, for some people their pet is company on a quiet night, for others the pet has seen them through their own emotional turmoil and is more than a pet – it's a member of the family. It's a very rewarding job, being able to help them.'

He was preaching to the converted: I know full well how much we all want the best for our animals, and how close to them we are.

Before I left the hospital, I got a progress report on the dogs I had met. Lola had passed her final check-up with flying colours. Archie had the operation on the tumour in his jaw and was making a full recovery. And luckily for Fudge and Andrew, the cancer in Fudge's leg had not spread, and Nick was confident that he could remove the tumour and save the leg.

It was an inspiring visit, and I really admire the pioneering work done by vets like Professor Fitzpatrick and Professor Bacon, as well as being totally in awe of their skills. I never doubted that we made the right decision for Dolly because of her age and the widespread cancer raging aggressively through her body. But I totally sympathise with owners who are prepared to travel miles and pay out large amounts to save their dogs, especially young ones. As every owner I spoke to said: 'Whatever the outcome, by coming here we feel we have done everything we possibly could do. We've given our dog the best chance.'

That's what we all, as dog owners, want.

CHAPTER 11

Dogs at War

I crouched down in a muddy trench, rain spattering my shoulders, and fumbled with a small green felt bag tied to the collar of an alert, patient Airedale terrier. Opening the bag, I stuffed a folded piece of paper into it.

'Go, Earnie, go!' I whispered to him.

As soon as I released his collar, Earnie, a typical curly-haired brown and black Airedale, took off at speed. He leapt out of the trench and tore across the field to another trench, where his owner, Karin Schnichels, was hiding. Spotting her immediately, Earnie leapt straight down into the trench to deliver the message.

We were filming for *Countryfile* as part of a special edition that went out on Remembrance Sunday; dedicated to the way life in the countryside was affected by the First World War. The programme covered the regeneration of the countryside where the battles were fought, the cemeteries of the war dead that are so beautifully maintained and the development of the first tanks in Lincolnshire, among other topics.

I found filming my segment was very moving: I looked at the way dogs, particularly Airedales, were

used in the First World War to carry important information from the trenches back to headquarters; risking
their lives to save human lives, acting with incredible
bravery as shells whined around them, dodging the
holes left by the heavy artillery bombardment, tearing
their flanks on jagged barbed wire, racing on despite
being hit by snipers' bullets. I felt very humble in the
safe surroundings of a farm field near Ipswich demon-
strating how those amazing dogs worked, and I was
well aware that I was many miles and lifetimes away
from the harrowing, appalling conditions of the French
battlefields where so many young soldiers perished.

It's important, a hundred years on, as we remember
the horrific conditions of that terrible war, not to over-
look how crucial dogs were to the war effort and how
courageously they worked – unquestioningly obedient
and willing to give their lives for mankind. Hearing
their stories, I was deeply moved by how much we owe
to these remarkable creatures – the dogs we have taken
into our lives and who reward us with loyalty beyond
imagination. I know, from working every day with my
own dogs, how valuable they are in my life, and in the
lives of any shepherd or farmer, how loyal they are and
how much they want to please. But my dogs have comfortable beds to sleep in at night, if they have an
accident they are whisked to a vet, and they live long,
fulfilled lives.

These trenches dogs, the ones who saved so many
lives, were far from the comfort of their homes, their

'Go on, throw it again'. Ella with Boo and Dolly

Dolly: I commissioned this lovely line drawing by artist Sophie Cotton as a birthday present to Charlie, after Dolly passed away

One man and his dog: On a walk with Dolly

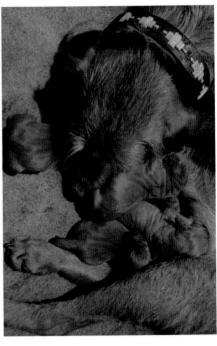

'Don't I look smart? But have they forgotten I'm a girl?' Boo does some modelling for the clothing brand, Joules

A beautiful litter of puppies for Boo

Six hungry pups

The latest edition to the family: Olive makes herself at home

'Come on, play with me.' Olive wants Boo to pay attention

Stand back! Peg cooling down in her water trough

Ashley Stamper with her sheepdogs

On location in New Zealand with *Countryfile*. Rhondda the terrier sits on the quad bike with the Huntaways

Clint Coventry, hunting hare with his eagles

Earnie, the Airedale

Allen Parton with Endal and EJ

Alan Stewart and his sled-dog team

Myrtle the whippet

A farmer and his dog

injuries were tended in rudimentary fashion, and as soon as they were fit they were back at the front line. Thousands died on active service, and thousands more were killed at the end of the war; put down when their help was no longer needed.

I didn't know of the work of dogs in the war until I made the programme, but it is one episode of *Countryfile* that has made an indelible impression on me. I interviewed author Isabel George, who has written extensively about the use of animals in warfare, and it really struck home when she told me that it was men like me – farmers, gamekeepers and shepherds – who were mainly chosen by the army to handle the dogs in the trenches, for the obvious reason that we work with dogs all the time.

We chose to stage the recreation of how messages were carried by dogs with an Airedale because that was the breed used more than any other. When I heard this, my immediate question was: why? Today we don't particularly think of Airedales as a popular working breed, but I was soon to learn what made them the right choice for the war effort 100 years ago.

At the start of the First World War, the British had not yet cottoned on to the idea that dogs were useful on the battlefield. There was only one working military dog, an Airedale with the 2nd Battalion of the Norfolk Regiment, and he was being used as a sentry. By contrast, the French army had 5,000 working dogs and the Germans 6,000. Ironically, many of the German army dogs had actually been bought in Britain in the years leading up to the conflict. As early as 1895, the German government was sending agents to Britain to buy large numbers of dogs, particularly collies, because of their intelligence and natural willingness to train and work.

The most important man in this story is Lieutenant Colonel Edwin Hautenville Richardson, who pioneered the use of dogs here (and whose training methods were taken up by the US army in turn, and who still influences dog training today). Edwin Richardson was the son of a gentleman farmer, so he grew up with a close knowledge of the land, and in particular, of dogs working on the land. He knew from an early age, as I did, that dogs are a vital extra worker, sometimes doing the work of more than one man around a farm. He also loved them, and I completely agree with the words he wrote in his book, published in 1920: 'As a family we have a way with dogs and all animals. What this exactly means is extremely difficult to define, but there seems to be in people this sense, a certain sympathetic confidence, to which the animal responds with a like attitude. This comradeship is very delightful, and brings much sweetness and happiness in life. One feels really sorry for those people who do not possess it, as certainly they deny themselves an immense amount of pleasure and innocent fun.'

I can't improve on what he said: he was clearly a man after my own heart. As a young man he was well educated, being sent abroad to become fluent in both German and French, and then on to Sandhurst to become a British army officer. After he married, Lt Col Richardson and his wife Blanche bought a farming estate in Scotland, where they raised their two sons in a household shared with lots of dogs.

It was while he was out shooting with friends before the war that Lt Col Richardson saw a shepherd selling one of his dogs to a German, and when he spoke to the foreigner he discovered he was going round the countryside buying up dogs for army service back in Germany. Intrigued, and already very keen on dog training, he and Blanche set about training their own dogs. Richardson made contact with dog-training schools in France, Belgium, Holland and Germany. He even went over to Germany to see collies being trained as Red Cross dogs for finding wounded soldiers. He bought one of the dogs and brought it back.

Convinced that dogs would be useful if Britain were to find itself at war, Lt Col Richardson started training his own dogs to carry messages, find wounded men on the battlefield, guard objects and act as sentries. There were army camps nearby, and he was able to train his dogs, unofficially, with the soldiers – all at his own expense.

The dogs were so good that various officers from the camps wrote to the War Office about their usefulness.

Other countries recognised how good these dogs were: when Russia went to war with Japan their army bought several Airedales from Lt Col Richardson, which resulted in him being awarded a Red Cross medal and given a gold watch by the Czar. He went on to supply dogs to Morocco, Bulgaria, India and Italy and even sent sentry dogs to guard the harem of the Sultan of Turkey!

However, back in Britain, despite many recommendations, including from Queen Mary, by the time the Great War broke out, he had only one Airedale working officially in military service, with the Norfolk Regiment. The police were gratefully recruiting dogs from him, including bloodhounds, collies and Airedales. But when he offered the services of his dogs to the army he was rebuffed: the War Office was too busy organising the shipping out to Europe of vast numbers of men, equipment and supplies, and there was no time or money to spend on dogs. The Red Cross were willing to use them, however, and found them an immense help leading them to men who were wounded, among the many dead.

Lt Col Richardson did not give up his belief that dogs had more to give; continuing to train his dogs and travelling to France to see how the French were using their dogs on the front line. He was constantly fighting to convince military bosses that dogs would be formidable allies for men fighting on the front line. Eventually, halfway through the war, he was asked to set up a training school for war dogs at Shoeburyness, Essex, and within a month 30 dogs were in the trenches – most of them collies, but also Airedales and German shepherd dogs. (It was during the First World War that German Shepherds became known as Alsatians, because anything with 'German' in the name was associated with the enemy.) Soon, the Airedales were performing so well that they became the breed most in demand.

Which brings me back to my question: what is it about Airedales that made them so suitable for this work? They are not a breed I had encountered much before, and I had no idea of their history.

Airedales are the biggest of the terrier breeds, known to their fans as the 'king of terriers'. They originate from the Aire Valley, in West Yorkshire, where, in the mid-nineteenth century, miners competed to breed a dog that was the best hunter and the best fighter. By selective breeding the Airedale evolved into a strong, brave, intelligent dog, loyal to his masters but quick to see off anyone he regarded as an enemy. It was a multi-purpose dog, very useful for retrieving during hunting (or poaching) expeditions, very happy to work in water, and with some herding skills, as well as its supremacy in dog fights. The downside is that they are not the easiest breed to train: you have to start early and persevere, so they are not recommended as family pets for anyone who is not prepared to put in the time and effort. But once they've been trained, they work superbly and willingly.

The main reason that Lt Col Richardson favoured them is because they are fearless. He assessed this by feeding all his dogs once a day, and a few minutes before their grub was served he threw several grenades into a nearby pit creating a loud noise. When the noise stopped the food was removed. For the first couple of days the dogs went hungry, until the bravest left their kennels and ran to the food. The ones who did well in this test, and were actually waiting for the noise that signalled food, were then trained to run through smoke, barbed-wire fences, across hurdles, through hedges and to work with the constant scream of shells from practice batteries, with heavy army vehicles passing to and fro. Local people volunteered to be the wounded, and as the dog approached they were told to fire blank cartridges.

Many other dogs showed as much courage as the Airedales, but no other breed was so consistently reliable. They are large enough to be able to leap wire, agile enough to dodge shell holes and their brown and black colouring was good camouflage in the mud of no man's land. Richardson found retrievers and Labradors were too compliant, not independent enough, and other breeds were too playful and could be distracted. Whereas Airedales, once given a task, were single minded and determined.

Once the War Office approved, the first two Airedales went out to France: Wolf and Prince, who carried messages for a battalion of the Royal Artillery. They were so successful that Richardson was inundated with requests for more.

The dogs travelled out to the battlefield with their handlers – known as keepers – who were the only ones allowed to feed them. This gave the dogs a huge incentive to get back to their handlers, who were based at headquarters, from wherever they were taken to on the front line. They were released with messages, and would run through the worst of conditions to make it back. Field telephones existed in the First World War, but reception was poor and the booming of artillery and wailing of shells made it impossible to hear. Men who carried messages had a very short life expectancy as they were a natural target for snipers. So dogs, when they finally arrived with the British troops, were invaluable.

One of the most difficult problems was to stop the soldiers in the trenches petting and feeding them: the presence of a dog in a trench was a huge boost to morale, lifting the spirits of young, homesick soldiers, as the dogs pushed wet noses into tired faces. But it was vital that the dog was kept alert and ready for duty, and any soldier caught sharing his rations with a dog was in serious trouble. There was a rule that no dog would spend more than 12 hours in a trench, to prevent him becoming too hungry and too comfortable with the soldiers there.

There are many tales of canine heroism, but the most famous is the story of Jack, an Airedale who rescued an entire battalion of the Sherwood Foresters that was surrounded and cut off without supplies. The message for help and reinforcements was put into his leather pouch, and off he went, running full pelt through the carnage of the battlefield.

A piece of shrapnel smashed his jaw, a shell tore open his back, and finally his forepaw was shattered by a sniper's bullet, but still he kept going, dragging himself the final three kilometres. When he reached headquarters he collapsed and died, but his message had got through, and reinforcements relieved the battalion. Many, many lives were saved by his incredible bravery and determination. I'm staggered when I think of it: how tempting it must have been to lie down and give up, but something inside him, some indomitable force, made him keep going. It's very moving to think of his remarkable determination.

While Jack's is perhaps the most spectacular story, there are many more of dogs who fulfilled their missions, time after time. One dog keeper recorded in his log: 'Boxer, a staunch, reliable Airedale, went over the top with the Kents. He was released at 5am with an important message. He jumped at me at 5.25am. A tip top performance, about four miles. Great dog!'

Another keeper wrote that his dog, Tom, was gassed and hit by shrapnel, but only needed two weeks to fully recover and be back at his post.

Because of my own close affinity with sheepdogs, I particularly like the story of Tweed, a large rough-coated sheepdog. When he arrived at the military dog school, Lt Col Richardson was not impressed as Tweed was slow to pick up the training and the colonel dismissed him as dim-witted. It was Blanche, the colonel's wife, who took over his training and in the end he served for six months, surviving Passchendaele. In May 1918, the Queen Victoria's Rifles were caught off guard by a surprise German attack near Amiens and pinned down by heavy shelling. If they did not hold the line, the Germans would break through and take Amiens, but they were low on ammunition and badly needed reinforcements. They stuffed a message into Tweed's leather pouch, and he sprinted off into the night. His keeper wrote later: 'He came through a Boche barrage, three kilometres in ten minutes. The French were sent up and filled the gaps and straightened the line, otherwise Amiens would be in the hands of the Germans.'

Six days later, Tweed made three night runs carrying messages that alerted headquarters that the Germans were preparing a raid. Lt Col Richardson said he was 'a dog not easily forgotten'.

After the War Office recognised the immense value of dogs on the battlefield, demand soon outstripped supply. Dogs were originally recruited from Battersea Dogs Home and other dog shelters, but eventually appeals were made to families to give up their pets. More than 7,000 family dogs were donated, a substantial contribution to the 20,000 dogs who served in the war. Sadly, because of the expense of keeping a dog, during the war when food was scarce many healthy dogs were put down, to Lt Col Richardson's annoyance: he felt that more would have been given to him if their owners had been told about his training school. Quite a few that did come to him were not in good enough health to be used. In his final dispatch of the war Field Marshal Haig, the British commander on the Western front, acknowledged their vital importance to the victory.

To quote Lt Col Richardson again: 'The trained dog regards himself highly honoured by his position as a servant of His Majesty, and renders no reluctant service. From my observation along this line I have, in fact, come to the conclusion that a dog trained to some definite work is happier than the average loafing dog, no matter how kindly the latter may be treated. I certainly found it to be the case with the army dog.'

Again, I can only agree: my sheepdogs are always ready and eager to work and seem to definitely prefer days when they have a job to do on the farm to simply being taken out for a walk. I've never owned a dog that does not have a purpose, whether it's for retrieving or working with sheep.

With the help of Earnie the Airedale we were able to illustrate the work of the amazing messenger dogs who worked in such terrible conditions for *Countryfile*. While obviously we could not reproduce the real conditions those dogs worked in, Earnie was able to show how fast and how obedient a well-trained Airedale is.

Earnie and his owner Karin Schnichels live in Surrey, and Karin takes him and her other three Airedales to obedience classes, where they compete against other breeds. Karin confirms my prejudice in favour of collies by admitting that when collies are in the competition, it is rare for any other breed to win, but she loves Airedales for their feisty spirits.

When Karin was asked why she thought Lt Col Richardson preferred Airedales to other breeds, she said: 'They are bloody-minded individuals, they like to do what they think is appropriate.' She believes they act on instinct and with bravado, never thinking about their own safety. 'They are tenacious, determined, brave, stubborn, agile, alert ... everything you would want from a dog that was going to war.'

When I met Earnie, and another of Karin's dogs, Denzell, who came along as an understudy for the filming, they immediately took to me, and I felt the same about them, with their tough, wiry coats and their intelligent faces. Denzell was so excited to meet me he bounced round me, wrapping his flexi lead around my legs, while seven-year-old Earnie was busy drinking a cup of tea which someone had unwisely left on the ground. I asked Karin about the background of Airedales, and she told me they were bred from Waterside terriers and Otterhounds: I can see the Otterhound in them.

Before we started filming, Karin made us all laugh when she pointed out that she is of German nationality, so that we were actually sending a message to a German trench. We were filming at Trench Farm, near Ipswich, in Suffolk, where there is a set of re-created trenches. Earnie stayed with me in one trench, which was built with similar wooden supports and duckboards as those that were used in the war, while Karin made her way to the other set of trenches lower down the field. Karin had made a green pouch, very similar to the ones used in the First World War, and I placed a note inside it, then told Earnie to go.

He shot out of the trench, covering the distance by the most direct route, avoiding the obstacles littered across the field to simulate the wartime conditions, and then leapt into the narrow trench where Karin was crouched. He virtually dropped like a stone, six feet down through the small opening. Unfortunately, the camera crew were expecting him to go to the sloping end of the trench, not leap in. We filmed again, and the second time he crashed into the crew in his determination to get to Karin as quickly as possible. Third time lucky, and we got the shots we needed.

Yes, I was only too aware of how staged and sanitised this was. But Earnie did his bit, and it was clear why Airedales had the characteristics that were needed for this vital work. There was one final, very poignant, moment, when I went across to Karin's trench and took the note out of Earnie's pouch, reading it with a lump in my throat.

'I have given my husband and my sons, and now that he is required, I give my dog, too.'

This was a real letter, sent by a woman who donated her pet dog to the training school for military dogs. Her sacrifice is almost too great for comprehension.

Lt Col Richardson continued to train dogs after the First World War, and by the outbreak of the Second World War there was no need to convince the military authorities of their worth in a theatre of war and they were used for detecting explosives, patrolling and guarding ammunition. Some were even parachuted into France during the D-Day landings under heavy artillery fire. Three thousand three hundred dogs served with the British military, and more than 200 were killed in action. Another 1,500 were put down after their military service ended. But the bravery of the dogs was recognised when, in 1943, the PDSA introduced the Dickin Medal, the animal equivalent of a Victoria Cross, to be awarded to the most courageous.

On the home front, the government again appealed to owners to give up their pets for war service, and a large number responded. For many of them, feeding a dog while living on reduced rations themselves was very difficult, and also very controversial: neighbours who were struggling to feed families were often openly critical of pet owners, believing dogs were eating valuable resources, and a great many dogs were put down.

I know about this for the most poignant of reasons. My dad, who throughout my life was my mentor and my hero, came into farming from an unusual background – so unusual that I and my sisters did not know the full story until after he had retired from the farm. We'd heard bits of it, but somehow it had never been very clear: no wonder, because it was a tangled and very moving story. After a little prompting, Dad wrote a long, detailed letter, with copies for me and my three sisters.

Dad's parents were an actress whose stage name was Billie Dell, and a very famous actor and comedian, Leslie Henson. My grandmother's fiancé had been recently killed in a motorcycling accident. Leslie, who was married at the time, swept into her life when they appeared together in a West End production, and he filled the gap in her life. When Billie became pregnant with my dad, Leslie rented a home for her, later buying a house. But he wasn't able to leave his wife, the actress Gladys Henson, even though he regularly spent time with Billie and their son.

Eventually, aware that Leslie (who was known to Dad as Lally) was never going to divorce his wife and marry her, Billie moved away, down to Bournemouth, and it was there that Dad acquired his first dog, a lovely big Great Dane called John. Dad adored John, and was completely devastated when, during the Second World War, his mother decided to hand him back to the kennels he came from because she couldn't stand the constant criticism from neighbours and passers-by for keeping a big dog when food was rationed. It must have been a very sad day for Dad.

There was some compensation, though, because by this time Billie had met and married my father's stepdad, Cyril, a fine man who Dad grew to love, and who after John was re-homed bought a little brindle bull terrier pup, Barney. This was another four-legged friend Dad became very close to. After the outbreak of war, Barney went with Cyril when he became a Bristol Blenheim bomber navigator, living with him at the RAF base but coming home on leave to Dad, who was eight or nine at this time, and Billie.

I'm going to quote from Dad's letter: 'One day, which I will never forget, the postman called with a telegram for Mum. Cyril was reported missing. Mum collapsed in tears and I held her in my arms, telling her that he was only missing. She seemed to know that she would never see him again.'

When Cyril's possessions were collected from the base, among them was Barney. Dad and he became inseparable and spent hours roaming together. Barney was a scrapper and Dad had to hold him tight on his lead when another dog came towards them. After a fight with a German shepherd he was reported to the police and an officer called at the house. Barney, who had been devoted to Cyril, loved any man in uniform, and made such a fuss of the constable that he was let off with nothing more than a warning to Dad to keep him under control.

On one occasion he probably saved Dad's life when they wandered on to the beach together. Barney went ahead, turning and barking at Dad leading him through the sand dunes. When they reached the road Dad saw the sign 'KEEP OUT. HEAVILY MINED.' Barney had guided Dad through, avoiding the mines.

Sadly, one day when Dad's father Lally was visiting, Barney attacked another dog so ferociously that Lally had to hit him with a stick to get him to let go, and Lally then insisted that Billie get rid of him. But it worked out OK for Barney: he was given to a seaplane pilot in the Fleet Air Arm, another man in uniform, and Dad and Billie later heard that he used to swim out to sea after the seaplane until it took off.

Leslie Henson finally divorced and married Billie in 1944, and Dad's birth certificate was changed to acknowledge Dad as Leslie's son. He and Billie had another son, the actor Nicky Henson, Dad's brother.

It's comforting to know that in Dad's tumultuous childhood, so very different from the secure idyll he and Mum gave to me and my sisters, he had the companionship of dogs. However, the stories of John and Barney underlined to me just how difficult it was to keep dogs as pets during the war. As I have learned to say goodbye to dogs when their lives come to a natural end, he had to say goodbye in very different circumstances. But I'm sure those early experiences with dogs as his companions – and the rabbits, chickens and geese he and his mother kept during the war – were the building blocks of his love of the outdoors and farming, and took him on a route in life that would never have been predicted by his show business family.

The *Countryfile* programme I made brought the story of how dogs are used in the armed forces right up to date. I visited the Defence Animal Centre at Melton Mowbray, where they carry out some of the most sophisticated military dog training in the world. The centre opened in 1946, initially to train dogs for the army, but now it also trains them for the RAF and the navy. So Lt Col Richardson's lesson was well learnt: dogs are an essential tool of modern warfare, and also for peacetime duties with all sections of the armed forces. Not just the military, either: the centre trains dogs for the UK Immigration Service, HM Prison Service, HM Revenue and Customs and other UK government agencies.

More than 250 dogs are trained there every year, with 150 there at any one time. After being cleared through security (and, yes, my car was given a thorough once-over by a sniffer dog), I met the officer in charge, Major Tom Roffe-Silvester, and, as I looked round the state-of-the-art facilities I commented that it was a far cry from the school that Lt Col Richardson set up, but that he would be proud to see his legacy.

I asked Major Roffe-Silvester whether dogs were still relevant today and he assured me they were needed more than ever. No amount of technology can completely supersede their skills. Just as quad bikes were once tipped to take over from sheepdogs, but are now recognised as a great addition to have on a farm, but certainly not a replacement for a dog that can work away from the shepherd and use its own initiative, so it is with military dogs. As Major Roffe-Silvester told me: 'We use dogs alongside the latest technology, and together that builds up a great toolbox in operations. Nothing can replace a dog's ability to follow a scent, and they are also more mobile.'

Nowadays, we have sophisticated ways of transmitting information, so dogs are no longer required to carry messages, but they are used to search vehicles for arms and explosives, to guard military bases, and to give soldiers warnings of IEDs (improvised explosive devices), ambushes and possible suicide bombers. As Dad realised after Barney led him safely through a minefield, dogs are brilliant at threading their way through danger, and one of their most valuable roles in conflict is to tell soldiers where bombs have been planted. Their sense of smell is off the scale compared with ours, and they can be trained to alert to almost anything.

The dogs most commonly trained for defence work are the Malinois, a type of Belgian shepherd, which look very similar to German shepherds but finer, and an alert, intelligent and strong breed. German shepherds are also trained for the same work. Springer spaniels, Labradors and a few cocker spaniels are used to search for explosives, drugs or other contraband. Training takes between nine weeks and 18 months, which impressed me: I know how many hours I put into training my sheepdogs.

I watched a demonstration as one of the Malinois was given the 'Attack' command, and immediately went after a man who was running away. The target was wearing a heavily padded 'bite arm', designed for these demonstrations, so that when the dog grabbed him it didn't do any damage. But I could easily see that without the protection the dog would have practically taken his arm off.

I asked his handler, who had him under complete control: 'How come the dog went for him, and not for me?'

'Because I pointed him at the target,' was the reassuring reply.

To get the dog to release the arm, the handler squeaked a little toy, and the dog immediately returned to his side. Another dog, also a Malinois, demonstrated sniffing out IEDs, the deadly improvised explosive devices which have caused so much loss of life and injury to our troops in recent years. He was on a long rope lead and he walked in a dead-straight line down a 40-metre sandy track, where a tiny piece of electrical wire had been hidden two inches down in the sand. The dog stopped, sat down and stared at the spot until his handler called him off with another squeaky toy. I was very impressed.

I was told how dogs have been used in every theatre of war since the Second World War, including the recent conflicts in Iraq and Afghanistan. I was thrilled to meet JJ, a boisterous, friendly yellow Labrador who was injured in Afghanistan. JJ was deployed to Afghanistan in 2011 with his handler, Corporal Phil Corlett, who trained alongside him at the Defence Animal Centre. JJ's job was to sniff out roadside IEDs. While he was working he fell down a deep well, breaking his back.

Unlike the dogs who served in the two World Wars, who would have been immediately put down, JJ was treated, flown back to Britain and given extensive physio at the veterinary and rehabilitation facility, which is on the same site as the training centre.

To the delight of both JJ and Phil, they were reunited as soon as he got back – a 'hugely emotional' moment, Phil says.

Now, happily, JJ has been adopted by Phil and his girlfriend Gina and is a very contented family pet, who likes nothing more than splashing through streams (well, he is a Labrador ...) on his daily walks. I was amazed to see how well he has recovered from such a severe injury, and relieved that we are now treating our hero dogs so well.

I ended my part of the Remembrance Day programme with the words:

'One hundred years later, the legacy of Lieutenant Colonel Edwin Richardson lives on.'

Dogs are still saving lives, day after day. We owe them so much. In the next chapter I will tell you about the remarkable work of two civilian dogs I have met who every day make their own contribution to keeping their owners safe and well.

CHAPTER 12

Assistance Dogs

I'm sure by now you've picked up that I think the world of my working sheepdogs. But I'm prepared to admit that they are not, in all cases, the right breed for every job, and that there are other dogs whose abilities in their own fields are up there with those of an elite trialling collie.

These are dogs who have been trained to help human beings in remarkable ways: assistance dogs. It blows my mind when I hear about dogs that have turned the lives around of so many people. Anyone who owns a pet dog knows the therapy value of having a wet-nosed, waggy-tailed mutt gazing up with eyes brimming with love. It is a statistical fact that people who have dogs are four times as likely to recover from cardiovascular disease, and dog owners have signifi-cantly smaller increases in heart rate and blood pressure in response to stress. Couples with dogs are less likely to split and divorce than non-dog owners. But these are just normal dogs, pet pooches with no special training, nothing but instinctive devotion and love for their owners. Imagine the impact if this instinct is harnessed to specific training?

Guide Dogs UK was the first dog-training charity I, and most people, became aware of, as we occasionally saw a steady, unruffled Labrador or retriever guiding a person with little or no sight through crowded streets, negotiating round all sorts of obstacles, patient and never distracted, even by other dogs. Today there are many more assistance dogs for a whole range of disabilities.

The first guide dogs were trained in Germany immediately after the First World War, to help ex-servicemen blinded in the trenches. It was not until 1930 that Britain began training its own dogs, a year after the idea took hold in America. And it was a lot longer before the idea of assistance dogs expanded to cover other disabilities. Now there are over 7,000 people in the UK who have a specially trained dog to help them with their disabilities, including deafness, epilepsy, diabetes, autism, stress, including post-traumatic stress, Addison's disease and life-threatening allergies. I've been privileged enough to see assistance dogs in action, and watching a dog work demonstrates their value much more effectively than any statistics.

From time to time, I am invited to give talks to different organisations, sometimes about my farming life, sometimes more specifically about my relationship with my working dogs. One such invitation came from the Vets4Pets organisation, which represents many vet practices across the country.

I gave my talk to a full house and was pleased with the reception I received. But I'm more than happy to admit that my contribution was completely eclipsed by that of the man who spoke after me. Everyone in the hall was bowled over by his story, and as I looked out from the stage I saw lots of tissues wiping away tears. I was not ashamed to have to dab at my own eyes, as his story was so moving. All the time he talked, a gentle yellow Labrador lay at his feet.

Allen Parton was badly injured in an explosion on board a ship in the first Gulf War in 1991, where he was serving as a naval officer. He had a catastrophic head injury, which paralysed him from the waist downwards: he could no longer read or write or talk, and, perhaps most important, he was unable to remember anything that happened before the explosion. He did not recognise his wife, Sandra, and had no knowledge of his two children. It was devastating for him and equally so for his family. When his children, Liam and Zoe, who were six and four at the time, visited him in hospital he did not know them, had no interest in them, and was trapped in an angry and despairing mood.

Despite five years in hospital and a long period of rehabilitation, during which he made two major attempts at suicide, Allen's condition showed no sign of improving, and his wife Sandra was, he says, a saint for looking after him. When he was in the rehab hospital one of the staff told Sandra that he would never speak again and suggested she should divorce him and get on with her own life without him, but she refused.

Eventually, Allen was living at home but going to a day centre for rehab, but there was little progress and the children became used to tiptoeing around his irritable temper.

Unable to work because of her full-time caring duties, but with the children in school and Allen at daycare, the house was calmer and Sandra decided to volunteer as a puppy walker for the charity Canine Partners, which pairs dogs with disabled people to help them perform everyday functions. Once a week she had to attend the local centre with the puppy she was helping to train.

'One day the bus that was taking me to daycare didn't turn up,' said Allen. 'Sandra was understandably annoyed that she was going to miss her puppy class, so she bundled me into the back of the car and took me with her. I was left in my wheelchair, completely unresponsive, at one end of the hall while the puppy walkers went about their training.

'At the other end of the hall was a yellow Labrador that had been returned to the centre for a career change – he wasn't working out as an assistance dog because he had a bit of an attitude problem. If he was asked to pick something up he'd give a look, as if as to say, "Why don't you do it yourself?" He was going to be socialised and rehomed as a pet.

'While I was slumped in my wheelchair, immersed in my own miserable world, the dog, Endal, picked up a toy and brought it to me, dropping it in my lap. He expected praise or a reward, but he got no reaction from me. It clearly hacked him off, so he went to the mocked-up supermarket (where the puppies are taught to help their disabled owners to shop) and he took a tin of beans off a shelf and dropped it into my lap. Still nothing. He brought more toys, more shopping. I did not respond, I did not know how to respond. This was a challenge to him.

'Eventually, as I and my wheelchair slowly disappeared under a mountain of things that the dog brought, I smiled. It was the first human reaction, apart from anger, that had crossed my face since the injury. Somehow, Endal had seen and unlocked in me something that no amount of rehab had managed.

'He came home with me that day and he stayed with me for the next 14 years, completely transforming my life and the life of my family. He broke my miserable, unhappy world apart with his waggy tail.'

Allen explained that Endal had no advanced training, but that he instinctively knew how to handle Allen's problems, eventually learning more than 900 different commands – far more than any sheepdog needs, even the best trialling dogs. He learnt to put Allen in the recovery position and cover him with a blanket if he collapsed. Endal would bark for a neighbour to help, and if nobody came he would go and find someone. If Allen became unconscious in the bath Endal would leap in and release the plug. For the first time since Allen came home from hospital, Sandra could go out and leave her husband, knowing he was in good paws.

It was after Allen involuntarily burped, which seemed to excite Endal, that Allen stuttered his first words.

'Endal did what five years of speech therapy had not achieved,' said Allen, who today talks fluently.

But much more than any physical help he gave, he 'found' the old Allen, the good-natured man who Sandra and the children knew before the injury.

'Before Endal came I was on a perpetual short fuse, angry with the children if they disturbed me, or if they smeared chocolate on my trousers. But Endal released the goofy, funny side of my personality. He once dragged a rhododendron bush into the house that had only been planted the day before, and I just laughed. I'd have gone ballistic before he came.

'One by one, he brought back my emotions. I learnt to hate, because I began to hate people who were cruel to animals. And I learnt to love again, not just him but my family. I had no memory of marrying Sandra, and it was important to me to do it again. Endal was my best man.'

Allen and Sandra could have had their marriage blessed in church, but Allen insisted he did not want a blessing on something he could not remember. It took an effort to get permission to marry again, with a complete ceremony, but they achieved it.

But the story that brought sobs from the audience was what happened one night, after Endal and Allen had been giving a demonstration at Crufts to raise awareness of the charity Canine Partners. They were staying at a hotel and Allen took Endal out to the car park for a final chance to relieve himself before bed, when they were both knocked down by a hit and run driver, and left unconscious.

'I know what he did because it was all recorded on CCTV,' said Allen. 'But I was unconscious throughout, so I wasn't aware of it at the time. When Endal came round he was clearly dazed, but after a few seconds he pulled me into the recovery position, and then fetched a blanket from the back of my wheelchair to cover me. Then he crawled under a car to retrieve my phone, and tried to rouse me. When he got no response he went to the hotel and raised the alarm, barking and leading people to me.'

Endal was voted Dog of the Millennium by the PDSA, and given the Dickin medal, commonly called the animal's VC, and normally awarded for valour in wartime. 'He qualified because my injuries were sustained in war,' said Allen.

One day, when Allen was struggling at a cashpoint machine, Endal jumped up, took the card, the money and the receipt and handed them to Allen. This became part of their normal routine. One day, a newspaper photographer was behind them in the queue and asked for permission to snap Endal doing it, and he featured in a national newspaper, becoming a star. He was used to launch chip and pin machines when they were introduced, taking all the fuss and flashing cameras in his stride. He was the first dog on the London Eye and the first dog to be invited into the cabin of a commercial aircraft. He even picked up a Gold Blue Peter badge.

For Allen, a wonderful moment came when his children, who are now grown up, invited him to speak at their school.

'I think until I got Endal I was an embarrassment, a father whose speech and behaviour were not normal. But Endal was the catalyst, he made them proud of me.'

Eventually, when he was nearly 15 years old and very arthritic, Endal had a fit and lost his balance. Allen phoned the vet who said he would come the following day. That night Allen stayed downstairs with the dog who had changed his life.

'I was cuddling him, telling him how grateful I was for the incredible journey he had taken me on. He had given me back my wife, my children, my life. When I left him asleep on the sofa you could almost see him thinking, "Thank goodness, now I can get some sleep ..." The vet came in the morning, and I held Endal on my lap while he died, peacefully. He had given me so much, and in his death he gave me another enormous gift. I cried like a baby, and it was the first time I had been able to cry since my injury: another emotion he had released in me.

'My life was like a jigsaw puzzle that was smashed to pieces in the Gulf War, and every day Endal patiently found a bit of the missing puzzle and put it back. I still can't walk, I still have problems, I still have days when I feel miserable, but everything positive that I have, I owe to that remarkable dog.'

When Endal died there was a young, 11-month-old puppy called EJ in the house, starting his training as an assistance dog. He had come to live with Allen when he was eight weeks old, and had learned from Endal to pick up his bowl, and all the other help that Allen needs on a regular basis.

'That day, the day of Endal's death, EJ picked up Endal's collar and his assistance dog jacket and he brought them to me. He knew it was his turn. And he has become a great addition to our family. He can do everything that Endal did, even using an Oyster card on the London underground.'

It was while thinking about the amazing second chance he got with EJ, a dog who took over from Endal so smoothly, that Allen came up with the idea for a charity to provide dogs just for injured servicemen, and that's how the charity Hounds for Heroes came into existence.

'I looked back at what a miserable, unresponsive lump I was. I didn't want to sit back and think "I'm alright, Jack". I realised how much I had been given by these two dogs, and how incredibly lucky I was to have a second dog of such quality. What made me special? There are 9,000 injured servicemen and women in the UK today. And I know from my own experience that not all the injuries are the ones you can see: there are physically fit men and women who are crippled with post-traumatic stress disorder, and for them a dog is just as much a lifeline as it is for those of us who struggle with a cashpoint machine.'

Allen's charity now has more than ten dogs out in the community, helping ex-servicemen, and there are more dogs being trained.

'Although I'm a Lab man myself, we also train golden retrievers because they are more sensitive. Labs career in with great enthusiasm and gusto, which is what I needed from Endal, but it's not always the right approach. There are men and women who have been injured so badly that there is not enough skin to stitch up the holes in their bodies, and they need very, very gentle dogs.

'One chap, a double amputee, came to our HQ with his mother and grandmother, who had persuaded him to come. He didn't want to be there and he said, "I don't want a dog near me". One of our best dogs, Rookie, who can put keys and pens into someone's mouth, can operate pedestrian lights, and knows 938 commands even from an electronic voice, quietly went up behind him and put his head on the guy's lap without him realising it, while he was still protesting about dogs hurting him. He changed his mind.'

Allen was a vice chairman of Canine Partners for 15 years, and Sandra worked there for 20 years.

'We are not in competition with them or any other charity. We just feel we give servicemen something they can relate to. We use military language: the puppies are "cadets", and they have names like Juno, Monty, Colonel, Flanders. We joke and banter in the way that service people are used to: there's plenty of black humour.

'We get a lot of support from the armed forces, and from people connected with them. It was very touching when a widow sold her husband's Second World War medals and his gold watch chain and gave us the proceeds.'

EJ has raised more than two-and-a-half million pounds for the charity, happy to appear in endless photoshoots, as well as taking care of Allen every day. The charity fully funds the costs of the dogs, never wanting a dog to be a luxury some injured serviceman cannot afford. By paying for food and vet's bills, they know the dogs are being well cared for. They get sponsorship from Petplan, the animal insurance company, and they get free medical supplies and food donated to them. The hotels where they hold conferences and training events have all given them the use of rooms free.

'I'm gobsmacked by how kind people are to us,' said Allen.

The charity places dogs with injured firemen, policemen, paramedics, and prison officers. 'We don't think the word "hero" exclusively applies to the military.'

Like I said, there wasn't a dry eye in the house when Allen told his story. He finished his talk by telling us: 'Endal picked me up from an abyss of despair, and took me to where I am now: confident, able to talk to anyone. I wouldn't be here talking to you if it wasn't for the love of a dog.'

I was so moved by what I heard, that when I got home I nominated Hounds for Heroes as our latest charity to be sponsored at Cotswold Farm Park, where we display collecting boxes. I couldn't think of a more deserving cause, or a better ambassador for it than EJ, who gave me an affectionate nudge when he came on stage with Allen.

The story of dogs like Endal and EJ make me realise how adaptable dogs are. My sheepdogs are working in much the same way as their ancestors, going back centuries. Despite modern technology, their role has hardly changed: they run across fields and hills, rounding up sheep. Yet assistance dogs have had to learn all about life in the twenty-first century, to be able to help with the everyday aspects of life for their human partners.

Another assistance dog I met is Archie, a miniature poodle (although he's large for the breed). He is a smashing chap, friendly but always keeping an eye on his owner, William Stavert, who was born profoundly deaf and uses Archie as his ears. I met them when I went on the Great British Dog Walk organised by the charity Hearing Dogs for Deaf People, where they were also walking, raising money for the charity which has helped him so much. I went on the walk with Charlie and Boo.

William says he knew as soon as he met Archie that there was a bond between them, and it's easy to see that they have become a very close partnership.

'Archie's an independent dog, he only comes to me for strokes and cuddles occasionally. But when we are outside he never leaves my side or lets me out of his sight.'

He has twice alerted William to potentially life-threatening situations: once when a faulty toaster was burning the bread and close to setting fire to it, and another time when William forgot that he had put something in the oven. After pawing at William to alert him, Archie is trained to lie down flat if the smoke alarm is going off.

'The kitchen was full of smoke, goodness knows what would have happened if Archie hadn't alerted me.'

Archie's training is for specific sounds. Every morning when William's alarm goes off, Archie wakes him. He also tells William when the doorbell rings, when the timer for the oven goes off and, most importantly, if the smoke alarm sounds.

He also alerts to fire alarms in public places. When William was working in a college his colleagues forgot to tell him that the fire alarm would be sounded to tell them all it was time for the two minutes' silence on Remembrance Day. Archie naturally barked and pawed at William when the alarm went off, and William, as usual, shouted 'What's that?' Archie lay flat, to signal it was danger: the fire alarm. It was only when a colleague signalled to them to be quiet because they were disturbing the silence that William realised what it was.

'If they'd told me first, I'd have taken Archie out of the room!' he said.

Archie even understands some of the sign language William uses every day – he knows the signs for 'food', 'bed', 'walk', 'car'.

As well as helping with William's inability to hear, Archie has brought other benefits to his life.

'He is a great companion. He makes me go out, and he helps me to meet people. I'd be completely lost without him. He gives me confidence. I love Archie.'

Before Archie came along, William had not had an easy life. He was at school at a time when sign language was not encouraged, and was even banned. The authorities believed that deaf children would do better in life, and be more included in society, if they could lip read and talk. It meant that William was sent away from his home in Malvern at an early age to a boarding school for deaf children, where signing wasn't allowed.

'But we did it in the evenings, when the staff weren't around,' he said. 'Then if someone came in we'd switch to speech.'

Today, he tells his story with the help of a British Sign Language interpreter, Deb Watkins. Deb and the other BSL interpreters are special people, completing a long and difficult training to become accredited. They are a vital link between deaf people and a hearing world, and Deb has interpreted in some unusual places, including an operating theatre, laboratories, sports fields, cruise ships and behind the scenes at weddings and funerals.

When William left school at 17, he was taken on for an engineering apprenticeship with the Ministry of Defence, at the Royal Signals and Radar Establishment. He says, 'It came as a shock, moving into a hearing world. I was only used to deaf peers, and I didn't know how to make friends or communicate.'

He received no help as he tried to learn alongside hearing apprentices, who often mocked him and were cruel. 'Even the lecturers refused to turn round from the blackboards so that I could lip read.'

After a near breakdown, social services became involved and helped William find a teacher for the deaf to interpret for him in college. He became the first person in adult education at that college to have specialist support.

He completed his apprenticeship, passed with flying colours, and worked at the RSRE for 18 years, until a round of redundancies led to a career change and he went to work as a deaf role model for deaf students in college.

'The students were as lost as I had once been, and I helped them adjust to living in a hearing world. All the tutors were hearing, so I would intervene in lectures to help deaf students understand.'

He also spent half his time working in a school with younger deaf pupils, until his role was phased out and he was made redundant. By this time, he had Archie, who was very popular at the school and the college, and created a lot of interest in hearing dogs. Being a poodle, Archie does not moult: this was vital when he was chosen for William, because working in a school meant that William could be in contact with pupils who might be allergic to dog hair.

It was William's sister who first persuaded him that having a dog would give him more independence. Her husband is blind, and consequently she knew about guide dogs and other assistance dogs.

'I wasn't sure, but it turned out to be the best thing ever,' said William.

Every year, Hearing Dogs for Deaf People places over 150 dogs with people who need them, and they are aiming to increase the figure to 200 by the year 2020.

Jay Elcock is a training team leader at the charity, and has worked there for the last ten years. 'We train the dogs to physically touch the people they are working with in order to alert them. It's the only reliable way, especially if the deaf person has their eyes closed. With big dogs it's a nose nudge, with smaller dogs they sit on the ground and put two front paws up onto the person's legs.

'When they have been alerted by the dog, the deaf person will use a hand gesture, which means "Where?" Then the dog leads them to the sound, or in the case of danger, like a fire alarm, a burglar alarm or a carbon monoxide detector, they will lie flat on the floor.' Just like Archie did.

Those who have hearing dogs are encouraged to use a portable timer for the cooker, so that the dog doesn't have to lead them to a potentially dangerous situation.

Jay recalled one dog owner who commuted into London to work every day, and on the way home, like so many others after a long day at work, had the habit of falling asleep on the train. So he set the timer every day so that it would go off and his dog would wake him up just before they got to the right station. After a while he realised that other people were regularly getting into his carriage, because they too wanted to be woken up and not go beyond their stop.

Another dog was desperately trying to alert its owner to danger, but she could not see anything wrong. Then she looked out of the window and realised that the burglar alarm at the next-door house was flashing, and she phoned the police. The dog had heard the alarm.

Dogs also help those who live with a deaf person. One deaf woman was alerted by her dog when her father, who was upstairs, suffered a heart attack. She phoned for an ambulance and got him to hospital in time to be saved.

A profoundly deaf mother of three children was able to let them play in the garden on their own for the first time after she got a dog: before that she had to be with them, because she would not hear them cry if they fell over. Now the dog fetches her whenever she is needed.

All the hearing dogs are taught to a high level of obedience and manners. I noticed that when I was walking with them there was no skittish misbehaviour, as you often see on dog walks. Of course, they all have to know how to behave in shops, cafés, on public transport – not the normal places for a pet dog.

The most popular dogs for training are the reliable breeds: Labradors, cocker spaniels, poodles and crosses, like cockapoos. Jay believes that any dog could be taught to do the job, but clearly some breeds are happier working than others, so it makes sense to train those.

I really approve of the way the charity trains and looks after its dogs. All the puppies stay with their mothers, living with foster families, until they are eight weeks old, then they go to live with a puppy socialiser, who introduces them to all the normal situations they will encounter with their deaf recipient: walking through a busy town street, going into public places like libraries and so on.

At about ten months old – it varies from dog to dog – they meet their potential new owners and begin their specific training for their lifestyle. They may have to get used to a household with children, or cats, they may have to go to an office every day and lie quietly. The next part of the training is a two-day overnight stay in their new home to see if the pair bond. If it all works out well, the deaf person does a week's course at a placement centre, working with their dog, and at the end of the week they go home together. There's more support at home – in fact, all the 800 dogs that the charity has working in Britain today are supported whenever they need help.

I learnt all this about the charity during the walk and at the end we saw an amazing demonstration, which brought home to me just how well these dogs work. The charity has a team of demo dogs, specially trained to work in front of crowds of people and even in television studios, but they essentially do the same job as a dog in a normal home.

A ring was set up in a field, with a room setting with a bed, a chair, a doorbell, an alarm clock, a telephone and a timer. I watched in wonder as an enthusiastic cocker spaniel alerted to every different sound, leading the person to the right noise every time, or lying flat in the general 'Danger!' alert.

I know how to train dogs to sounds: that's what shepherds do with their dogs. We teach them voice commands and whistle commands. These dogs were reacting in exactly the same way that Peg does when I tell her to 'come by', or 'stop'. She hears the sound, and she obeys.

But if a sheepdog gets it wrong, the worst that happens is a few swear words from the farmer or shepherd and another go at it. These dogs can never get it wrong, because the people they live with depend on them so completely, and sometimes they are saved from life-threatening situations by them.

I am full of admiration for these dogs, and all the other assistance dogs who have transformed the lives of so many people. They do it out of devotion and loyalty, and they enjoy it: that's the most striking thing about all working dogs. They love to be needed and wanted, and they are happy when they have a job to do.

CHAPTER 13

How Bright Are My Dogs?

I didn't watch a lot of television when I was a child as there were always far more interesting things to do outside, following Dad around the farm. But on a wet afternoon there was one programme I really enjoyed: the TV films about Lassie, the amazing dog that always came to the rescue, performing feats of great daring and endurance to bring help when it was needed.

It never occurred to me that the dog's skills were exaggerated, and achieved by clever editing. After all, I lived with highly intelligent sheepdogs, and I had no doubt they were capable of similar exploits should the occasion arise. If ever I was going to round up a gang of baddies, a dog would fetch help for me. If ever I was stranded by a raging torrent, a dog would swim for help. If ever I needed a dog to leap through the air and knock down a criminal, or drag an injured person from a burning building, a dog could do it for me. And that dog, of course, would be a collie. We had Labradors as house dogs and gundogs, but I knew from a very early age that collies were the ones with the brains, who would share these amazing adventures with me. Just like Lassie.

Lassie, as she appeared on screen, was a rough collie. At least, from her first appearance in cinemas in 1943 through to her last appearance in 2007, she was played by many rough collies, most of them direct descendants of the original, Pal, who shared the screen with a very young Liz Taylor, and most of them male. 'She' starred in nine feature films, a TV series that ran for 18 years, a radio series and animated cartoons.

Why was a collie chosen for the part of this amazing dog? I'm not exactly impartial, because of my love for the breed, but even without my bias, it's a no brainer. It's an accepted fact in the canine world that collies are the brightest, most intelligent and agile dogs. There are now dog shows that hold agility and flyball classes labelled ABC, standing for Anything But Collies, in order to give other breeds a chance. If there's a collie or two in the class – and up to 95 per cent of the entrants to the large dog category at agility shows are collies – they invariably take the top spots. They are fast, the right shape, and good at jumping, plus they are the brainiest of all the breeds.

But how do we know this? I have my own experience to go on, but that's not scientific. I understand my own dogs and what they can do, but I don't understand how their intelligence works, and whether or not it can be compared to human intelligence.

So when *Countryfile* wanted to look into a new intelligence test for dogs, I was very happy to take Peg, my super-bright sheepdog, and our Hungarian wire-haired

Vizsla, Boo, a lovable buffoon of a house dog, along to be put through their paces. To make up a threesome for the trial, I also took Millie, our collie/kelpie cross farm dog. They made up a good cross section: Peg who (not really thanks to me, but because of her previous owner) is a highly trained ex-trials dog; Millie, who is a sweet, good-natured hardworking sheepdog trained to the level we need on a farm, but not as refined as Peg in her abilities; and Boo, who is completely lovable, knows how to behave, but has never struck me as particularly bright.

The test has been devised by Dr Rosalind Arden, who is a research associate at the centre for Philosophy of Natural and Social Science at the London School of Economics. Rosalind normally researches cognitive abilities (known to you and me as intelligence) in humans, but she is very interested in exploring differences in intelligence in non-human species, like dogs.

She told me why she has chosen to work with dogs, rather than other animals: 'Dogs are charismatic, they are not stressed by working with us, they are easy to work with, fun, and they enjoy doing the tests.'

The intelligence test involves giving the dogs six different tasks, and under scientific conditions each task would be carried out twice by each dog. But my dogs were doing the tests as a demonstration for the cameras, so we only put them through five of the tests; enough, Rosalind said, to get a relative score for their intelligence. Her major university study, done with 68 working border collies, set out to demonstrate that the bright dogs who excel at one task will also be reasonably good at the other tests, even though the tests are completely different. This tallies with how intelligence works in humans, and has long-reaching implications for the study of the relationship between high IQ and dementia (dogs can also get dementia in old age).

More relevant for me and others who rely on dogs for work, the tests will also be able to give a guide to how trainable a dog will be, from a very early age.

Apart from the scientific importance of the test results, I was simply intrigued to see how my dogs would fare. I was pretty sure Peg would come out best, but she did not get off to a flying start ...

The first test set out to see how long a dog faced with a bowl of food behind a mesh barrier would take to work out that it needed to go round the barrier to get its reward. It sounds simple to us, but dogs see the world differently, and this 'Detour Barrier Test' is a good starting point.

To my great surprise, Peg appeared to linger, looking around, before making her way round the barrier to the food. In contrast, both Millie and Boo did it very quickly, and scored better times than she did.

'My guess is that Peg is being very vigilant, looking around in case she should be heading off to round up sheep,' said Rosalind, as we were in a field where there are often sheep grazing. 'That's why we need to do other tests.'

It is true that collies are cautious by nature, always looking for possible problems. That's part of their intelligent makeup, and it has saved many a shepherd who has not spotted a problem that the dog has seen, and taken steps to solve without any human command. But it meant Peg, surprisingly, came last in this test, probably because she had higher priorities on her mind than food.

The next test was similar, but with a much longer mesh barrier between the dog and the food, necessitating a much longer detour. Peg and Millie both did it in a very impressive 12 seconds. Boo decided to run off with a stick, and it took her twice as long – that's my girl ...

The next test demonstrated whether dogs react to social cues. In other words, do they take instructions from human beings, by watching what the person wants them to do? I had two bowls of food, one either side of me, and I pointed firmly at one of them. When Peg was released she went straight to the bowl I was indicating. Millie appeared to be more confused, and ate the food in the other bowl. Boo came good, following my pointing hand and eating from the bowl I was gesturing towards.

In fairness to Millie, she is not a dog I work with regularly or feed, although she knows me well enough around the farm, so perhaps the other two had the advantage of being more used to me serving their grub.

But in the next test, again Millie didn't do too well, and this one was nothing to do with her familiarity with me. Two bowls of food were put down, one containing substantially more food than the other one. The test aims to show if dogs can discriminate between quantities. Peg went straight to the fuller bowl, whereas Millie went to the smaller amount and began eating it. Boo, who likes her food, made sure she went for the larger portion.

The final test was the hardest, a lot more elaborate. Two hay bales formed a passageway into a three-sided mesh cage. In front of the cage was a plate of food. Each dog was led into the cage, and then when released had to go backwards out of the cage, around the hay bales and round to the front of the cage to get the food. It took a lot more working out.

Peg sorted it out in a flash, and backed out, ran round and scoffed the food in five seconds flat. Millie, after a very slight pause, did the same, clocking a time that was only a second longer than Peg's. Boo showed her true colours, jumping on the hay bale as I led her in, then looking very confused when she saw the food. It didn't take her too long – she reversed out and ran round – but in her enthusiasm ran beyond the food and had to come back to it. All in all, nine seconds, four more than Peg.

Now the results were in, and Rosalind did the maths and gave me the final scores: Peg, nine; Millie, seven; and Boo not far behind with six.

It was exactly the order I thought they would come in, and it confirmed my belief that Peg would do very well. But I was agreeably surprised that Boo didn't completely lose the plot.

'Boo doesn't have a terribly low IQ, does she?' I asked Rosalind.

'No,' she replied, not too convincingly. 'Besides, IQ is only one thing, and we love our dogs for lots of different reasons.'

That's true, and we didn't choose our wire-haired Vizslas for their MENSA ratings. But putting the dogs through the test was fun, they enjoyed it, and I discovered how their skills vary. I'm all for anything that helps us understand dogs better, because the more we know the better we can work with them, and if Rosalind and her colleagues can use their studies into dog intelligence to help human beings, that's great.

Rosalind explained to me that scientists have known for some time that brighter people tend to live longer, but it is tricky to investigate because human beings make so many different lifestyle choices, like whether we smoke, how much we drink, the amount we eat and whether or not we exercise.

'Dogs, on the other hand, are basically teetotal,' she said. 'They don't touch pipes, cigars or mess around with recreational drugs – lots of things that muck up our findings in human reports can be very much better studied in non-human animals.'

By studying a cohort of border collies, all working dogs, it's a good chance to get a fairly even playing field. And because dogs, like humans, can get dementia, which interferes with their behaviour and brain structure, it could lead to a better understanding of why some dogs are more likely to get it than others, with possible ramifications for humans.

Of course, this work is very much in its infancy, and Rosalind and her colleagues at both the LSE and Edinburgh University are working on perfecting the IQ test. But so far their findings show that dogs that do best on the detour tests – finding their way round the barriers to the food – also did better on the choice tests, when they chose a fuller bowl of food or when they chose to interact with the human pointing them to one particular bowl. So those dogs are overall more intelligent, not just suited to one task, and the hope is that this will lead to more understanding of the evolution of intelligence.

As for me, well, I'm just delighted to have my faith in Peg confirmed.

Stanley Coren, a Canadian Professor of Psychology and the author of *The Intelligence of Dogs*, has done a lot of work on how dogs think and why. His interest was triggered when, as a student, he saw an example of a dog's ability to reason. The family pet, Penny, a boxer cross, had done something wrong and Stanley's mother was so angry with her she hurled a bunch of keys at the dog, hitting her in the rump and causing her to yelp. Stanley, who walked into the kitchen at the end of this scene, rescued Penny by suggesting she come with him to his room. As they were leaving the kitchen Penny made a wide detour round the keys, which were lying where they had fallen. As she reached the doorway, she dashed back, picked up the keys, carried them to another room and hid them behind a sofa, pushing the keys with her nose until they were out of sight.

Professor Coren concluded that Penny was actually using reason. She was hiding the keys that had been used to punish her, having reasoned that they could be used against her again. At the time that Stanley Coren watched Penny's behaviour, the general belief in the scientific community was that dogs don't have conscious reasoning abilities, even though many pet owners have similar stories to demonstrate that they do.

I'll quote just one, and it's not about a pet dog, but about a stray bitch who gave birth to nine puppies. When they were two weeks old the forest where the puppies were born, in Chile, was engulfed by a forest fire. Unable to carry all of her dogs to safety, the mother dug a deep hole, placed all the puppies into it, then dragged a sheet of metal from a nearby landfill site and covered them. She stayed close by, and when the fire was brought under control she led firefighters to her underground shelter. After publicity, all the pups were adopted. But, again, the mother showed a great deal of insight and reasoning.

Lots of research has been carried out on perception, awareness, memory and learning in dogs, and experts have found that dogs have very high interpersonal intelligence, higher than that of other intelligent mammals like the great apes and much higher than their own wild relatives, like wolves.

Interpersonal intelligence shows that a person, or an animal, has social skills and can relate to others. Dogs definitely relate to the humans around them, often showing preferences, and a recent study in Japan has shown that dogs even remember people who have been unfriendly towards their owners. They look to humans for help when they face a problem they cannot solve, whereas captive-raised dingoes do not, even though they are just as smart as dogs at solving the other problems.

Of course, other animals, including apes and wolves, live in societies where they relate to each other because there is a pack order, and they all know and accept the hierarchy. They learn from each other: a puppy set a simple task with a reward at the end of it will learn the task 15 times more quickly if an older dog demonstrates it than if left to its own devices, and it's roughly the same success rate if a human demonstrates it.

But the relationship between domestic dogs and humans goes beyond the pack mentality. Dogs are the only animals that can discriminate emotional expressions on human faces. Without being aware of it, humans tend to look at the right-hand side of another person's face, because that's the side that most expresses emotion. Dogs also look at this side, interpreting signs of anger, happiness and irritation in exactly the same way that we do. The fact that dogs don't look at any particular side of another dog's face shows that they use this behaviour just with humans, where there is a point to it.

Another type of intelligence is linguistic, the ability to understand and use language. While dogs don't talk in words, they certainly understand many and can express themselves to their owners. Professor Coren estimates the average dog knows 160 words or phrases. Seems a lot to me, and I'm not sure Boo would have such a big vocabulary, but clearly many dogs do.

A border collie called Chaser is believed to have the largest vocabulary of any animal in the world. Chaser has been taught by her owner, a Professor of Psychology in America, to correctly identify over a thousand different toys by their name, and to retrieve the right one when asked to do so. I'm convinced that it's not the word they understand but the sound. As people we can understand the same word spoken in many different accents, pitches and tones, whereas a dog needs consistency of tone.

Dogs also understand body language and hand signals. Although chimps and other primates have been taught similar language skills, dogs of all breeds pick up words and gesture, often without any structured teaching.

Spatial intelligence is the ability to recognise places and remember them relative to other places. In other words, to have a mental map of the world. Dogs remember where the dog food is stored, where their bed is, which way to go when they are taken out for a favourite walk. What's more, they have a spatial memory. Take a dog back to a place it used to live, or where a relative lives, and it will instantly know its way around, even if it hasn't been there for years.

Another type of intelligence is logical-mathematical. Well, dogs clearly don't do algebra and fractions (and plenty of us humans never really got the hang of them!) but dogs are able to make logical choices – just as the dogs in Rosalind's intelligence test did when they went to the large bowl of food not the smaller one. Some dogs also have rudimentary counting skills, and it is more than likely that a bitch with pups has a mental count of them, so she knows when one is missing.

Professor Coren carried out a major study into which breeds of dog are the most intelligent. Nearly half of all the obedience judges in North America filled in a questionnaire for him and added their own comments. From their information he assessed 140 different breeds of dog, and ranked them from 1 to 79 for obedience and working intelligence. Of course, as he points out (and so did the judges) there are exceptions in any breed: dogs that do better or worse than their breed would suggest. Mixed-breed dogs are harder to place on charts, as it all depends what genes they inherited from which parents.

Different research shows that, generally speaking, a mixed-breed dog will behave most like the breed it looks like. For example, a poodle/Labrador cross that looks more like a poodle is likely to have more behaviour traits of a poodle. But of course, some dogs are 'bitzers' – bits of this and bits of that – so their behaviour and character can only be judged on an individual basis.

So for the purpose of his list, Professor Coren has only assessed pure breeds. And guess what? Top of the list, numero uno, is the border collie. Out of 199 judges who assessed the breeds, 191 put the border collie in the top ten, so there was a great deal of overall consistency. At the bottom of the list too, where the ditzy but loveable Afghan hound took the wooden spoon, 121 of the judges assessed it in the bottom ten.

How did the other dogs in my life fare? Labradors came in at number seven, and springer spaniels at 13. As for Vizslas (and the list did not differentiate between smooth and wire-haired), they came in at number 25. According to Stanley Coren, dogs ranked in the top ten will start to understand commands after less than five goes, and will remember them with ease. He said: 'These are clearly the top breeds for intelligence and seem to learn well, even with inexperienced or relatively inept trainers.'

Dogs ranked from 11 to 26 are 'excellent' working dogs, but they may respond a bit more slowly when the handler is further away: 'Nevertheless, virtually any trainer can get these breeds to perform well.'

I don't want to sound smug, but it's no surprise to me to find border collies in top place. But there is a note of caution to be sounded: the Border Collie Rescue charity says that intelligence in dogs is a double-edged sword. Working dogs like Peg are fine: they have plenty of scope for exercise and to use their active brains. But the charity warns: 'Having a smart dog means waging a continual intellectual war with your dog, trying to out-smart them. Put in a gate, and they figure out how to get over or under it.' These are dogs that can lift latches and even turn doorknobs, and they need a lifestyle that allows them to burn off their tremendous energy and work their restless brains.

Before I end this chapter, I want to share one very heart-warming story with you, that takes me right back to my early love of Lassie, and demonstrates the intel-ligence of dogs. Two rough collies (probably not pedigrees but definitely collies from the look of them) called Panda and Lucy, escaped from their home in Ukraine and spent two days stranded on a railway track after Lucy was injured and could not move. Panda, a male dog and the larger of the two, stayed close to her, and every time a speeding train approached he lay down next to her and nudged her head flat, so that the train rattled over them. He never left her side, and was so fiercely protective that locals had to call in dog rescue experts to get them off the tracks.

'I saw a train approaching, and felt sick,' said Denis Malafeyev, a volunteer from a rescue centre who was contacted by a train engineer about the plight of the dogs. 'The male dog also heard it, came close to the female and lay down next to her. Both of them pushed their heads to the ground and let the train pass. He had been doing this for two days, and keeping her warm. I don't know what to call it: instinct, love, friendship, loyalty?'

I'd say it is all of those. But I'd add bravery and intelligence. The dogs were rescued, Lucy was treated, and they were returned home. That's collies for you.

CHAPTER 14

They Also Serve ...

I set out from Aviemore in my Land Rover, bumping along a narrow, icy track, pine forest closing around me, hoping I was going the right way. Eventually, when I was beginning to seriously wonder if this was the route, I came to my destination: the Cairngorm Sleddog Centre. The centre, the home of Alan and Fiona Stewart, feels about as remote as you can get in this crowded isle of ours. It's five miles from Aviemore, but they're a lonely five miles, with no other habitation around.

As soon as I realised I was in the right place, I paused to take in the landscape. The centre is in the foothills of the beautiful Cairngorm mountains, the highest, coldest and snowiest range in Britain. The Caledonian Forest, which used to extend over much of Scotland and stopped the Roman invaders in their tracks, may now be reduced to only 1 per cent of its original size, but it is still dense here. I was struck by how crisp and clean the air is, and how the intense wintry light sharpened the colours of the hills, the snow and the pines.

Alan Stewart came out to meet me; a friendly, energetic man whose life story is just as breath-taking as the scenery. He runs the centre, and he was going to take me on one of the most exhilarating experiences of my life, riding behind a team of 12 Alaskan huskies, being filmed for *Countryfile*.

Alan is, by anyone's standards, a tough guy. He spent more than 18 years as a member of a deep-sea diving team, working all over the world as well as on the North Sea oil rigs, and he still works in the industry as a dive rep for an oil company, monitoring the dive teams working for them.

'Working under the sea, you are at the sharp end,' he said. 'If you make a mistake, you are not coming back. You work at great pressure for four months of the year. So when you are back on land it can be boring, when you are used to that pressure and excitement. I am very lucky: I found something just as exciting and rewarding to fill the rest of my life.'

That something was dog racing with Alaskan huskies, an interest that consumes Alan, his wife Fiona and their son John. Alan has been running and breeding sled-dogs for 26 years, and he and Fiona have lived at their remote home for 18 years.

'I was working in a deep saturation diving team, living at a depth of 500 feet in a pressurised container no bigger than a medium-sized van for 26 days at a time. I was reading about dogs, and luckily my super-intendent was interested, and was happy to let me have blocks of time off to go to America to learn about it properly. I went over to Minnesota and worked at the kennels of a well-known sled-dog guy. It was unpaid work, but I got six or seven weeks' training from him at a time.'

When he felt he really knew the sport, Alan started to buy his own team of dogs.

'I've always bought from the best sled-dog racers, usually from one kennels in Montana, and I know the great, great grandfathers of most of my dogs.'

While he is away working, the job of looking after the dogs falls to Fiona. She is responsible for feeding them, supervising their medical care and taking care of the pups. She runs the admin for the centre, taking bookings and liaising with local hotels. She's also, like Alan and John, a musher, and has competed at the top level in the UK. ('Musher' is the name given to sled-dog racers, and it's believed to come from the French word 'marche', meaning 'walk', used by the original French settlers in the icy wilds of Canada, where travelling with sleds and dogs was a skill learnt from the indigenous people.)

Alan's dogs are magnificent to look at, and I immediately fell in love with their wonderful thick coats and their intelligent eyes. The dogs live outside in kennels made from old whisky barrels.

'They're not domesticated. You can't train them to walk on a lead or sit. They're athletes, born to run,' he says.

Alan's dogs are all Alaskan huskies, descended from those dogs who were a vital form of transport in the wild and inaccessible terrain of North America and

Canada, and who were used by the prospectors and miners in the Klondike gold rush days of the 1890s, a time which inspired Jack London's famous novel, *The Call of the Wild*, about the tough life of a sled-dog.

The word 'husky' comes from 'huskimos', which was the name English sailors in the eighteenth century gave to all indigenous people in the far north (a corruption of the work 'eskimo'), and by the early nineteenth century the name had transferred itself to the dogs.

Alaskan huskies are mongrels, bred specifically as sled-dogs, and first recorded in the late 1800s. They are a mix of Alaskan Malamutes and Siberian huskies, with genes from pointers and Salukis to increase speed, and a contribution from Anatolian shepherd dogs to give them a solid work ethic. Some may have greyhound blood, and some are part wolf. They are smaller and leaner than other sled-dog breeds, and because of their mixed heritage they come in different colours and with different markings. On the whole they are good with other dogs and gentle with people. They are now the fastest breed of sled-dogs, and the favourites for competitive sled-dog racing.

The first sled-dogs were Alaskan Malamutes, which probably evolved in Mongolia about 30,000 years ago, when humans migrated and trained them to pull sleds carrying their belongings. Malamutes are larger and stronger than Alaskan huskies, not bred for speed but for pulling strength. They were used in rural communities in Alaska, Canada, Lapland, Siberia, Norway,

Finland and Greenland for mail deliveries, and for transporting supplies.

Other sled-dogs include the Canadian Eskimo dogs, used by the indigenous Thule people of Arctic Canada. They were used for pulling sleds, but also by the Inuits for hunting seal, musk ox and polar bears. Greenland dogs are another Eskimo breed that have high endurance, but are not noted for speed. Samoyeds, bred by the native Samoyede people of Siberia, are all-purpose dogs which haul sleds, herd reindeer and hunt. The Siberian husky is smaller than a Malamute, although there is a strong resemblance between the two breeds. They can pull large loads, but not for such long distances as the Malamutes.

The last mail delivery by dog sled was in 1963, because planes had taken over, highways had been built for trucks, and snowmobiles were being used for local transport. But the dogs live on in remote communities, and, of course, in the kennels of mushers like Alan, since dog-sled racing has become an international sport, and is particularly popular in Canada and the USA.

As well as racing dogs on snow, Alan's dogs also pull wheeled carts, which is what I rode in. There simply isn't enough snow to always run sleds, even in the Cairngorms.

Alan's dogs run in teams of 12, and he changes around their positions, so that every dog gets the opportunity to lead. The worst position is to be the wheel dogs, close to the cart or the sled, and they need to be calm and steady and not worried about the wheels immediately behind them.

Travelling at great speed behind a team of dogs through the forest tracks was a peak experience for me, something I will never forget. We moved at an astonishing, bone-shaking speed, and it was inspiring to see these strong, willing dogs straining to run as fast as they could, working together as a team and clearly loving it as much as I did, confirming my oft-stated belief that dogs are happier when they have a real job to do.

Alan has raced dogs all over the world, competing at the highest level of the sport in the USA, Chile, Argentina and Europe. He was the first and only UK musher to take sled-dogs over the UK's second highest mountain, Ben Macdui.

But the star of the family – and of all British sled-dog racing – is Alan and Fiona's son, John, who has raced and trained dogs since he was six. As a junior he dominated all the British events, and travelled with Alan to major events all around the world, spending six weeks in the remote Chilean mountains at the age of ten. From the age of 18 he has lived and worked in the USA and Canada with the world's greatest mushers. He and his wife Liz, also a professional musher, live in remote Wyoming. Prize money in the big events can be as high as $250,000, and John's greatest success to date is coming second in the gruelling 700-mile Wyoming

Open race. Like his dad, he is a commercial deep sea diver when not racing dog teams.

John has taken part in the most famous dog-sled race in the world: the legendary Iditarod. Alan suggested I might consider taking part in the race. I think I was tempted for a few seconds, then the reality of what it means hit home and I firmly shook my head. No thank you. It's a gruelling endurance test that lasts for two weeks, covers 1,150 miles, and is known as 'the last great race on earth'. Teams race through blizzards and gale-force winds that can bring the temperature down to minus 73 degrees Celsius. People have been known to veer off course, get lost and die in those conditions – not for me, thanks!

The race has been run every year since 1973, but its roots stretch back much further. The Iditarod Trail was used by indigenous people, and then by Russian fur traders, followed by gold-rush miners. Dog sleds were used all year round to deliver mail, firewood and supplies, because the seaports were closed for vicious winters which lasted from October to June.

Sled-dog racing became a popular winter sport, and in 1908 a man called 'Scotty' Allan started the All-Alaska Sweepstakes race, which covered 408 miles. Scotty is a great hero of Alan's, and the Cairngorm Sleddog Centre includes a small museum dedicated to him. Scotty was a local lad – well, he was born in Dundee, only 60 miles away from Alan's home – who was sent out to South Dakota in the early twentieth century by the local laird to deliver a valuable Clydesdale horse. Scotty saw an opportunity and stayed in the States running his own dog-sled transport business. He was an acclaimed musher, winning the race he established three times in the early 1900s, and setting up a famous breeding kennel for Alaskan huskies. He only returned to Europe to deliver dog teams to help carry supplies to the Allied troops fighting the Germans in the First World War. After the war, Scotty returned to the wilds of North America, where he became a successful businessman and politician, and never came back to Scotland.

'We brought a bit of him home,' said Alan. 'To me, he is the founder of sled-dog racing, and I wanted him to be honoured in his home country.'

Sled-dogs were also used in the Second World War, transporting munitions and laying telephone wires. Teams of dogs also towed sleds to find survivors when planes went down. As a military historian said: 'Dogs were eminently more economical than horses. Two dog teams could do the work of five horses in formidable terrain ... Although it may seem that dog sleds are an obsolete mode of transport ... sled dogs are still far superior to aircraft and track vehicles, a dog requires no repair shops or spare parts ... In one of the most desolate and inhospitable regions on earth, the dog is still a man's best friend.'

The most celebrated and moving story of mushing in Alaska, and one that is honoured every year when the

Iditarod is run, is the Great Race of Mercy, one of the most gallant feats ever performed by dogs for their human masters. In the winter of 1924–25 the small town of Nome, in Alaska, was threatened with a diphtheria epidemic. The doctor, Curtis Welch, had placed an order for diphtheria antitoxin a few months earlier, but the shipment did not arrive before the port at Nome iced up and closed to shipping for the winter. In several weeks over the winter Dr Welch treated children for tonsillitis, four of whom died. He was increasingly convinced he could have a diphtheria epidemic on his hands, and when he had two confirmed cases in children, both of whom also died, the mayor of Nome arranged an emergency town meeting, and the whole town was quarantined, to prevent the epidemic spreading. Dr Welch sent radio telegrams to all other towns in Alaska, alerting them to the threat, and also to the US Public Health Service in Washington.

'An epidemic of diphtheria is almost inevitable here. Stop. I am in urgent need of one million units of diph-theria antitoxin. Stop. Mail is the only form of transportation. Stop.'

When the serum was obtained from west coast hospitals it had to be shipped to Seattle and then on to Seward, before it could begin the journey across Alaska. But a smaller supply was at Anchorage hospital; not enough to defeat the epidemic but sufficient to hold it at bay until the larger shipment arrived. It was taken by train to Nenana, 674 miles from Nome.

Dr Welch calculated that the serum would only last for six days in the brutal winter conditions, with temperatures at an all-time low and snow drifts and high winds burying the route and making the going tough. The dog sleds would have to travel by night as well as day, and make record-breaking times to get there, on a route that offered no protection from blizzards, and included a 42-mile stretch across the shifting ice of the Bering Sea.

A relay of the best dog teams in Alaska set off. Most of the dog mushers were direct descendants of native Athabaskans, the indigenous people who were the original dog mushers, and who now worked for the mail delivery service.

It was a brutal run. One musher arrived with half of his face blackened by frostbite, having made a run of 52 miles – double the 25 that makes for 'an extreme day's mush' and the third-longest leg of the relay. Another musher had to have hot water poured over his hands to get them off the sled's handlebar. The teams travelled by day and night. One of the mushers had to take over pulling the sled himself after two of his dogs died.

The longest section was run by Leonhard Seppala with his lead dog Togo, and they travelled 91 miles into an oncoming storm with gale-force winds and a wind chill of minus 65 degrees. Twelve-year-old Togo led the team across the sea ice in the dark, using his sense of smell to keep them on course. After feeding the dogs and resting them for six hours, they set off again in the teeth of a blizzard, climbing 1,500 metres up Little McKinley Mountain, before passing the serum on to the next runner. The dogs were near collapse, and Togo was never able to race again.

The final stage was taken by a musher called Gunnar Kaasen with his lead dog Balto. When his sled flipped over in the storm he nearly lost the cylinder of serum, and had frostbitten hands through groping for it on his hands and knees in the dark. They ran a total of 53 miles, the second-longest leg.

When the serum was triumphantly delivered, not one vial was broken, and it was thawed and ready for Dr Welch to use about seven hours after arriving. The whole trip had taken five days and seven and a half hours, a world record achieved in ferociously bad conditions. Several dogs died during the trip, but the people of Nome were saved. The death toll was five or six, but Dr Welch estimated that as many as a hundred more died in the camps of indigenous people outside the town, where no medicine was available. A second run was made by many of the same mushers when the rest of the serum arrived, but the time pressure was not so acute, even though weather conditions were still appalling. Critics had argued that transportation by plane would have been better, but on this second delivery, when a plane was to be used to carry half the delivery, it failed to take off on two consecutive days because of the conditions, and even the greatest advocates of technology over dogs had to concede that the dogs were the only way the serum would have made it in time.

All the mushers received letters from the president and a gold medal. Balto became the greatest star, and there is a statue of him in New York's Central Park, with the inscription 'Endurance. Fidelity. Intelligence'. Among mushers, though, the greatest respect is given to Leonhard Seppala, who with Togo did the longest and most difficult leg of the run, and apparently Seppala died unhappy that Balto was getting the credit: 'I never had a better dog than Togo. His loyalty, stamina and intelligence could not be improved on. He was the best dog that ever travelled the Alaska trail,' he said.

The Iditarod Trail race today does not follow the route taken by the dogs delivering the serum, but the race commemorates the bravery of the men and dogs who saved the town. The Leonhard Seppala Humanitarian Award is given every year to the musher who provides the best care for his dogs during the race.

The modern Iditarod race was started to encourage the preservation of sled-dogs. The traditional Iditarod trail was becoming overgrown and forgotten, until a man called Joe Redington started clearing it to work as a hunting guide. He was depressed that the invention of the snowmobile had almost wiped out the role of the sled-dog in ten years. He and an associate, Dorothy Page, started a 25-mile race to encourage owners to keep and breed these fantastic dogs, and a few years later the race expanded, and mushers and their dog teams were running the full Iditarod.

I'm full of huge admiration for Alan's son John who has done the race, and all the other mushers who face the unforgiving conditions of the trail each year. But I think I made the right decision to give it a miss ...

When I visited Alan, as well as the huskies he had a German pointer, Buster, who used to run with the dog teams. Buster had another job: when Alan bred a litter of puppies, once they were weaned they were taken from their mothers (who went back into harness to pull sleds) and they roamed free, with the pointer rounding them up and keeping them safe. He even took them swimming in the river. Alan explains, 'No husky puppy goes into harness until it is 18 months old, and they never go on a lead. With Buster with them, I always knew they were safe.'

Alan now has another dog who also has a vital role at the centre. Arnold is an Australian blue heeler, also known as an Australian cattle dog, a breed that is used for rounding up and driving cattle in the outback. Arnold has a different job from Buster: he takes the old huskies out for walks. There are four or five old ones, no longer able to join the sled teams, so Arnold rounds them up and, with a walkie-talkie round his neck so that Alan can communicate with him, trots off with them for a walk. As soon as the old dogs spot Arnold they are ready to go. 'The walkie-talkie means I can keep my voice low, because you never raise your voice to huskies,' Alan says. Alan told me he'd wanted a blue heeler because he'd seen them when he worked in Australia years before. I'd seen them, though I'd never worked with them, but I understood why he liked them. They are a tough, energetic breed, known for their incredible loyalty to their masters. Alan intended to import one from Australia, but then he found out about a breeder in Italy. He rang her while he was out on an oil rig, and she told him he could do her a great favour if he was prepared to take a heeler who had not worked out in its home in England because it was too excitable.

Now Arnold has definitely found his niche. He lives outside Alan and Fiona's cottage, on a long line.

'We need a guard dog because we are in the middle of nowhere, and he alerts us to trouble. There is an osprey nest near to us, and we have had thieves trying to steal the eggs.'

As well as the ospreys there are plenty of other rare breeds around Alan's home: 'The cottage we live in once belonged to the man who introduced reindeer to Britain,' he says. The herd of reindeer in the Cairngorms is the only wild herd in the country.

The isolation of the life is normal for Alan and Fiona, and they both love it.

'Not many people can understand why we do it. Even the ones who want to take up sled-dog racing find it harder than they imagined. Many of them go into it because they like the look of it, but 80 per cent of the people who take it up only last two or three years. I feel sorry for people who do it as a hobby, as they miss most of the pleasure of having dogs, and I feel sorry for the dogs, because they need to run. The courses we organise are meant to show people the reality of it, so they don't go into it with romantic notions. It's hard work.'

I know better than most people the amount of time and energy that you need to have working dogs, but Alan's kennels are on a much bigger scale than anything I have ever dealt with. Because the centre is winding down, through lack of snow, Alan now has only 26 dogs, but there were 36 when I was there.

'We knew global warming was happening, but we never expected it to come this quickly. I used to have my dogs in training mode for seven months of the year, and I could take clients out all that time. Now the season is down to four months. It was too warm to take the dogs out last Christmas Day, and even John, living in Wyoming, has had to take the dog teams up to Alaska to find snow. I used to be able to take a sled across the mountains, but I can't now.'

I enjoyed my visit to Alan and Fiona so much that I seriously considered having one of their puppies. As well as the dog-sled teams, Alan showed me two-wheeled scooters that are pulled by one dog, and I loved the idea of being able to zoom about being towed by one of these beautiful animals.

When I got home I had a quick reality check. Life on a farm is always very busy, and when I add on my *Countryfile* filming, there is no spare time left. A sled dog requires regular running, and, unlike all my other dogs, it could not wander around the farm with me. I got in touch with Alan and told him that I wouldn't be able to give the dog the life it deserved and needed.

It is very sad that Alan's centre is winding down. But Alan is never going to put his feet up in front of the fire: he's found himself another high-adrenalin sport, racing specialised off-road vehicles. And sled-dog racing is such a big sport in North America and Canada that the future of these fantastic dogs is assured, at least as long as there is enough snow.

I knew before I reached Alan's remote centre that I was going to love his dogs. Not only is the breed beautiful to look at, but they are the sort of dogs I relate to: working dogs with a strong purpose in life.

But I have to admit I was very pleased when I met another breed, the Yorkshire terrier, to have my prejudices overturned. Yorkshire terriers are cute little things, with a reputation as handbag dogs, wearing ribbons in their hair and posing prettily with their little heads cocked to one side.

Not my type of dog, I thought. And then I met David Ward and his two little Yorkies, Sika and Turtle, when I was making a series of programmes for *Countryfile* on county breeds. In each county I went to, I met and found out about the animals that originate there. In Yorkshire I met Swaledale and Wensleydale sheep, a

Cleveland Bay horse, large white pigs and, finally, Yorkshire terrier dogs.

I came away with a new respect for these tough little fellows. They were originally working dogs just as much as my sheepdogs or the Alaskan huskies, although nowadays far more are kept as companion dogs. I discovered they punch well above their weight in terms of ferocity, stamina and loyalty, and they've got a big attitude for such a little dog. What's more, in a survey of dog owners, it's apparently Yorkie owners who are the happiest, so the little fellas obviously bring a lot of pleasure with them.

They were bred for ratting in the textile and woollen mills of Yorkshire. They were small enough to get behind the large looms, and brave enough to corner and take on any rodent, shaking it to death.

'They're lightning quick, and they can get into all the nooks and crannies,' David told me. 'And they are not frightened of anything. They're a big dog in a small body. They'll tackle any dog that they think is threatening them – don't be deceived by the ribbon in their hair.'

In the 1800s there was an influx of Scottish labourers into Yorkshire, looking for work. It was the time of the Industrial Revolution, and factories and mills were springing up all over the county. The labourers brought with them small terrier dogs of non-descript breeds, which were great hunters and ratters. They'd been used in Scotland for hunting animals that lived in burrows and dens, like badgers and foxes. The dogs were carried in the pockets of the hunters and then released into the dens of the wild animals, fighting fiercely with their cornered prey. They were encouraged to bark, so that the hunters would know where to dig to catch the quarry and retrieve their dogs. They were famous for standing their ground, and were so determined they would risk their lives in the struggle rather than give up.

They found a natural home in the mills, and also down the coal mines of Yorkshire. Cats were used for catching mice, but rats are often too large and vicious for a cat to handle. The dogs were also useful in the overcrowded slums that sprung up to house the mill-workers, again keeping the rat population down. There are no records of what breeds these small dogs from Scotland were, but it is believed they were Clydesdale, Paisley and Skye terriers, which interbred with other small dogs. The dogs' history and lineage was of little importance to the mill workers: all they wanted was a good ratting dog that they could take hunting as well. It wasn't until 1874 that the breed was given the official name of Yorkshire terriers, affectionately known as Yorkies.

In the Victorian era they were adopted as pets, and became the pampered pooches that many people like me mistakenly thought was their true calling. It's easy to see why they became so popular in the salons of Victorian England: they are small, cute, fond of attention and easy to train. As the breed has been bred to be even smaller, they don't need very large amounts of exercise, which makes them an ideal town dog, but they are bright, and they definitely keep their owners on their toes if they don't get enough mental stimulation. In Stanley Coren's book, *The Intelligence of Dogs*, the Yorkie comes in at number 27, an 'above average working dog', and the highest ranked of all the terriers.

David, who converted me to them, uses his when he goes shooting, to stalk deer and rabbits. He showed me how they worked in the mills by taking them into a barn and turning them loose among some bales of hay, where they darted about, looking for rats or other vermin. I could see how useful they were, and how families must have relied on them to keep rats away from their homes. Unlike my soft-mouthed gundogs, the spaniels, Labradors and Vizslas that I am used to, these little fellas have a terrier instinct to shake anything they chase down, to stop the rat or other prey biting them. You can see this in the way they shake newspapers (I've got a friend whose terrier regularly shreds her daily paper and her post) or dog toys.

Now, whenever I see a Yorkie, even if it has a ribbon in its hair, I don't dismiss it as a handbag dog, or an old lady's petted pooch: I see it for the spirited little working dog that it really is.

It's not only through *Countryfile* that I meet other breeds of dogs, and discover their histories. Just as I had never really given much thought to Yorkies before I met them, similarly I didn't know much about whippets until they came into my life through some very good friends of ours. Now I know what wonderful dogs they are, and how they have also been bred for centuries to help out their owners, including in a very surprising way.

Whippets were a multi-purpose dog to their peasant owners in the north of England and Wales. They are sighthounds, the sort of dogs that hunt by keeping their prey in view, and then overpowering it with their great speed and agility. They were very useful for bringing in rabbits for the family pot. They are able to detect motion faster than many other breeds, so the slightest rustling in a hedgerow will send them off in pursuit before their owner or another dog would have spotted anything.

The name 'whippet' comes from an early seventeenth-century word meaning to 'move briskly', which we still use in the abbreviated form of 'whip'. For example, we talk of the wind 'whipping across the fields'. Whippets look like small greyhounds, and that's exactly where they come from: when a greyhound pup was too small for the landowner to use for stag hunting, it was given back to the peasant who bred it. Sadly, the small pup was often maimed, by having a tendon in its leg cut or a toe removed, because under the forest law peasants could not own hunting dogs. The dogs defied their disabilities and were still used for poaching hares and rabbits, and ratting. When the forest law was repealed these small greyhounds became very popular, and by the time of the Industrial Revolution they were well established in northern parts of the country, where they were prized for their speed. From their basic use, providing food for the table, developed sports such as hare coursing and racing against other dogs, and a whole betting culture evolved around them. Race tracks were established and whippet racing was a very popular Sunday outing for the whole family. There is today a very well established whippet-racing calendar, all across the country.

But there was another use for whippets, which surprised and fascinated me. In the days before central heating, when bedrooms of peasant cottages or industrial slums were cold enough to have ice inside the windows, and poverty meant there were not always enough blankets to keep children warm, whippets became furry hot water bottles, put into the beds of toddlers and small children. They were perfect for the job, not shedding hair to trigger allergies, and being delighted to burrow under the covers.

It's a great tribute to the gentle nature of whippets that parents trusted them with this vital job. It must have been a huge comfort to many a child to snuggle up to sleep with their own permanent source of heat. I can remember how much I loved sharing my bed with Nita (although she never came under the covers). For these children, there was not only the companionship of the dog, but the vital warmth of its body.

·

It's possible the instinct to climb under the covers was bred into them, or it may simply be because they are naturally skinny, with no extra layer of fat, and their coat is thin with no soft underfur, so they enjoy the warmth of the bed covers and of the human being they are snuggled up against. It's definitely something they still want to do, as any whippet owner will tell you.

My friend David Bridgwater and his wife Lucy have actually bought a bigger bed – going from double to king size – to allow room for their whippet Molly. Now there's love for you.

David was a top horse jockey, riding over 500 winners, coming second in the Grand National and second in the jockey's championship one year, and is now a successful race-horse trainer. He and Lucy have had whippets for over 20 years, often several at a time, but until his children grew up and moved out, the dogs shared their beds. Now that George is at university and Poppy is an apprentice jockey with Andrew Balding (brother of Clare), Molly has decided that she needs to sleep with David and Lucy.

'She used to share Poppy's bed, and if Poppy wasn't around she slept with George. Now she snuggles under our duvet, right inside the bed.'

It was Lucy who originally chose whippets as a family pet, although David says: 'They say owners choose dogs that look like them – well, I like to think that once upon a time I was a whippet ...'

I came to know David and Lucy when Poppy and my daughter Ella became best friends when they were really young and at school together. It was in David's yard that I first encountered whippets. He told me what great pets they make:

'They are never aggressive, very placid. They're easy to train, they don't moult, they are great with children, other dogs and brilliant around horses and other animals.'

Molly and her predecessors spend their day in the farm yard at David's stables, and he has found their gentle presence is a good, calming influence on the race horses he trains. He also has two Dobermans, Stan and Maud, who live in the yard, as guard dogs, and a collection of other free-range animals, including cats, chickens, two pygmy goats and my namesake, Adam the goat. Adam came originally from my farm, and David chose the name for that reason 'and also because there is a slight ginger tint in his coat'.

I gave David the goat after one of his two pet sheep died.

'When the children were toddlers I took them to see lambs being born at a nearby farm,' he said. 'The farmer moved one newborn lamb into a corner. When I asked why, he said there were too many for the ewe to feed, and they had too many to bottle-feed. So I thought it would be fun for the children if we took it home and bottle-fed it ourselves. A minute or two later another one was put in the corner, so we took that one, too. Then I left quickly before we ended up with any more ...'

David found the sheep were great companions for the race horses, which can be highly strung. When one of the sheep died young, he asked me if I could provide a companion. That's where Adam, a Boer cross goat from Cotswold Farm Park came in.

'He's very much part of the family, along with Libby and Lulu, the two pygmy goats. He's quite an old man by now, but he's not showing much sign of ageing. On a sunny day there's a spot in the yard where all the animals go to sunbathe, and you see them all cuddled up together: goats, cats, dogs and even the chickens. Molly the whippet is always in the mix, she loves snuggling up to the others.'

Since I met David and Lucy's whippets I have encountered another beautiful whippet. Doris Churchley is another family friend: she used to look after our children when Charlie and I were working, and now she moves in to look after our dogs and cats when we go away on holiday. She's part of the family.

When Doris decided she wanted her own dog, she was tempted to have a Labrador: 'That's the breed I grew up with, but I wanted something smaller. I wanted a gentle, placid, loyal dog that likes other animals, because I work with horses. I didn't think of whippets at first, but when I looked into them I realised they fitted the bill completely.'

I remember when Doris brought her puppy, Myrtle, to introduce her to us. She was tiny, and so lovely to look at, a beautiful slate-grey colour with blue eyes. I can easily understand why anyone falls in love with them.

Like David and Lucy, Doris has to share her bed with Myrtle: 'She's under my duvet at the first opportunity. She sleeps curled up by my back, or in the crook of my legs. And, unlike a hot water bottle, she is still warm in the morning. She also loves pregnant women: she lies across their bumps. She's great with children, following them around devotedly. I can understand why they were used to keep children warm in bed, because they love children, and they give off a lot of heat.'

When Doris house-sits for us, Myrtle gets on well with our dogs. 'Dolly, the old Vizsla, used to ignore her, but Boo really loves her. They run around together. She likes all other dogs except other whippets: she gets jealous if I show any attention or affection to another whippet.'

Using dogs for warmth is not confined to whippets: many of today's lap dogs started life as 'comforters', or mobile hot water bottles. However cute dogs like Cavalier King Charles spaniels are, they were only partly chosen as fashion statements. They, and all the other small breeds, enjoyed a lot of popularity among the landed gentry, not only for keeping their owners warm, but also because it was believed they attracted fleas away from their human hosts, back in the days when hygiene wasn't what it is today. Parasites were no respecter of titles or wealth: every seventeenth-century lord and lady had a problem with fleas and lice, and dogs were adopted as allies in the never-ending struggle against infestations, in the belief that the fleas would jump ship onto the dog.

It's probably the most bizarre instance of a job for a dog that I've ever heard about. But it shows that even the smallest, cutest toy dog was, in its own weird way, a working dog. They also serve who only sit on a lap ...

Afterword

How can I summarise my love for dogs? They are so much part of my life and family, and always have been, that it is impossible to think of an existence in which they were not there. I've known a wonderful procession of them, all with different merits and, if I'm honest, sometimes with different faults. But all faithful, loyal, and as devoted to me as I have always been to them.

I'm up early in the morning because of my work on the farm, and the first greeting I get for the day ahead is from the Vizslas in the kitchen, enthusiastic and energetic, thrilled to see me. Then it's outside to let Peg and Pearl out, and another round of tail wagging and sheer delight at the prospect of what lies ahead.

They are workmates, companions, and the greatest friends anyone can have; unquestioning, non-judgmental, and asking for nothing more than food and a bed and as much love as their owner can give them.

I hope in this book I have given a glimpse into not just how much they mean to me, as an individual and as a farmer who relies on them, but how much dogs give, endlessly, to the whole human race. They are our greatest allies.

I, for one, appreciate everything they have brought to my life. I am grateful to you all, my wonderful dogs.

Index

AH indicates Adam Henson.

Adam the goat 295, 296
Afghanistan 38, 234
Agricultural Training Board 76
Ainsdale, Southport 150–4
Airedale terrier 213–27
Akita 9
Alaska, U.S. 276, 279, 280–7
Alaskan husky 274–88
  ancestry/history of 275–7
  characteristics of breed 276
  Great Race of Mercy and 280–4
  name 276
  sled-dogs 274–88 *see also under*
    individual race name
Alaskan Malamutes 276–7
Aletsch glacier, Alps 148
All-Alaska Sweepstakes race 279
Allan, 'Scotty' 279–80
Andrews, Becky 62, 64
Andrews, Duncan 35, 44, 47–8, 50,
  57, 58–9, 62, 63–4, 101, 169
Animal Magic (television
  programme) 23–4, 111
Archie (dog with tumour in jaw)
  207, 211
Archie (miniature poodle) (assis-
  tance dog) 248–50, 252, 253
Arden, Dr Rosalind 259–60, 262,
  263, 264, 268
armed forces, dogs used in 213–35
  Countryfile Remembrance Sunday
    special 213–15, 224–7, 231–5
  First World War 214–27
  modern day use of 38, 231–5
  Second World War 227–31
Arnold (Australian blue heeler)
  285–6
assistance dogs ix, 237–56
  disabled people and 239–48

guide dogs 238
hearing dogs 248–56
therapy value of 237, 239–48,
  250
Auroch cattle 112
Australia:
  AH travels to in gap year 44,
    47–59, 60, 61, 62, 79, 113, 169
  Countryfile in 105–7, 195
  kelpies and *see* kelpies
  Maremma sheepdog initiative in
    132–4
Australian blue heeler 285–6

Bacon, Professor Nick 205, 209,
  210–11
Bagley, Matt 167–8
Bagot goats 112
Bala, North Wales, first sheepdog
  trial held in (1873) 145–6
Balmoral Castle, Scotland 144
Balto (Alaskan husky) 283, 284
Balwen sheep 157
Barney (bull terrier) 1, 229, 230,
  232
Barney (yellow Labrador) 2, 3, 6
Barnyard Safari (television
  programme) 24
Barry, Steve 96, 97, 98–9, 100, 103,
  108
Bath and West Show 203
Battersea Dogs Home 223
bearded collies 77
Belalp, Alps 148
Belted Galloway cattle 110
Bemborough Farm 18–19, 21, 97,
  111, 148, 170, 175–6, 199
  AH business partner at 47 *see*
    also Andrews, Duncan

Bemborough Farm (*Continued*)
AH childhood and *see* Henson, Adam
AH commitment to taking over 60, 63
AH takes over from father 63
Cotswold Farm Park and 23 *see also* Cotswold Farm Park
dog bed in downstairs loo 35–6, 61
Joe Henson takes over tenancy of 2
number of sheep at 48
Ben (springer spaniel) 7, 10, 30, 45
Ben Macdui, Scotland 278
bilberry 158
Bill (collie) 25, 61
Birkdale chorus (Natterjack toads) 152
Black Ox Bank 126
Black Welsh sheep 157
Blackface sheep 159
Blease, Tom 168
Bloodhound 179
Bob (kelpie) 47, 49–52, 53–5, 56, 57, 59, 60, 79, 169
Bonang Tommy (kelpie) 64, 70
Boo (Hungarian wire-haired Vizsla) vii, ix, 132, 188–90, 191–4, 195, 196, 204, 248, 258–9, 260, 261, 262, 263, 267, 297
border collie vii, viii, 15, 16, 21, 147
ancestry/history of 20, 113–15, 138–48
appearance 20, 21, 95–6
assistance dogs 237
breeding from 90–1
castration/spaying 19–20
character traits 25–8, 76–9, 103
choosing 80–3, 97
comparing working and non-working dogs 164–5
dog shows and 146, 147
family pet, as a 25–8
'hand trained' 101–2
hearing 20
'hyper' nature of 26–7
intelligence 25–6, 76–9, 103, 257–64, 267, 269, 270–1
kelpie and 50–1, 54, 59, 60, 65
life expectancy 93
love their own space 98

male and female, choosing between 18–19
name 20, 142
ready-trained, taking on 98–103
rehoming of 25–8, 79
'strong eye' 21–2, 76–7
suitability for life as sheepdog 76–7
tail position 82
training 17–18, 75–9, 83–9, 90–1, 92–3, 95, 98–103
wartime and 216, 217, 218, 219, 225
water and 151
weight 132
Welsh collie and 21–2, 77
whistle commands 99–103
Border Collie Rescue 26–7, 270
Bowden Kirk 166
Boxer (Airedale) (war messenger dog) 222
Braveheart (film) 37
Bray, Sophie 153–4
break-ins, dogs and 4, 175–6
Brecon Beacons 119
Bridgwater, David 294, 295–6, 297
Bridgwater, George 294
Bridgwater, Lucy 294, 295, 296, 297
Bridgwater, Poppy 294, 295
Bristol School of Veterinary Science 71
British Sign Language (BSL) interpreters 250–1
British Veterinary Association 6
Bronze Age, shepherding in 139
Bryher 62–3
Bundy (kelpie) 60–2, 64–9, 70, 72, 75, 76–7, 79, 82, 83, 87, 88
Buster (German pointer) 285
Buster (springer spaniel) (explosives detection dog) 38
Buttington Clump 46, 73, 91, 203
Bye, Rebecca 191

Caio, Wales 121–2
Cairngorm Sleddog Centre, Aviemore, Scotland 273, 275, 279, 285, 287, 288
Cairngorms, Scotland 273, 277, 286
Caledonian Forest, The, Scotland 273

Canada 132, 184, 275–6, 277, 278, 288
Canadian Eskimo dogs 277
cancer, dogs/animals and 200–11
Canine Partners 240, 243, 246
Cap (border collie) 80
Carlo (border collie) 15–17, 18, 21, 23, 25, 95
Castlemilk Moorit sheep 113
Cavalier King Charles spaniels 37–8, 297
Charles, Prince 111, 163
Chaser (border collie) 267
Chatsworth Estate, Derbyshire 35, 190–1
Chemmers (black Labrador) 1–3
Cheviot Hills, Northumbria 159, 162–4
chocolate, pets eating 40
Churchly, Doris 296–7
Cilycwm, Wales 125
Clarke, Richard 41–2
Cleveland Bay horse 289
Clydesdale terrier 290
cocker spaniel 36, 232–3, 254, 255
collie:
    ancestry/history of 20, 113–15, 138–48
    appearance 20, 21, 95–6
    assistance dogs 237
    different types of 21
    'eye' 21–3, 76–7
    hearing 20
    intelligence 25–6, 76–9, 103, 257–64, 267, 269, 270–1
    kelpie and 50–1, 54, 59, 60, 65
    name 20, 142
    Queen Victoria love of 137, 144–5
    rehoming of 25–8, 79
    training 17–18, 75–9, 83–9, 90–1, 92–3, 95, 98–103
    wartime and 216, 217, 218, 219, 225
    water and 151
    weight 132
    see also individual collie breed
Colyer, Richard Moore 121–2, 123–4, 125–6
Combe, Iris 118
Coren, Stanley 264–5, 267, 268, 269; The Intelligence of Dogs 264, 291
Corlett, Corporal Phil 234

Cotswold Farm Park 23, 63, 91–2, 95, 109–10, 111, 120, 132, 134–5, 141, 149, 248, 296
Cotswolds Lions sheep 141
Cotswolds, wool trade and 141, 142
Cotton, Sophie 203
Countryfile (television programmme) vii, ix, 95, 138, 147, 195, 287
    'Adam's Farm' pieces 192
    AH begins working for 91
    Ainsdale, Peg rounds up Herdwick sheep on beach at 150–4
    Ashley Stamper, AH meets shepherd 159–67
    Boo (Hungarian wire-haired Vizsla) pregnancy scanning 192
    Border Collie Rescue, AH visits 27
    cancer in dogs item 204
    cattle in Australia, AH rounds up on horseback 105–7
    county breeds, series of programmes on 288–91
    Dick Roper and problems of taking on a ready-trained dog feature 101
    drover's road, AH follows for three days 91–2, 119–27
    Hafod y Llan farm, AH visits 155–9
    intelligence test for dogs feature 258–63
    New Zealand, programmes from (2016) 169–73
    Newton Rigg college, AH and Peg visit 167
    Olive meets sheep for first time 196–7
    One Man and His Dog competition 75–6, 146, 168
    pet food industry, AH investigates 41
    Remembrance Sunday special 213–14, 215, 224–7, 231–5
    Swiss Alps, AH joins shepherds of 148
    Tintagel, AH helps introduce sheep to 149
    Tracie Rickman, AH interviews gamekeeper 177

Countryfile (*Continued*)
  Valley of the Rocks feral goats
    annual check-up, AH joins
    148–9
  Young Farmer of the Year
    Award 168
Coventry, Clint 178, 181–3, 184–6,
  187, 193, 194
Crown of St Stephen 180
Crufts 79, 146, 243
Crusades 112
'cur' 142–3
Cynographia Britannica 117
Cyril (stepfather of Joe Henson)
  229

D-Day landings 227
Dark Green Fritillary butterfly 152
Darwin, Charles 130
Dell, Billie (Harriet Collins)
  (grandmother) 228, 229,
  230–1
dementia, dogs and 260, 264
Denzell (Airedale) 225
detection dogs 38, 227, 231, 234
Detour Barrier Test 260–1
Dewar, Pete 53, 55, 57–8, 66
Dexter cattle 110
Dickin Medal 227, 243
dingo 50–1, 266
Doberman 295
dogs:
  advantages of having as pet
    vii–viii
  AH love for 299–300
  ancestry/evolution of viii, 113–15
  children, special bond with 32–3
  human bond with viii–ix
  intelligence 257–71
  loyalty 7–10
  mourning of companions 38–9
  rehoming 7–8, 25–7, 78–9, 82, 240
  sheepdog *see* border collie; collie
    and sheepdog
  see also under individual function,
    breed and dog name
Dolly (Hungarian wire-haired
  Vizla) 183–4, 186–8, 189, 193,
  199–205, 208, 211, 297
drones, herding sheep with 165
droving dogs 21, 22, 115–27, 135
dune helleborine 152

eagles, hunting with 184–6, 194
Earnie (Airedale) 213–14, 224–7
Edinburgh University 264
EJ (Labrador) (assistance dog) 245,
  247, 248
Elcock, Jay 252–3
Emmie (Hungarian wire-haired
  Vizsla) 186
Endal (Labrador) (assistance dog)
  240–5, 246, 247–8
English pointer 179
Ettrick Shepherd (James Hogg)
  143–4
Exmoor ponies 110

Farmers Weekly 70
farming:
  birth of British 139
  future of British 163, 168
  Henson family entry into 159,
    228, 230–1
Fenn (border collie) 75, 80–91, 100
Fido (street mongrel) 9
First World War (1914–18) 141, 238;
  dogs used in 213–27, 280
Fitzpatrick, Professor Noel 204–5,
  206–9, 211
Fitzpatrick Referrals, Godalming,
  Surrey 204–5
Fitzpatrick Referrals Oncology
  and Soft Tissue hospital,
  Guildford 205–7
flyball 79, 146, 258
foods, pet 40–3
foot and mouth crisis 91
Forthglade pet foods 42–3
Fox, Meryl 96, 97, 98, 99, 100, 107
Frost (Hungarian wire-haired
  Vizsla) 191
Fudge (Labradoodle) 209, 211

Galina (eagle) 184
geese, droving 119–27
George, Isabel 215
German pointer 176, 178, 285
German shepherd 5, 78, 131, 176, 191,
  219, 229, 232
German wire-haired pointers 179,
  186
Gibson, Mel 37
global warming 287
Gloucester cows 109

Gloucester Old Spot pigs 109
goats v, 91, 112–13, 114, 115, 129, 135, 137, 139, 140, 148–9, 295, 296
golden eagle 185–6, 194
golden retriever 246
Great British Dog Walk 248, 255
Great Dane 1–2, 228–9
Great Race of Mercy 281
Greenland dogs 277
Greyfriars Bobby (Skye terrier) 9
guard dogs ix, 4, 15–16, 20, 35, 81, 113, 117, 131, 175–6, 177, 286, 295
guardian dogs 127–35, 139
guide dogs 39, 238, 252 see also assistance dogs
Guide Dogs for the Blind Association, The 39
Guide Dogs UK 238
Guinevere (Old English sheepdog) 128–9, 131
Gulf War (1991) 239, 244
gundogs ix, 7, 10–11, 18, 38, 40, 101, 176, 177, 184, 190, 257

Hachiko (Akita) 9
Hafod y Llan farm, Snowdonia 155–9
Haig, Field Marshal 224
Hawling Manor 7
Hearing Dogs for Deaf People 248, 252–6
heath dog violet 152
Henson, Adam:
  agricultural college, Devon 35
  birth 2
  boarding school and A-levels 13, 31–2, 34–5
  Chatsworth Estate, Derbyshire, works at 35, 190
  childhood 1–46
  Countryfile and see Countryfile
  decides future lies at Bemborough Farm 60, 63
  dogs and see under individual breed and dog name
  family and see under individual family member name
  gap year travelling (Australia/ New Zealand) 35, 47–60, 64, 169
  moves into bungalow on Bemborough Farm 60–1

sheepdog training 79, 83–9, 98–104
  takes over Bemborough Farm 63–4
  Vets4Pets, gives talk to 238–9
Henson, Alfie (son) 72, 73, 85, 132, 175, 188–90, 196, 203
Henson, Becca (sister) 1, 29, 30
Henson, Charlotte 'Charlie' (wife) 63, 68–9, 70, 72, 90, 93, 98, 104, 132, 175, 176, 178, 181, 186–7, 188, 189, 190, 194, 195, 201, 202, 203, 248, 296
Henson, Ella (daughter) 72, 85, 92, 132, 175, 188, 189, 193, 203, 295
Henson, Gill (Mum) 6, 11, 29, 36, 39, 61, 128, 199
  AH childhood and 13, 14, 16, 29, 30, 31, 32, 36, 39, 43, 230
  AH first dog and 30, 31, 32
  Chemmers (black Labrador) and 1–2, 3
  family dogs and 1–2, 3–4, 6, 11, 14, 16, 29, 30, 31, 32, 36, 39, 43, 128
  meets and marries husband 1–2
Henson, Gladys (first wife of Leslie Henson) 228
Henson, Joe (Dad) 76, 105
  AH childhood and 3–4, 6, 7, 8, 10–12, 13, 14, 15, 16–18, 20, 21, 22–5, 29, 30–1, 32, 37, 39, 53, 54, 257
  AH takes over Bemborough Farm from 63
  Barney (bull terrier) and 229–30, 232
  Cotswold Farm Park, establishes 110
  death of 199–200
  entry into world of farming 159, 228, 230–1
  first dog, John (Great Dane) 228–9
  meets and marries wife 1–2
  parents and childhood 228–31
  provides animals for Braveheart 37
  Rare Breeds Trust and 109, 110–11
  receptive to AH new ideas for Bemborough Farm 59–60, 61
  sheepdogs, training of 15, 17–18, 20, 21, 22–3, 24–5
  television work 23–4, 111

Henson, Leslie ('Lally') (grandfather) 17, 57, 228, 230
Henson, Libby (sister) 1, 2, 3, 4–5, 6, 7, 29, 43, 44, 199–200
Henson, Lolo (sister) 1, 29–30
Henson, Nicky (uncle) 17, 230
Herdwick sheep 150–1, 154
Hidcote, Mr 7–8
Highland cattle 110, 112
Hounds for Heroes 245–7, 248
house dogs 4, 10, 13, 33, 40, 61, 72, 98, 177, 178, 187, 257, 259
Hungarian wire-haired Vizsla vii, ix, 175–97, 291, 299
  AH and family acquire 177–9, 181–3, 186–7, 188–90, 194–6
  appearance 177–8, 183–4, 193
  breeders 181–6
  breeding 187–8, 191–3
  buying 177–9, 181–3, 186–7, 188–90, 194–6
  cancer and 201–2
  character 177–8, 181, 187
  choosing puppies 194–5
  eagle hunting and 186
  gundog 190, 191
  history of 178–80
  intelligence 258–63, 269
  life expectancy 202
  selling 193–4
  sensitivity 187
  smooth-haired Vizsla and 178–80, 181
  usages 177–8
  weight 132
  see also under individual dog name
Hungary 179–80

Iditarod/Iditarod Trail, the 279–85
Industrial Revolution 289, 293
intelligence, dog 257–71
  breeds and 268–9
  collies 257–8, 269
  conscious reasoning abilities 264–6
  how dogs think 264–5
  interpersonal intelligence 266–7
  Lassie 257–9, 270
  linguistic intelligence 267
  logical-mathematical intelligence 268
  spatial intelligence 268

testing 258–67
Inuits 277
Iraq 38, 234
Irish setter 179
Iron Age pigs 111–12

Jack (Airedale) (war messenger dog) 221–2
Jack Russell 8, 171–2
Jacob sheep 110
Jake (springer spaniel) (detection dog) 38
Jemima (black Labrador) 11, 12–14, 32, 33, 38–9, 40
Jemima (goose) 123, 124
JJ (armed forces sniffer dog) 234
John (Great Dane) 1–2, 228–9, 230
Jones, Dafydd 121–2
Jones, Daniel 156, 157
Jones, David 126

Kaasen, Gunnar 283
Katanning, Western Australia 47–59
kelpie (Australian sheepdog) 49–57, 59, 60–73, 75, 76–7, 79, 106, 147, 162, 169, 259
kelpie-collie cross 65–7, 69–70, 71–3, 75
Kennel Club 6, 36, 69, 145, 176, 202
kennel, choosing 97–8
King, John 89, 92, 188

Labradoodle 209
Labrador 66, 78, 169, 177, 200, 209, 220, 291, 296
  appearance 11
  armed forces use of 234
  assistance dogs 238, 239, 240–8, 254
  bark/break-ins and 4
  cancer in 209–10
  diet/love of food 6, 11–13, 40–1, 176
  Gill Henson and 1–3
  gundogs 190, 210
  hip dysplasia 5–7
  house dog 4, 40
  intelligence 257, 269
  mating and colour of 2–4
  search dogs 232–3
  tail 4
  weight 6, 11–13, 40
  see also under individual dog name

Lady (Hungarian wire-haired Vizsla) 186
Laing, Peter 120, 121, 123, 124, 125, 127
Lake District 154
Lakeland fells 150
Land Rover vii, 25, 163–4
Land Rover Discovery Sport 163
lap dogs 137, 297–8
Lassie (television/film dog) 257–9, 270
Leonhard Seppala Humanitarian Award, The 284
Libby (pygmy goat) 296
Little penguin 132–3
Llandovery, Wales 119, 121, 126–7
Lloyds Bank 126
Lola (Labrador) 210–11
London School of Economics (LSE): centre for Philosophy of Natural and Social Science 259–64
London, Jack: *The Call of the Wild* 276
longhorn cattle 110
Lucy (rough collie) 270–1
Lulu (pygmy goat) 296

Magyars 179–80
Malafeyev, Denis 270–1
Malinois (type of Belgian shepherd) 232, 233
Maremma sheepdog 131–5
Marsh, Alan 'Swampy' 133, 134
Mary, Queen 218
Maud (border collie) 90–2, 93, 95, 100, 120, 122, 124, 127
Maud (Doberman) 295
Meadow, Tony 153–4
Megan (Welsh collie) 21, 22–3
Mercer, Dave 151–2, 153
Merino sheep 48, 52, 113
Merlin MacDonald (springer spaniel) 37
MI5 180
microchipping, puppies and 182–3
Middle Island, South Victoria 132–4
Millie (collie/kelpie cross) 259, 260, 261, 262, 263
Ministry of Defence 159, 162, 251
Molly (collie) 153–4

Molly (whippet) 294, 295, 296
Monty (collie cross) 205–6
Morris, Johnny 23–4, 111
mouflon, wild (sheep) 112, 113
Myrtle (puppy) 297

National Nature Reserve 150
National Trust 155, 156, 158
Natterjack toads 152
Natural England 150, 151
Neave, John ('Uncle John') 63, 76
Neolithic man 112
New Zealand 44, 133, 168–73, 195
New Zealand Huntaways 147, 168–73
Newton Rigg college, Cumbria 167, 168
Nita (Benita) (springer spaniel) (AH first dog) 29–36, 38–40, 43–6, 61, 176, 189, 190, 293
Noble (collie of Queen Victoria) 145
Nome, Alaska 281, 283
Norfolk sheep 110
Norfolk Regiment, 2nd Battalion 215
Nouvet, Sabine 158–9

Oddball (Maremma sheepdog) 133–4, 135
Old English sheepdog 128–9, 131
Olive (Hungarian wire-haired Vizsla) vii, ix, 195–7, 204
One Man and His Dog competition 75, 146, 168
Opočno, Czech Republic 184
Otterhound 225
Owen, Arwyn 156

Page, Dorothy 284–5
Paisley terrier 290
Pal (rough collie) (Lassie) 258
Panda (rough collie) 270–1
Parton, Allen 239–48
Parton, Sandra 239–40, 242, 246
pastoral dogs 115, 127–35 *see also* guardian dogs
Pat (border collie) 23, 24
PDSA:
  Dickin Medal 227, 243
  Dog of the Millennium 243
Pearl (border collie) vii, 92–3, 95, 100, 115, 175, 189, 204, 299

Peg (border collie) vii, viii, 147, 196, 204, 255, 299
  AH bond with viii–ix, 107–8, 299
  AH first sees 95–6
  AH takes ownership of 96–7
  Ainsdale, herding of sheep on beach at 151, 153–4, 163
  ancestry/evolution viii–ix, 115, 138, 147–8
  appearance 95–6
  breeding from 107
  Countryfile location shooting and 107, 108, 151, 153–4, 156, 157–8, 167, 258–64
  Hafod y Llan farm, visit to 156, 157–8
  intelligence testing 258–64, 270
  jumping in the water trough 104
  kennel 97–8
  Newton Rigg college, visit to 167
  Olive and 196
  trialling 103–4
  weight 132
  whistle commands 98–103, 255
  work on farm/adaptability 104–5, 107
Penguin Preservation Project 133
Penny (boxer cross) 264–5
Peters, Derek 180
Petplan 247
pheasant shoots 10–11, 34, 184, 186, 190
pig dogs 172–3
pigs 111–12, 172–3, 289
Pilgrim Fathers 37
poodle 179, 209, 248, 252, 254, 269
Portland sheep 110
Prince (Airedale) (war messenger dog) 220–1
Prince's Countryside Fund 163–4
puppy farms 66, 181–2

quad bikes 60, 92, 97, 159, 162, 164, 168, 172, 232
Queen (ex-trialling dog) 24–5
Queen Victoria's Rifles 223

rare breed farm animals 23, 63, 109–12, 141, 154, 157, 286 *see also under individual breed name*
Rare Breeds Survival Trust 109, 110–11

Raven (black Labrador) 39–40, 43, 61, 176
Red (kelpie) 62–3, 64
Red Cross dogs 217, 218
Red Poll cattle 154
Redington, Joe 284–5
Remembrance Sunday 213
Rhondda (Jack Russell) 171–2
Richardson, Blanche 217, 223
Richardson, Lieutenant Colonel Edwin Hautenville 216–17, 218–21, 223, 224, 225, 227, 231, 234
Rickman, Tracie 177
Robertson, Bill 51–2
Roffe-Silvester, Major Tom 231–2
Rogers, Anne 205–6
Romans 36, 140–1, 273
Romney sheep 170
Ronnie Barker (kelpie) 66–7, 69–70, 71–3, 175
Rookie (golden retriever) 246
Roper, Dick 75–82, 84, 85, 86–7, 88–9, 90, 92, 96, 97, 100, 101–3, 107–8, 168
Rottweiler 4, 176
rough collie 258, 270–1
Roy (collie of Queen Victoria) 145
Royal Agricultural Society 109
Royal Agricultural University, Cirencester 203
Royal Artillery 220–1
Royal Signals and Radar Establishment (ESRE) 251
RSPCA 120

Samoyeds 277
Schnichels, Karin 213, 225, 226–7
Scott, Anita 177, 184, 187, 194, 195
Scrimgeour, Derek 167
seaside centaury 152
Second World War (1939–45): dogs and 179, 180, 227–31, 234, 247, 280
Seppala, Leonhard 282, 284
Sharp (collie of Queen Victoria) 145
sheep:
  brain 105
  drenching 48–9, 52, 53, 54–5, 57
  drovers and 115–17
  evolution of 113
  hefted 155

rare breed 24, 110, 112–13, 157
  see also under individual breed
  name
rustlers 129–30
shearing 47, 49–50
wool trade development and 140,
  141
sheepdog:
  ancestry/history of 20, 113–15,
    138–48
  castrating/spaying 19–20
  different types of herding 147
  droving dogs see droving dogs
  male and female, difference
    between 18–19
  pastoral dogs see pastoral dogs
  training 17–18, 75–9, 83–9, 90–1,
    92–3, 95, 98–103
  see also border collie and under
    individual type of sheepdog
sheepdog trials 19, 22, 24, 64, 70,
  75–6, 77, 80, 86–7, 96, 99, 102,
  103–4, 145–6, 165, 167, 168, 237,
  241
shepherd/shepherding viii, ix
  castration/spaying, attitudes
    towards 19–20
  Countryfile features or
    programmes on, see
    Countryfile
  history of 137–48
  Newton Rigg college course
    dedicated to sheep dog
    handling 167–8
  rogue dog and 197
  sheep rustling and 130
  training of sheepdogs 17–18,
    75–9, 83–9, 90–1, 92–3, 95,
    98–103
  young people and 159–68
  see also sheepdog; sheepdog
    trials and under individual
    sheepdog breed
Sherwood Foresters 222
Shetland cattle 154
Siberia 276, 277
Siberian huskies 276
Sika (Yorkshire terrier) 288
Sirrah (dog of Ettrick Shepherd)
  143–4
Skye terrier 9, 290
sleddog/sleddog racing 273–88

Sledge (kelpie collie cross) 69
smooth-coated collies 144–5, 147
sniffer dogs ix, 231 see also detection dogs
Snowdonia 154–9
Soay sheep 24, 110, 113, 149
Sophie Cotton Limited 203
spaniel 7, 30–8, 43–6, 61, 78, 138,
  177, 189, 190
  ancestry/history of 36–8
  armed forces work 232–3
  assistance dogs 254, 255
  character 33, 176, 187
  drug and explosive detection 38
  energy and enthusiasm 33
  gundog 33–4, 291
  intelligence 269
  lap dogs 297
  name 'spaniel' 36
  retrieve and flush, ability to 38
  sense of smell 33–4, 38
  springers and cockers separated
    36
Spratt, James 41
springer spaniel 7, 30–1, 33–4,
  36–8, 176, 232–3, 269
St Bernard 114, 131
Stamper, Ashley 159–67
Stan (Doberman) 295
Stavert, William 248–52
Stewart, Alan 273–8, 279, 280,
  285–7, 288
Stewart, Fiona 273, 274, 275, 278,
  286, 287
Stewart, John 274, 275, 278–9, 285,
  287
Stewart, Liz 278
sticky stork's-bill 152
stockmen 18, 25, 69, 77, 89, 92, 107
Supervet (television programme)
  204
Swaledale sheep 288

Tammy (springer spaniel) 43–4
Tamworth pig 112
Tassle (black Labrador) 4–5, 6–7
Tato (collie) 154
terrier breeds 219 see also under
  individual breed name
Thule people 277
Tintagel, Cornwall 149
Togo (Alaskan husky) 282–3, 284

Torddu, or Badger face sheep 156–7
Torwen sheep 157
Treatise of Englishe Dogs, The 36
Trench Farm, Suffolk 226
trialling *see* sheepdog trials
Trudy (Labrador) 7, 10–11
Tui (kelpie-collie cross) 69
Turtle (Yorkshire terrier) 288
Tweed (rough-coated sheepdog)
    (war messenger dog) 222–3

Vaccine Induced Autoimmune
    Disease 71
Varro, Marcus Terentius 141
Vets4Pets 238–9
Victoria, Queen 137, 144–5, 146

Wales, Prince of *see* Charles,
    Prince
Walker, Pam 166
Wallace, William 37
war messenger dogs 213–27
War Office 217, 218, 220, 223
Ward, David 288, 289, 291
Ward, Matt 149
wartime, dogs in 213–35
    Countryfile Remembrance
    Sunday special 213–14, 215,
    224–7, 231–5
    First World War 214–27

modern day 231–5
Second World War 227–31
Waterside terriers 225
Watkins, Deb 250–1
Weimaraner 4
Welch, Dr. Curtis 281–3
Welsh black cattle 21, 126, 171
Welsh collie 21–2, 23, 77, 115, 147
Welsh mountain sheep 156
Wensleydale sheep 288
whippets 292–4, 295, 296–7
Whipsnade Zoo 109
White Park cattle 110, 112
wild boar 111–12
Wilkes, Ben 27
Windsor Castle 144
Windsor Home Park 145
Wolf (Airedale) (war messenger
    dog) 220–1
wolves viii, 84, 113–14, 266, 276
wool trade, birth of 140, 141
Wyoming Open race 278–9

yard dogs 49, 60, 77
yellow bartsia 152
Yorkshire terrier 288–91, 292
Young Farmer of the Year Award,
    Countryfile 168

Zoological Society of London 109

Picture credits:

Page 9, courtesy of Sophie Cotton. Page 13, courtesy of Clint Coventry.
Page 14, courtesy of Karin Schnichels. Page 14, courtesy of Allen Parton.
Page 15, courtesy of Alan and Fiona Stewart. Page 15, courtesy of Doris
Churchley. Page 16 by Jude Edginton. All other pictures are from the
author's personal collection.